FRIDAY NIGHT LIGHTS

H G Bissinger has won the Pulitzer Prize, the Livingston Award, the National Headliner Award and the American Bar Association's Silver Gavel for his reporting. He is the author of the highly acclaimed *A Prayer for the City*, and is a contributing editor at *Vanity Fair*. He lives in Philadelphia.

H. G. Bissinger

FRIDAY NIGHT LIGHTS

*A Town, a Team,
and a Dream*

YELLOW JERSEY PRESS
LONDON

Published by Yellow Jersey Press 2005

15 17 19 20 18 16

Text copyright © 1990 by Henry Bissinger
Afterword copyright © 2000 Henry Bissinger
Photographs copyright © Rob Clark Jnr

First published in the United States of America by
Da Capo Press, 2000

First published in Great Britain in 2005 by
Yellow Jersey Press

Yellow Jersey Press
Random House, 20 Vauxhall Bridge Road,
London SW1V 2SA

Addresses for companies within The Random House Group Limited
can be found at:
www.randomhouse.co.uk/offices.htm

The Random House Group Limited Reg. No. 954009
www.randomhouse.co.uk

Grateful acknowledgement is made to the following for permission to reprint previously published material:

Excerpts from *Autumn Begins in Martin's Ferry, Ohio* by James Wright © 1962 James Wright by permission of
University Press of New England. Excerpts from the lyrics to *Lay Your hands on Me* by Jon Bon Jovi and Richie
Sambora © 1988 Bon Jovi Publishing/New Jersey Underground/PRI Music, Inc by permission of PRI Music, Inc.
Excerpts from the lyrics to *Somewhere* from *West Side Story*, lyrics by Stephen Sondheim and music by Leonard
Bernstein © 1957 Leonard Bernstein and Stephen Sondheim by permission of Jalni Publications. Excerpts from the
lyrics to *Headed for the Future* by Neil Diamond, Tom Hensley, and Alan Lindgren © 1986 by Stonebridge Music, by
permission of Stonebridge Music. Excerpts from the lyrics to *I'm into Something Good* by Gery Goffin and Carole
King © 1964 by Screen Gems-EMI Music, Inc, by permission of Warner/Chappel Music, Inc.

A CIP catalogue record for this book
is available from the British Library

ISBN 9780224076746

The Random House Group Limited supports The Forest Stewardship
Council® (FSC®), the leading international forest-certification organisation.
Our books carrying the FSC label are printed on FSC®-certified paper. FSC is
the only forest-certification scheme supported by the leading environmental
organisations, including Greenpeace. Our paper procurement policy can be
found at www.randomhouse.co.uk/environment

Printed and bound by
CPI Group (UK) Ltd, Croydon, CR0 4YY

To Howard, whom I miss.
To Sarah, Gerry and Zachary, whom I love.

In the Shreve High football stadium,
I think of Polacks nursing long beers in Tiltonsville,
And gray faces of Negroes in the blast furnace at Benwood,
And the ruptured night watchman of Wheeling Steel,
Dreaming of heroes.

—From "Autumn Begins in Martins Ferry, Ohio,"
by James Wright

PHOTOGRAPHS BY ROB CLARK JR.

Contents

PUSH FOR THE PLAYOFFS

POST-SEASON

Preface

MAYBE IT WAS A SUDDENLY ACUTE AWARENESS OF BEING "thirtysomething." Maybe it was where I lived, in a suburb of Philadelphia, in a house that looked like all the other ones on the block. Or maybe it was my own past as an addicted sports fan who had spent a shamelessly large part of life watching football and basketball and baseball. I just felt something pulling at me, nagging at me, a soft voice telling me to do it, to see for myself what was out there and make the journey before self-satisfaction crept in for good.

The idea had been rattling in my head since I was thirteen years old, the idea of high school sports keeping a town together, keeping it alive. So I went in search of the Friday night lights, to find a town where they brightly blazed that lay beyond the East Coast and the grip of the big cities, a place that people had to pull out an atlas to find and had seen better times, a real America.

A variety of names came up, but all roads led to West Texas, to a town called Odessa.

It was in the severely depressed belly of the Texas oil patch, with a team in town called the Permian Panthers that played to as many as twenty thousand fans on a Friday night.

Twenty thousand . . .

I knew I had to go there.

You drive into Odessa the first time and become immersed in a land so vast, so relentless, that something swells up inside, something that makes you feel powerless and insignificant. Pulling onto Highway 80, there is row after row of oil field machinery that no one has use for anymore. Farther on down comes a series of grimy motels that don't have a single car parked in front of them.

You come to the downtown, and even though it is the middle

xi

of the afternoon there isn't another soul around. So you just walk in silence, past a couple of big buildings belonging to the banks, past a closed-down movie theater with the words THE END in crooked letters on the marquee, past a beige brick building where the old lettering saying JCPENNEY is still there, past a few restaurants and a lot of pawnshops.

Farther east, past the gas stations and fast-food joints and the old civic center that looks like a brooding frown, there is a different Odessa. It is almost suburban, with a shiny mall and comfortable ranch houses, many of which have FOR SALE signs planted in the front lawns. Driving back south there is still another Odessa, called the Southside. It is across the tracks, and it is an area of town predominantly for minorities.

Turning around again, heading north on Grandview back into those plains, there is a feeling of driving into the fathomless end of the earth. And then it rises out of nowhere, two enormous flanks of concrete with a sunken field in between. Gazing into that stadium, looking up into those rows that can seat twenty thousand, you wonder what it must be like on a Friday night, when the lights are on and the heart and soul of the town pours out over that field, across those endless plains.

I visited Odessa in March of 1988. I met the coach of the Permian Panthers and relayed to him the intent of my journey, to live in Odessa for a year and spend a season with his football team. I talked to others, but mostly I just drove and looked.

It became apparent that this was a town where high school football went to the very core of life. From the glimpses of the Southside and the FOR SALE signs and the unwanted machinery filling up the yards of Highway 80, it also became apparent that this was a town with many other currents running through it as well.

There seemed to be an opportunity in Odessa to observe not simply the enormous effect of sports on American life, but other notions, for the values of Odessa were ones that firmly belonged to a certain kind of America, an America that existed beyond the borders of the Steinberg cartoon, an America of factory towns and farm towns and steel towns and single-economy towns all trying to survive.

What were the attitudes toward race? What were the politics, and as the 1988 election approached, what did people want from their president? In a country that was having more and more difficulty teaching its young, what was the educational system like? What did people hold on to as they watched their economic lifeblood slip from them? What did they hold on to as they watched their country slip from them? What had happened to their America?

My heart told me that I would find the answers to all these questions in Odessa, not because it was a Texas town, but an American one.

I left my job as a newspaper editor for the *Philadelphia Inquirer* in July 1988 and moved to Odessa two weeks later. The following month I met the members of the 1988 Permian Panther football team, and for the next four months I was with them through every practice, every meeting, every game, to chronicle the highs and lows of being a high school football player in a town such as this. I went to school with them, and home with them, and rattlesnake hunting with them, and to church with them, because I was interested in portraying them as more than just football players, and also because I liked them.

I talked with hundreds of people to try to capture the other aspects of the town that I had come to explore, the values about race and education and politics and the economy. Much of what I learned about the town came from these interviews, but some of it naturally came from the personal experience of living there, with a wife and five-year-old twin boys. Odessa very much became home for a year, a place where our kids went to school and we worked and voted and forged lasting friendships.

It was in Odessa that I found those Friday night lights, and they burned with more intensity than I had ever imagined. Like thousands of others, I got caught up in them. So did my wife. So did my children. As someone later described it, those lights become an addiction if you live in a place like Odessa, the Friday night fix.

But I also found myself haunted by something else, the words of a father with a son who had gone to Permian and had later become a world-class sprinter in track.

He saw the irresistible allure of high school sports, but he also saw an inevitable danger in adults' living vicariously through their young. And he knew of no candle that burned out more quickly than that of the high school athlete.

"Athletics lasts for such a short period of time. It ends for people. But while it lasts, it creates this make-believe world where normal rules don't apply. We build this false atmosphere. When it's over and the harsh reality sets in, that's the real joke we play on people. . . . Everybody wants to experience that superlative moment, and being an athlete can give you that. It's Camelot for them. But there's even life after it."

With the kind of glory and adulation these kids received for a season of their lives, I am not sure if they were ever encouraged to understand that. As I stood in that beautiful stadium on the plains week after week, it became obvious that these kids held the town on their shoulders.

Odessa is the setting for this book, but it could be anyplace in this vast land where, on a Friday night, a set of spindly stadium lights rises to the heavens to so powerfully, and so briefly, ignite the darkness.

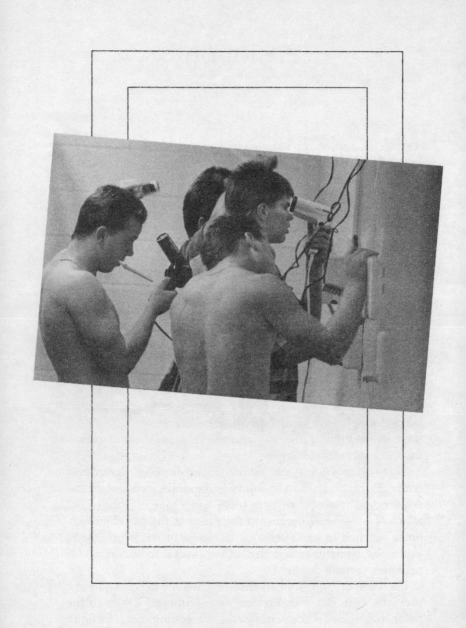

Prologue

IF THE SEASON COULD EVER HAVE ANY SALVATION, IF IT COULD
ever make sense again, it would have to come tonight under a
flood of stars on the flatiron plains, before thousands of fans
who had once anointed him the chosen son but now mostly
thought of him as just another nigger.

He felt good when he woke up in the little room that was his,
with the poster of Michael Jordan taped to the wall. He felt
good as he ate breakfast and talked to his uncle, L.V., who had
rescued him from a foster home when he had been a little boy,
who had been the one to teach him the game and had shown
him how to cut for the corner and swivel his hips and use the
stiff arm.

L.V. still had inescapable visions of his nephew—Boobie
Miles as the best running back in the history of Permian High
School, Boobie as the best high school running back in the
whole damn state of Texas, Boobie as belle of the ball at Nebraska or Texas A & M or one of those other fantastic college
casinos, Boobie as winner of the Heisman. He couldn't get
those dreams out of his head, couldn't let go of them. And neither, of course, could Boobie.

There were still some questions about the knee, about how
ready Boobie was after the injury two months earlier that had
required arthroscopic surgery (they had a tape of it that L.V.,
who was out of work because of the slump in the oil field, sometimes watched in the afternoon darkness of the living room,
just as he sometimes watched other pivotal moments of his
nephew's football career).

The Cooper Cougars had thrashed Boobie pretty badly the
previous week down in Abilene, headhunting for him to the
point that he had to be restrained from getting into a fistfight.

1

But he had held up under the physical punishment, two or three or four tacklers driving into him on many of the plays, the risk always there that they would take a sweet shot at his knee, smash into that still-tender mass of cartilage and ligament with all their might and see how tough the great Boobie Miles really was, see how quickly he got up off the ground after a jolting *thwack* that sounded like a head-on car collision, see how much he liked the game of football now as fear laced through him and the knee began to feel as tender to the touch as the cheek of a baby, see how the future winner of the Heisman felt as he lay there on the clumpy sod with those Cooper Cougars taunting through the slits in their helmets:

Com'on, Boobie, you tough motherfucker, com'on, let's see how
tough you are!
Com'on, get up, get up!
You ain't nothin' but a pussy, a goddamn pussy!

He had made it through, he had survived, although it was clear to everyone that he wasn't the same runner of the year before, the instinct and the streak of meanness replaced by an almost sad tentativeness, a groping for feeling and moments and movements that before had always come as naturally as the muscles that rippled through his upper torso.

But there was a fire in his belly this morning, an intensity and sense of purpose. This game wasn't against a bunch of goody-two-shoes hacks from Abilene, the buckle of the West Texas Bible Belt. It was against Midland Lee—Permian's arch-rivals— the Rebels, those no-good son-of-a-bitch bastard Rebels—under the Friday night lights for the district championship before a crowd of fifteen thousand. If Permian won, it was guaranteed a trip to the most exciting sporting event in the entire world, the Texas high school football playoffs, and a chance to make it all the way, to go to State. Anybody who had ever been there knew what a magic feeling that was, how it forever ranked up there with the handful of other magic feelings you might be lucky enough to have in your life, like getting married or having your first child.

After tonight, Boobie knew the fans would be back in his corner extolling him once again, the young kids who were counting off the years until their own sun-kissed moment excitedly whispering to one another as he walked down the street or through the mall. *There he is! That's Boobie! There he is!* The bigtime college recruiters would come charging back as well, the boys from Nebraska and Texas A & M and Arkansas and all the others who before the injury had come on to him as shamelessly as a street whore supporting a drug habit, telling him in letter after letter *what a fine-looking thing* he was with that six-foot, two-hundred-pound frame of his and that 4.6 speed in the forty and how sweet he would look in a uniform in Norman or College Station or Fayetteville and how he should just *stick with me, sugar, I'll take good care of you*. They would all be there pleading for him, just as they had before the knee injury, before his dreams had so horribly unraveled.

He felt good when he left the little white house that he lived in, where a green pickup truck sat in the bare, litter-strewn yard like a wrecked boat washed up on the shore. He felt good as he made his way out of the Southside part of town, the place where the low-income blacks and Mexicans lived, and crossed the railroad tracks as he headed for Permian over on the northeast side of town, the fancy side of town, the white side of town.

He felt good as he walked into the locker room of the Permian field house that morning and pulled on his jersey with the number 35 on it. He felt good at the pep rally as he and his teammates sat at the front of the gym in little metal chairs that were adorned with dozens of black and white balloons, the decorations making them look like little boys attending a gigantic birthday party. The wild cheering of the entire student body, two thousand strong, above him in the bleachers, the sweet hiss of the pom-poms from the cheerleaders, the sexy preening of the majorettes in their glittery black costumes with hair as intricately laced as frozen drizzles of ice and their tender Marilyn

3

Monroe smiles, the way the lights dimmed during the playing of the alma mater, the little gifts of cookies and candy and cakes from the Pepettes, the pandemonium that broke loose when defensive back Coddi Dean gave the last lines of his verse—

The moral is obvious, it's plain to see
Tonight at Ratliff Stadium, we're gonna stomp on Lee!

—all these things only energized Boobie Miles even more. The feeling came back to him now, the cockiness, the "attitude" as his teammates liked to call it, the self-confidence that had caused him to gain 1,385 yards the previous season and knock vaunted linebackers semi-unconscious. As he sat there, surrounded by all that pulsating frenzy, he could envision sitting in this very same spot a week from now, acknowledging the cheers of the crowd as he picked up the Superstar of the Week award from one of the local television stations for his outstanding performance against the Rebels.

"A person like me can't be stopped. If I put it in my mind, they
can't stop me . . . ain't gonna stop me.
"See if I can get a first down. Keep pumping my legs up, spin out
of it, go for a touchdown, go as far as I can."

That's right. That's how it would feel again, getting that ball, tucking it under his arm, and going forever like someone in the euphoria of flight. Nothing in the world could ever be like it. No other thing could ever compare, running down that field in the glow of those Friday night lights with your legs pumping so high they seemed to touch the sky and thousands on their feet cheering wildly as the gap between you and everyone else just got wider and wider and wider.

After the pep rally he went to class, but it was impossible to concentrate. He sat there in a daze, the messages of algebra and biology and English lost to him. Like most of his other teammates on game day, he couldn't be bothered with classes. They were irrelevant, a sidelight to the true purpose of going to

Permian High School: to play football for the Panthers. Only one thought crossed his mind as he sat in those antiseptic, whitewashed classrooms until the middle of the afternoon, and it didn't have anything to do with schoolwork. He desperately wanted to perform well against Midland Lee, to break tackle after tackle, to be Boobie once again.

He didn't seem like a high school football player at all, but an aging prizefighter who knew that if he didn't get a knockout tonight, if he didn't turn his opponent's face into a bloody pulp, if he didn't sting and jab and show the old footwork, he was done, washed up, haunted forever by the promise of what could have been. Could he regain his former footing as a star? Or at the age of eighteen, was he already a has-been?

He felt good as he left class for the day and had a few hours to kill before it was time to go to the field house to suit up.

He felt good.

After classes ended, Jerrod McDougal walked out of school into the parking lot. It didn't take him long to find his black Chevy pickup, perhaps the tallest object in all of Odessa with the thirty-three-inch Desert Dueler treads that made it hard to get into without a stepladder. He climbed inside the cab amid the clutter of cassettes and paper cups. He found what he was looking for and did the same thing he did every Friday afternoon in those lousy waning hours before game time.

The pounding of the drums came on first, then the scream of "Hey!", then the sound of a guitar like that of ten-inch fingernails sliding up and down a blackboard, then explosive sounds moving back and forth between the speakers. There were more guttural yells, more screeching snippets of guitar, then the sudden, ominous wail of an organ that kept building and building and made his heart beat a little faster.

The guitars dug into his ears and the lyrics poured into his veins like liquid fire, the louder the better, the angrier the better, every sound aimed to strike right at the top of the skull and just rattle up there for a little while, get trapped in there, like a ball bouncing repeatedly off a wall:

Lay your hands on me
Lay your hands on me
Lay your hands on me
Lay your hands on me
Lay your hands on me

Thank God for Bon Jovi.

McDougal closed the tiny eyes of his face and leaned his head against the back of the seat. He waited to see if the feeling would be there, as it had been a couple of weeks ago when Permian had beaten the hell out of the Bulldogs, had taught them a thing or two about having the fucking nerve to step on the same field with the Panthers, the Boys in Black. And it was, yes it was, a series of chills shooting down his back straight to his spine like lightning splitting a tree, a tingling feeling that both reassured and excited him. And at that moment, at that very moment, he knew there was no way that Permian could lose to Midland Lee tonight, no fucking way, not as long as he was alive.

It was all that mattered to him, not because it was a ticket to anything or a way out of this town that held as many secrets as the back of his hand. Long before, when he had stopped growing at five nine, he had put away all lofty dreams of playing for the University of Texas, or anywhere else for that matter. He knew that all he was, when you got to the core of it, was an offensive tackle with a lot of heart but little natural ability.

After the season there would be plenty of time to think about college and careers and all that other stuff that a high school senior might want to start thinking about. But not now, not when the most important moment of his life was about to take place. Friday night is what he lived for, bled for, worked so hard for. It sure as hell wasn't school, where he shuffled from one creampuff course to another. It wasn't the prospect of going into the oil business either, where he had watched his father's company, built with sweat and tears, slide through the continued depression in oil prices.

6

I'm a fighter, I'm a poet
I'm a preacher
I've been to school and
Baby, I've been the teacher
If you show me how to get
Up off the ground
I can show you
How to fly and never
Ever come back down

Thank God for Bon Jovi.

The tingling sensation stayed with him, and he knew that when he stepped on that field tonight he wouldn't feel like a football player at all but like someone much more powerful entering a glittering, barbaric arena.

"It's like the gladiators" was the way he once described it. "It's like the Christians and the lions, like Caesar standing up there and saying yay or nay. There's nineteen thousand fans in the stands and they can't do what you're doing, and they're all cheering for one thing, they're cheering for you. Man, that's a high no drug or booze or woman can give you."

He pulled back into the school parking lot. He left his pickup and entered the locker room of the field house where everything had been laid out the night before with the meticulousness of a Christmas display window, the shoes and the shoulder pads and the socks and the pants all in their proper places, the helmets fresh and gleaming from the weekly hand cleaning by one of the student trainers.

Mike Winchell hated these moments in the field house, wandering around in his uniform as the minutes dripped away with excruciating slowness. Secretly he wished that he could be knocked out and not wake up until five minutes before game time when there was no longer any time to dwell on it. He was the quarterback and that gave him a certain status, because just about everybody in town knew who the quarterback was and the novelty of having his picture in the local paper had worn

7

off long ago. But with all the responsibilities—learning the audible calls and the three-play packages, not getting fooled by
that overshifted defense the Rebels liked to run—it was hard
not to feel overwhelmed.

He awoke early that day, in the darkness of the shabby house
on Texas Avenue that shamed him so much he wouldn't even
let his girlfriend enter it. In silence he had carefully wrapped
up some toast and bacon in paper towels so he would have
something to eat when he got to school. Then he got his mother
up so she could drive him there since, unlike most kids at
Permian High School, he didn't have his own car. They barely
said anything to each other, because he hated questions about
the game. When she dropped him off she whispered, "Good
luck," and then left.

Once he got to school he had to go to the pep rally, where his
long, angular face, framed by balloons, had a look of delicate
sadness as haunting as a Diane Arbus photograph. It was a fascinating face, Huck Finnish, high-cheekboned, yet somehow
devoid of expression, the eyes flat and deadened against the
roar and tumult that surrounded him, impervious to it, unable
to react.

He welcomed going to class afterward, finding relief in the
equations spread across the blackboard in algebra II, glad to
have something else filling his head besides the thousand and
one things that were expected of him. But outside class the
pressure intensified again, the Lee game hovering over him like
a thundercloud, the incessant questions of the students as he
walked through the halls driving him crazy and offering him
no escape.

Everyone seemed uptight to him, even the teachers who
always dressed up in black on game day. When he walked
through the halls of school during the season it wasn't as a
proud gladiator, but instead he seemed enveloped in an almost
painful shyness, his head ducked to the side and his eyes shifting furtively, fending off questions with one-word answers, es-

8

pecially hating it when people came up to him and asked, "Do y'all think you're gonna win?"

He had first started as a junior, and back then he had been so nervous that the butterflies started on Tuesdays. In the huddle his hands shook. Teammates looked at him and wondered if he was going to make it. But this season he was leading the district in passing and had cut his interceptions down to almost none. A big game against the Rebels would be further vindication, further proof that he had what it took to be a college quarterback in the Southwest Conference.

There could have been other options for him. During the season he had gotten a letter from Brown expressing interest in him because he was not only a decent quarterback but a good student. But for Winchell, who had never been east of the Texas-Louisiana border, the mere idea scared him to death. Rhode Island? Where in God's name was *Rhode Island*? He looked on a map and there it was, halfway across the earth, so tiny it could move into West Texas overnight and no one would ever know it, taking its anonymous place beside Wink and Kermit and Notrees and Mentone.

"Hell, Brown, that might as well have been in India" was the way he put it. He had read about the Ivy League in the sports pages and seen a few of those games on ESPN where the caliber of play wasn't too bad but it sure as heck wasn't football the way he had grown up to understand football. He also got a nibble of interest from Yale, but when he tried to imagine what these schools were like, all he could think of was people standing around in goofy sweaters with little *Y*'s on the fronts yelling, "Go Yale, beat Brown."

A series of meetings was held in the field house, the five Permian coaches trying to pound in the game plan against Lee one more time. Afterward, as part of a long-standing tradition, all the lights were turned off. Some of the players lay on the floor or slumped against concrete posts. Some listened to music, the tinny sound from their headphones like violent whispering in a serious domestic spat. Winchell, who had gone over the audible calls in his mind yet again, agonized over the wait. It was the worst part of all, the very worst. After several minutes the lights came back on and he and his teammates boarded the yellow school buses waiting outside.

With the flashers of a police escort leading the way so there wouldn't be any wait at the traffic lights, the caravan made its way to Ratliff Stadium like a presidential motorcade.

The sound of vomiting echoed through the dressing room of the stadium, the retching, the physical embodiment of the ambivalence Ivory Christian felt about what he was doing and why he was there. Droplets of sweat trickled down his face as he lay in front of the porcelain. None of the other players paid much notice. They had heard it before and gave little half-smiles. It was just Ivory.

There was so much about football he hated—the practices, the conditioning, the expectations that because he was a captain he had to be Joe Rah-Rah. He wasn't sure if he cared about beating Midland Lee. He wasn't sure if he cared about winning the district championship and getting into the playoffs. Let other players dream their foolish dreams about getting recruited by a big-time school. It wasn't going to happen to him and he figured that after the year was over he would enlist in the Marines or something, maybe buy a Winnebago so he could get out of this place and drive around the country without a care in the world, where no one could get to him.

But the game had a funny hold on him. The elemental savagery of it appealed to him and he was good at it, damn good, strong, fast, quick, a gifted middle linebacker with a future potential he didn't begin to fathom. Severing from it, letting it go, was not going to be as easy as he thought it would be, particularly in Odessa, where if you were big and strong and fast and black it was difficult not to feel as if the whole world expected you to do one thing and one thing only and that was play football. And despite the grim detachment with which he seemed

10

to approach almost everything, he seemed scared to death at the thought of failing at it. He loved it and he hated it and he hated it and he loved it.

After he had finished vomiting, he reappeared in the dressing room with a relieved smile on his face. He had gone through the catharsis. He had gotten it out of his system, the ambivalence, the fear.

Now he was ready to play.

Every sound in the dressing room in the final minutes seemed amplified a thousand times—the jagged, repeated rips of athletic tape, the clip of cleats on the concrete floor like that of tap shoes, the tumble of aspirin and Tylenol spilling from plastic bottles like the shaking of bones to ward off evil spirits. The faces of the players were young, but the perfection of their equipment, the gleaming shoes and helmets and the immaculate pants and jerseys, the solemn ritual that was attached to almost everything, made them seem like boys going off to fight a war for the benefit of someone else, unwitting sacrifices to a strange and powerful god.

In the far corner of the dressing room Boobie Miles sat on a bench with his eyes closed, his face a mixture of seriousness and sadness, showing no trace of what this pivotal night would hold for him. Jerrod McDougal, pacing back and forth, went to the bathroom to wipe his face with paper towels. Staring into the mirror, he checked to make sure his shirt was tucked in and the sleeves were taped. He straightened his neck roll and then put on his gloves to protect his hands, the last touches of gladiatorial splendor. It looked good. It looked damn good. In the distance he could hear the Midland Lee band playing "Dixie," and it enraged him. He hated that song and the way those cocky bastards from Lee swaggered to it. His face became like that of an impulse killer, slitty-eyed, filled with anger. Mike Winchell lay on the floor, seduced by its coldness and how good it felt. His eyes closed, but the eyelids still fluttered and you could feel the nervousness churning inside him.

In the silence of that locker room it was hard not to admire these boys as well as fear for them, hard not to get caught up in the intoxicating craziness of it, hard not to whisper "My God!" at how important the game had become, not only to them, but to a town whose spirits crested and fell with each win and each loss. You wished for something to break that tension, a joke, a sigh, a burst of laughter, a simple phrase to convince them that if they lost to the Rebels tonight it wasn't the end of the world, that life would go on as it always had.

Gary Gaines, the coach of Permian, called the team to gather around him. He was a strikingly handsome man with a soft smile and rows of pearly white teeth somehow unstained, as if by divine intervention, from the toxic-looking thumbfuls of tobacco snuff that he snuck between front lip and gum when his wife wasn't around to catch him. He had beautiful eyes, not quite gray, not quite blue, filled with softness and reassurance. His message was short and sincere.

"Nobody rest a play, men. Don't coast on any play. You're on that field, you give it everything you got."

Across the field, in the visitor's dressing room, Earl Miller, the coach of the Rebels, gave similar advice in his thick Texas twang that made every syllable seem as long as a sentence.

"First time you step out on that field, you go down there as hard as you can and bust somebody."

Brian Chavez's eyes bulged as he made his way to the coin toss with the other captains. On one side was Ivory Christian, belching and hiccuping and trying to stop himself from retching again. On the other was Mike Winchell, lost in a trance of intensity. The three of them held hands as they walked down a ramp and then turned a corner to catch the first glimpse of a sheet of fans dressed in black that seemed to stretch forever into the desert night. The farther they moved into the stadium field, the more it felt as if they were entering a fantastic world, a world unlike any other.

The metamorphosis began to take hold of Chavez. When the

12

game began and he took the field, his body would be vibrating and his heart would be beating fast and every muscle in his body would become taut. He knew he would try to hit his opponent as hard as he possibly could from his tight end position, to hurt him, to scare him with his 215-pound frame that was the strongest on the team, to make him think twice about getting back up again.

It was the whole reason he played football, for those hits, for those acts of physical violence that made him tingle and feel wonderful, for those quintessential shots that made him smile from ear to ear and earned him claps on the back from his teammates when he drove some defensive lineman to the sidelines and pinned him right on his butt. He knew he was an asshole when he played, but he figured it was better to be, as he saw it, an "asshole playin' football rather than in real life."

He had no other expectations beyond the physical thrill of it. He didn't have to rely on it or draw all his identity from it. "I played because I like it," he once said. "Others played because it was Permian football. It was their ticket to popularity. It was just a game to me, a high school game."

As the number-one student in his class, his aspirations extended far beyond the glimmer of expectation that a Texas school, any Texas school, might be willing to give him a football scholarship. He had set his sights differently, zeroing in on a target that seemed incomprehensible to his family, his friends, just about everyone. He wanted to go to Harvard.

When he tried to imagine it, he thought it would be like stepping into a different world, a world that was steeped in history and breathtaking and so utterly different from the finite world of Odessa, which spread over the endless horizon like the unshaven stubble of a beard. When he visited it his senior year, he sat by the window of his hotel and watched the rowers along the Charles with their seemingly effortless grace, the strokes of their oars so delicate and perfectly timed as they skimmed along the water past the white domes and the red brick buildings and all those beautiful trees. It didn't seem real to him when he gazed out that window, but more like a painting, beautiful, unfathomable, unattainable.

But now he wasn't thinking about Harvard. Every bone in his body was focused on beating Midland Lee, and he felt so absolutely confident that he had already ordered a DISTRICT CHAMPS patch for his letter jacket. As the coin was being thrown into the air by one of the officials he stared across at Quincy White, Lee's bruising fullback. At that moment Brian felt hatred toward the Rebels, absolute hatred, and he wanted to prove he was the best there was on the damn field, the very best.

The team left the dressing room and gathered behind a huge banner that had been painstakingly made by the cheerleaders. It took up almost half the end zone and was fortified by the Pepettes with pieces of rope like in some scene of war from the Middle Ages. It became a curtain. The players congregated behind it in the liquid, fading light, yelling, screaming, pounding each other on the shoulder pads and the helmets, furious to be finally set loose onto the field, to revel in the thrilling roar of the crowd.

The fans couldn't see the players yet, but they could hear them bellowing behind that banner and they could see their arms and knees and helmets push against it and make it stretch. The buildup was infectious, making one's heart beat faster and faster. Suddenly, like a fantastic present coming unwrapped, the players burst through the sign, ripping it to shreds, little pieces of it floating into the air. They poured out in a steady stream, and the crowd rose to its feet.

The stillness was ruptured by a thousand different sounds smashing into each other in wonderful chaos—deep-throated yells, violent exhortations, giddy screams, hoarse whoops. The people in the stands lost all sight of who they were and what they were supposed to be like, all dignity and restraint thrown aside because of these high school boys in front of them, *their* boys, *their* heroes, upon whom they rested all their vicarious

14

thrills, all their dreams. No connection in all of sports was more intimate than this one, the one between town and high school.

"MO-JO! MO-JO! MO-JO! MO-JO!"

Chants of the Permian monicker, which was taken from the title of an old Wilson Pickett song and stuck to the team after a bunch of drunken alumni had yelled the word for no apparent reason during a game in the late sixties, passed through the home side. The visitor's side answered back with equal ferocity:

"REB-ELS! REB-ELS! REB-ELS!"

Each wave of a Confederate flag by a Lee fan was answered by the waving of a white handkerchief by a Permian fan. Each rousing stanza of "Dixie" by the Lee band was answered by an equally rousing stanza of "Grandioso" by the Permian band, each cheer from the Rebelettes matched by one from the Pepettes. Nothing in the world made a difference on this October night except this game illuminating the plains like a three-hour Broadway finale.

Permian took the opening kickoff and moved down the field with the methodical precision that had made it a legend throughout the state of Texas. An easy touchdown, a quick and bloodless 7–0 lead. But Lee, a twenty-one-point underdog, came back with a touchdown of its own to tie the game. Early in the second quarter, a field goal gave the Rebels a 10–7 lead.

Permian responded with a seventy-seven-yard drive to make it 14–10. Chris Comer, the new great black hope who had replaced Boobie Miles in the backfield, carried the ball seven of nine plays and went over a thousand yards for the season.

Earlier in the season, Boobie had cheered on Comer's accomplishments with a proud smile. As the season progressed and Comer became a star while Boobie languished, the cheers stopped.

He made no acknowledgment of Comer's score. He sat on the bench, his eyes staring straight ahead, burning with a mixture of misery and anger as it became clear to him that the coaches had no intention of playing him tonight, that they were willing to test his knee out in meaningless runaways but not in games that counted. His helmet was off and he wore a black stocking cap over his head. The arm pads he liked still dangled from his jersey. The towel bearing the legend "TERMINATOR X" from the name of one of the members of the rap group Public Enemy, hung from his waist, spotless and unsullied. The stadium was lit up like a dance floor, its green surface shimmering and shining in the lights, and his uniform appeared like a glittering tuxedo loaded down with every conceivable extra. But it made him look silly, like one of those kids dressed to the nines to conceal the fact that they were unpopular and couldn't dance a lick. He sat on the bench and felt a coldness swirl through him, as if something sacred inside him was dying, as if every dream in his life was fleeing from him and all he could do was sit there and watch it disappear amid all those roars that had once been for him.

With 2:27 left in the half, Winchell threw the finest pass of his life, a sixty-yard bomb to Lloyd Hill, to make the score 21–10. But then, with less than ten seconds left, Lee scored after connecting on a forty-nine-yard Hail Mary pass that unfolded like a Rube Goldberg drawing, the ball fluttering off the hands and helmets and shoulder pads of several Permian defenders before somehow settling into the hands of a receiver who had never caught a varsity pass in his life. Lee's try for a two-point conversion failed.

The score was 21–16 at halftime.

The Permian players came off the field exhausted, in for a fight they had never quite expected. The gray shirts they wore underneath their jerseys were soaked. Winchell, who had taken a massive hit in the first half, felt dizzy and disoriented. They grabbed red cups of Coke and sat in front of their locker stalls trying to get their breath, the strange Lee touchdown at the end of the half a weird and scary omen. There was hardly a sound, hardly a movement. The players seemed more shell-shocked

16

than frantic, and few even noticed when Boobie flung his shoulder pads against the wall.

In a furious rage he threw his equipment into a travel bag and started to walk out the door. He had had it. He was quitting at halftime of the biggest game of the year. He couldn't bear to watch it anymore, to be humiliated in those lights where everyone in the world could stare at him and know that he wasn't a star anymore, just some two-bit substitute who might get a chance to play if someone got hurt.

None of the varsity coaches made a move to stop him; it was clear that Boobie had become an expendable property. If he wanted to quit, let him go and good riddance. But Nate Hearne, a black junior varsity football coach whose primary responsibility was to handle the black players on the team, herded him into the trainer's room to try to calm him down, to somehow salvage what little of his psyche hadn't already been destroyed.

Boobie stood in the corner of the darkened room with his arms folded and his head turned down toward the floor, as if protecting himself from any more pain. "I quit, coach, they got a good season goin'," he said, his tone filled with the quiet hurt of a child who can't process the shame of what has happened except to run from it.

"Come on, man, don't do this."

"Why'd [Gaines] play me the last weekend and the weekend before that?"

"I know how hard it is. Don't quit now. Come on."

"That's why I'm gonna quit. They can do it without me."

"Everything's gonna be all right. Everybody knows how it feels to be on the sidelines when he should be out there."

"Could have hurt [my knee] last week, could have hurt it the week before. He didn't think about it then."

"You'll be all right. Just hang tough for now. The team needs you. You know we need you. Use your head. Don't let one night destroy everything."

"Why not just quit?"

"This is one game. We got six games down the line."

"Six games to sit on the sidelines."

"We're almost there and now you want to do this, don't do this."

"Next week it ain't gonna be a new story because I ain't gonna play. Just leave me alone, and I'll get out of here."

"You can't walk off now, in the middle of a game. You just can't walk off in the middle of a game."

"I'm just gonna leave because I ain't gonna sit on the sidelines for no one. I see what it's all about.

"What's it all about?"

"I'm a guinea pig."

It went on a little longer, Hearne's heartfelt understanding in contrast to the attitude of most of the other members of the Permian football staff who derided Boobie, who had grown weary of his emotional outbursts and privately called him lazy, and stupid, and shiftless, and selfish, and casually described him as just another "dumb nigger" if he couldn't carry a football under his arm.

Reluctantly, Boobie left the trainer's room and walked back out to the dressing room. Without emotion, he put on his hip pads and shoulder pads. Carefully, meticulously, he tucked his TERMINATOR X towel into the belt of his pants and put that ridiculous costume back on again because that's what it was now, a costume, a Halloween outfit. He went back out on the field, but it no longer had any promise. When players tried to talk to him, he said nothing. The Rebels scored early in the fourth quarter on a one-yard run to take a one-point lead, 22–21. The Lee band broke into "Dixie" and the taunting chant, now stronger than ever, resumed:

"REB-ELS! REB-ELS! REB-ELS!"

With about six minutes left Permian moved to a first and ten at the Lee 18, but the drive stalled and a thirty-yard field goal was blocked.

Permian got the ball back at its own 26 with 2:55 left in the game, but instead of confidence in the huddle there was fear. Chavez could see it in the eyes of the offensive linemen. He tapped them on the helmet and said, "Com'on, let's get it, this is it." But he could tell they weren't listening. The game was slipping away.

They were going to lose. They were goddamn going to lose and everything they had worked for for the past six years of their lives, everything they cared about, was about to be ruined.

Winchell, after the glorious touchdown pass he had thrown, now seemed hunted by failure. His face was etched in agony, the passes coming off his hand in a tentative, jerky motion, thrown desperately without rhythm. The Lee fans were on their feet. There was the incessant beat of the drums from the band. Both sides were screaming their hearts out.

"REB-ELS! REB-ELS!"

"MO-JO! MO-JO!"

How could a seventeen-year-old kid concentrate at a moment like this amid the frenzy of fifteen thousand fans? How could he possibly keep his poise?

With a third and ten at the Lee 41, flanker Robert Brown broke free down the left sideline after his defender fell down, but the ball was thrown way out of bounds.

"Fuck! Winchell!" screamed starting linebacker Chad Payne from the sidelines as the ball fluttered helplessly beyond Brown's grasp. With a fourth and ten, another pass fell incomplete.

It wasn't even close.

Jerrod McDougal watched as the Lee players fell all over each other on the field like kittens. He watched as they spit contemptuously on the field, *his* field, goddammit, his fucking field, defiling it, disgracing it, and never in his life had he felt such humiliation. Some gladiator he was, some heroic gladiator. In the dressing room he started to cry, his right hand draped tenderly around the bowed head of linebacker Greg Sweatt, who was sobbing also. With his other hand he punched a wall. Chavez and Winchell sat in silence, and Ivory Christian felt that creeping numbness. With a three-way tie for first and only one game left in the regular season, now Permian might not get into the state playoffs. But that wasn't potentially devastating to Ivory. There had to be something else in life, if only he could figure out what it was.

Boobie officially quit the team two days later. But no one paid much attention. There were a lot more important things to worry about than that pain-in-the-ass prima donna with a bad knee who couldn't cut worth a crap anymore anyway. There were plenty more on the Southside where he came from.

The loss to Lee sent Odessa into a tailspin, so unthinkable, so catastrophic was it. As in a civil war, goodwill and love disintegrated and members of the town turned on each other.

Gaines himself was distraught, a year's worth of work wasted, the chorus against him only growing stronger that he was a very nice man who wasn't a very good coach when it counted. When he got back to the field house he stayed in the coaches' office long past midnight, still mulling over what had happened and why the eighteen-hour days he had spent preparing for the Rebels had not paid off. The idea of a team with this kind of talent not making the playoffs seemed impossible, but now it might happen. And if it did, he had to wonder if he would be in the same job next year.

When he went home late that night, several FOR SALE signs had been punched into his lawn, a not-so-subtle hint that maybe it would be best for everyone if he just got the hell out of town. He took them and dumped them in the garage along with the other ones he had already collected. He wasn't surprised by them.

After all, he was a high school football coach, and after all, this was Odessa, where Bob Rutherford, an affable realtor in town, might as well have been speaking for thousands when he casually said one day as if talking about the need for a rainstorm to settle the dust, "Life really wouldn't be worth livin' if you didn't have a high school football team to support."

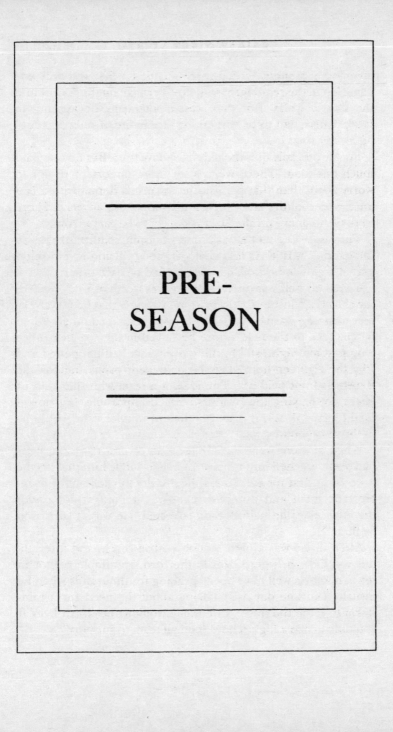

PRE-
SEASON

CHAPTER 1

Odessa

In the beginning, on a dog-day Monday in the middle of August when the West Texas heat congealed in the sky, there were only the stirrings of dreams. It was the very first official day of practice and it marked the start of a new team, a new year, a new season, with a new rallying cry scribbled madly in the backs of yearbooks and on the rear windows of cars: GOIN' TO STATE IN EIGHTY-EIGHT!

It was a little after six in the morning when the coaches started trickling into the Permian High School field house. The streets of Odessa were empty, with no signs of life except the perpetual glare of the convenience store lights on one corner after another. The K mart was closed, of course, and so was the Wal-Mart. But inside the field house, a squat structure behind the main school building, there was only the delicious anticipation of starting anew. On each of the coaches' desks lay caps with bills that were still stiff and sweat bands that didn't contain the hot stain of sweat, with the word PERMIAN emblazoned across the front in pearly thread. From one of the coaches came the shrill blow of a whistle, followed by the gleeful cry of "Let's go, men!" There was the smell of furniture polish; the dust and dirt of the past season were forever wiped away.

About an hour later the players arrived. It was time to get under way.

"Welcome, guys" were the words Coach Gary Gaines used to begin the 1988 season, and fifty-five boys dressed in identical gray shirts and gray shorts, sitting on identical wooden benches, stared into his eyes. They listened, or at least tried to. Winning a state championship. Making All-State and gaining a place on the Permian Wall of Fame. Going off after the season to Nebraska, or Arkansas, or Texas. Whatever they fantasized about, it all seemed possible that day.

Gaines's quiet words washed over the room, and in hundreds of other Texas towns celebrating the start of football practice that August day there were similar sounds of intimacy and welcome, to the eastern edge of the state in Marshall, to the northern edge in Wichita Falls, to the southern edge in McAllen, to the western edge in El Paso. They were Gaines's words, but they could have come from any high school coach renewing the ritual of sport, the ritual of high school football.

> *"There's twelve hundred boys in Permian High School. You divide that by three and there's four hundred in every class. You guys are a very special breed. There are guys back there that are every bit as good as you are. But they were not able to stick it out for whatever reason. Football's not for everybody. But you guys are special.*
>
> *"We want you all to carry the torch in the eight-eight season. It's got to mean somethin' really special to you. You guys have dreamt about this for many years, to be a part of this team, some of you since you were knee-high. Work hard, guys, and pay the price. Be proud you're a part of this program. Keep up the tradition that was started many years ago."*

That tradition was enshrined on a wall of the field house, where virtually every player who had made All-State during the past twenty-nine years was carefully immortalized within the dimensions of a four-by-six-inch picture frame. It was enshrined in the proclamation from the city council that hung on a bulletin board, honoring one of Permian's state championship teams. It was enshrined in the black carpet, and the black-and-white cabinets, and the black rug in the shape of a panther. It was enshrined in the county library, where the 235-page history that had been written about Permian football was more detailed than any of the histories about the town itself.

Of all the legends of Odessa, that of high school football was the most enduring. It had a deep and abiding sense of place and history, so unlike the town, where not even the origin of the name itself could be vouched for with any confidence.

Odessa . . .

There had been no reason for its original existence. It owed its beginnings to a fine blend of Yankee ingenuity and hucksterism, its selling the first primordial example of the Home Shopping Network.

It was invented in the 1880s by a group of men from Zanesville, Ohio, who saw a great opportunity to make money if only they could figure out some way to get people there, to somehow induce them into thinking that the land bore bountiful secrets, this gaping land that filled the heart with far more sorrow than it ever did encouragement, stretching without a curve except for the undulating trough off the caprock where the once-great herds of buffalo had grazed for water. What Odessa lacked, and one look informed the most charitable eye that it lacked a fantastic amount, the speculators from Ohio would make up for on the strength of their own imagination. With fourteen thousand arid acres to sell, truth in advertising was not something to dwell over.

The Zanesville syndicate looked at all the best natural qualities of the country and decided to attribute them to Odessa whether they were there or not. Through brochures and pamphlets it conjured up a place with weather as wonderful as Southern California's and soil as fertile as that of the finest acre of farmland in Kansas or Iowa.

"Splendid cities will spring up all along the railroads that traverse the plains, and immense fortunes will be made there in a few years, in land business ventures, you will see the most remarkable emigration to that section that has occurred since the days when the discovery of gold sent wealth-seekers by thousands into Colorado," Henry Thatcher boldly forecast in the *Chillicothe Leader* in 1886.

If that wasn't enough to make someone leave southern Ohio,

Odessa was also promoted as a utopian health spa with a $12,000 college and a public library, and a ban on alcohol. Those suffering from consumption, bronchitis, malaria, kidney, bladder, or prostate problems, asthma, or rheumatism would be welcomed with open arms, according to a promotional pamphlet.

Those who were failures, near death, didn't like working, bad with money, or cheap politicians were specifically not welcome, the same pamphlet said. The statement appeared to exclude many of the people who might have been interested in such a place.

The great Odessa land auction took place on May 19, 1886. The Zanesvile boys, careful to the last drop, actually held it 350 miles to the east, in Dallas. Historical accounts of Odessa do not accurately indicate how many settlers bought lots. But about ten families, German Methodists from western Pennsylvania around Pittsburgh, hoping to realize the utopian community so grandly talked about, did arrive.

They tried to fit in with the ranchers and cowboys who were already there, but it was not a good match. The Methodists found the ranchers and the cowboys beyond saving. The ranchers and the cowboys found that the Methodists did nothing but yell at them all the time.

As part of its commitment, the syndicate went ahead and built a college for the Methodists. It was constructed around 1889 but burned mysteriously three years later. Some said the college was set afire by cowboys who disliked being told by the Methodists that they could not drink, particularly in a place that cried out daily for alcohol. Others said it was burned by a contingent of jealous citizens from Midland because the Odessa college was competing with a similar institution that the sister city had built. Finally, there were those who said the college was burned down simply because it was something the damn Yankees had built the natives of the city when no one had asked for it. Given the later attitudes of Odessa, all these theories are probably true. A hospital was also built, but most settlers ignored it and instead relied on such tried-and-true home remedies as cactus juice and a wrap of cabbage leaves for the chills, a plaster made out of fresh cow manure for sprains, and buzzard grease for measles.

Contrary to all the boasts of the land's fertility, it was virtually impossible to farm anything because of the difficulty of getting water. Instead, Odessa eked out a living from the livestock trade, all dreams of utopia gone forever when the town's first sheriff, Elias Dawson, decided that the ban on alcohol constituted cruel and unusual punishment and became the proprietor, along with his brother, of the town's first saloon.

The first murder in Odessa occurred late in the nineteenth century when a cowboy rode into a water-drilling camp one afternoon and demanded something to eat from the cook. The cook, described as a "chinaman," refused, so the cowboy promptly shot him. He was taken to San Angelo and put on trial, but the judge freed him on the grounds that there were no laws on the books making it illegal to kill a Chinaman.

For more casual entertainment, a couple of cowboys gathered up all the cats they could find one day, tied sacks of dried beans to their tails, and then set them loose downtown to scare the daylights out of the horses and the citizens milling about. In later times it was hard not to get caught up in the frivolity of those great practical jokers, the Wilson brothers, whose professional standing as doctors didn't mean they were above grabbing unsuspecting townsfolk into the barbershop and shaving their heads.

By 1900, Odessa had only 381 residents. By 1910 the population had increased to 1,178. Most of those inhabitants depended on ranching, but various droughts made survival almost impossible because of the lack of grazing land for cattle. The ranchers became so poor they could not afford to buy feed, and many cattle were just rounded up and shot to death so the stronger ones could have what little grass was left.

Nothing about living in Odessa was easy. Finding a scrubby tree that could barely serve as a Christmas tree took two days. Even dealings with cattle rustlers and horse thieves had to be compromised; they were shot instead of hanged because there weren't any trees tall enough from which to let them swing.

A flu epidemic hit in 1919, filling up the only funeral home in town, which was part of the hardware store. It so severely overran the town that there weren't enough men well enough to dig the graves of those who had died. Medical care was at best a kind of potluck affair. The one doctor who settled in Odessa during this period, Emmet V. Headlee, used the dining room of his home as an operating room. He performed the operations while his wife administered the anesthetic.

By 1920 the population had dropped back down to 760, and it was hard to believe that Odessa would survive. But ironically, the Zanesville elite was right in its fanciful prediction that Odessa was bubbling with a bounty of riches.

Unknown to anyone when it was founded, the town was sitting in the midst of the Permian Basin, a geologic formation so lush it would ultimately produce roughly 20 percent of the nation's oil and gas. With major oil discoveries in West Texas in the early and mid-twenties, the boom was on, and Odessa was only too eager to embrace the characteristics that distinguished other Texas boom towns of the period: wild overcrowding, lawlessness, prostitution, chronic diarrhea, bad water, streets that were so deep in mud that teams of oxen had to be called in to pull the oil field machinery, and a rat problem so severe that the local theater put out a rat bounty and would let you in free if you produced twelve rat tails.

Odessa established itself as a distribution point for oil field equipment and experienced more growth in a month than it had in ten years, inundated by men who were called simply boomers. They came into town once a week, their skin scummy and stinking and blackened from oil and caked-on dirt, to get a bath and a shave at the barbershop. Young children ogled at them when they appeared because it was unimaginable, even by the standards of children, to find anyone as dirty as these men were.

From 1926 on, Odessa became forever enmeshed in the cycles of the boom-and-bust oil town. It made for a unique kind of schizophrenia, the highs of the boom years like a drug-induced euphoria followed by the lows of the bust and the realization that everything you had made during the boom had just been lost, followed again by the euphoria of boom years, followed again by the depression of another bust, followed by another boom and yet another bust, followed by a special prayer to the Lord, which eventually showed up on bumper stickers of pickups in the eighties, for one more boom with a vow "not to piss this one away."

There was a small nucleus of people who settled here and worked here and cared about the future of the town, who thought about convention centers and pleasant downtown shopping and all the other traditional American mainstays. But basically it became a transient town, a place to come to and make money when the boom was on and then get as far away from as possible with the inevitable setting in of the bust. If a man or woman wasn't making money, there wasn't much reason to stay.

Hub Heap, who came out here in 1939 and later started a successful oil field supply company, remembered well the single event that embodied his early days in Odessa. It was a torrent of sand, looking like a rain cloud, that came in from the northwest and turned the place so dark in the afternoon light that the street lamps suddenly started glowing. Nothing escaped the hideousness of that sand. It crept in everywhere, underneath the rafters, inside the walls, like an endless army of tiny ants, covering him, suffocating him, pushing down into his lungs, blinding his eyes, and that night he had no choice but to sleep with a wet towel over his face just so he could breathe.

Odessa also became tough and quick-fisted, filled with men

who hardly needed a high school diploma, much less a college one, to become roughnecks and tool pushers on an oil rig. They spent a lot of time in trucks traveling to remote corners of the earth to put in a string of drill pipe, and when they went home to Odessa to unwind they did not believe in leisurely drinking or witty repartee. More often than not, they did not believe in conversation, their dispositions reflecting the rough, atonal quality of the land, which after the droughts consisted mostly of the gnarled limbs of low-lying mesquite bushes. Outside of the oil business, the weather (which almost never changed), and high school football, there wasn't a hell of a lot to talk about.

J. D. Cone, when he came here from Oklahoma in 1948 to become a family practitioner, went on house calls with a thirty-eight pistol stuck into his belt after the sheriff told him it was always a good idea to be armed in case someone got a little ornery or disagreed with the diagnosis. Right after he arrived, he went with a friend to the notorious Ace of Clubs. Everything was fine until mid-evening, Cone remembers, when it was time for the nightly revue and beer bottles started flying through the air. No one except Cone thought much about it. It did reinforce for him his initial impression of Odessa, when all he could see as he drove into town the first time was the red cast of the clouds from a winter storm. At night there was the equally eerie sight of the gas flares, huge fissures of fire coming from the oil rigs where natural gas, an unwanted burden back then, was being burned off.

"This must not be planet earth," Cone told his partner. "This must be hell."

But it wasn't. It was just Odessa.

During the next boom period in the seventies and eighties, Odessa made a telltale leap into the twentieth century. A branch of the University of Texas was built and a new suburban-style mall opened, but the hearty, hair-trigger temperament of the place still remained intact. Differences of opinion were still sometimes settled by vengeful retribution, resulting in the kinds of brutal, visceral crimes that were supposed to take place in cities of several million, not in one of barely over a hundred thousand. Not surprisingly, most of these grisly killings occurred during the height of the boom, when money and madness overran much of the town.

In 1982, the thirty-seven murders that took place inside Ector County gave Odessa the distinction of having the highest murder rate in the country. Most agreed that was a pretty high number, but mention of gun control was as popular as a suggestion to change the Ten Commandments.

A year later, Odessa made national news again when someone made the fateful mistake of accusing an escaped convict from Alabama named Leamon Ray Price of cheating in a high-stakes poker game. Price, apparently insulted by such a charge, went to the bathroom and then came out shooting with his thirty-eight. He barricaded himself behind a bookcase while the players he was trying to kill hid under the poker table. By the time Odessa police detective Jerry Smith got there the place looked like something out of the Wild West, an old-fashioned shoot-out at the La Casita apartment complex with poker chips and cards and bullet holes all over the dining room. Two men were dead and two wounded when Price made his escape. His fatal error came when he tried to break into a house across the street. The startled owner, hearing the commotion, did what he thought was only appropriate: he took out *his* gun and shot Price dead.

It was incidents such as these that gave Odessa its legacy.

In 1987, *Money* magazine ranked it as the fifth worst city to live in in the country out of three hundred. A year later *Psychology Today*, in a ranking of the most stressful cities in the country based on rates of alcoholism, crime, suicide, and divorce, placed Odessa seventh out of 286 metropolitan areas, worse than New York and Detroit and Philadelphia and Houston. Molly Ivins, a columnist for the *Dallas Times Herald*, described Odessa as an "armpit," which, as the *Odessa American* pointed out, was actually quite a few rungs up from its usual anatomical comparison with a rectum. And there was the description in Larry McMurtry's *Texasville*, which simply called Odessa the "worst town on earth."

But none of that seemed to matter. Oil promised money through work on drilling rigs and frac crews and acidizing units, and it meant people were willing to live here whatever the deprivation. What pride they had in Odessa came from their very survival in a place they openly admitted was physically wretched.

Whether it was true or not, most people said they had first come out here during a sandstorm, meaning their first taste of Odessa had literally been a mouthful of gritty sand. They carried that mouthful with them forever, rolling it around with their tongues every now and then, never forgetting the dry grit of it. It reminded them of what they had been through to forge a life and a community and that they had a right to be proud of their accomplishments.

It was still a place that seemed on the edge of the frontier, a paradoxical mixture of the Old South and the Wild West, friendly to a fault but fiercely independent, God-fearing and propped up by the Baptist beliefs in family and flag but hell-raising, spiced with the edge of violence but naive and thoroughly unpretentious.

It was a place where neighbor loved helping neighbor, based on a long-standing tradition that ranchers always left their homes unlocked because you never knew who might need to borrow something or cook a meal. But it was a place also based on the principle that no one should ever be told what to do by anyone, that the best government of all was no government at all, which is why most citizens hated welfare, thought Michael Dukakis, beyond having the irreversible character flaw of being a Democrat, was the biggest damn fool ever to enter politics, considered Lyndon Johnson an egocentric buffoon responsible for the boondoggle of the 1964 Civil Rights Act, and saw the federal government's effort to integrate the Odessa schools in the fifties and sixties and seventies and eighties not as social progress but as outrageous harassment.

At times Odessa had the feel of lingering sadness that many isolated places have, a sense of the world orbiting around it at dizzying speed while it stood stuck in time—350 miles from Dallas to the east, 300 miles from El Paso to the west, 300 miles from the rest of the world—still fixed in an era in which it was inappropriate for high school girls to be smarter than their boyfriends, in which kids spent their Saturday nights making the endless circles of the drag in their cars along the wide swathes of Forty-second Street and Andrews Highway, in which teenage honor was measured not by how much cocaine you snorted, but by how much beer you drank.

But Odessa also evoked the kind of America that Ronald Reagan always seemed to have in mind during his presidency, a place still rooted in the sweet nostalgia of the fifties— unsophisticated, basic, raw—a place where anybody could be somebody, a place still clinging to all the tenets of the American Dream, however wobbly they had become.

In the summer twilight, against the backdrop of the enormous sky where braids of orange and purple and red and blue as delicately hued as a butterfly wing stretched into eternity, young girls with ponytails and freckles went up and down neighborhood streets on their roller skates. As the cool breeze of night set in, neighboring families pulled up plastic lawn chairs to conduct "chair committee" and casually meander over the day's events without rancor or argument or constant one-upmanship. On other nights, parents gently roused their children from bed near the stroke of midnight so they could sit together by the garage to watch a thunderstorm roll in from Big Spring, gliding across the sky with its shimmering madness, those angular fingers of light cutting through the night in a spectacle almost as exciting as a Permian High School football game.

There were many people in Odessa who, after the initial

33

shock, had slowly fallen in love with the town. They found something endearing about it, something tender; it was the scorned mutt that no one else wanted. They had come to grips with the numbing vacantness of the surroundings, broken only by the black horses' heads of oil pumpjacks moving up and down with maniacal monotony through heat and wind and dust and economic ruin.

There were also those who had grown weary of it and the oft-repeated phrase that what made it special was the quality of its people. "Odessa has an unspeakable ability to bullshit itself," said Warren Burnett, a loquacious, liberal-minded lawyer who after roughly thirty years had fled the place like a refugee for the coastal waters near Houston. "Nothing could be sillier than we got good people here. We got the same cross-section of ass-holes as anywhere."

There were those who found it insufferably racist and those who didn't find it racist at all, but used the word *nigger* as effortlessly as one would sprinkle salt on a slab of rib eye and worried about the Mexicans who seemed to be overtaking the place. There were those who had been made rich by it, and many more who had gone broke from it in recent times. But they seemed gratified, as Mayor Don Carter, who was one of those to go big-time belly up, put it, to have taken a "chance in the free enterprise market."

There were a few who found its conservatism maddening and dangerous and many more who found it the essence of what America should be, an America built on strength and the spirit of individualism, not an America built on handouts and food stamps. There were those who found solace in the strong doses of religion poured out every Wednesday evening and Sunday morning by its sixty-two Baptist churches, nineteen Church of Christ churches, twelve Assembly of God churches, eleven Methodist churches, seven Catholic churches, and five Pentecostal churches. And there were those like Burnett, who saw religion in Odessa used not to reinforce religious beliefs at all but as an excuse for people to come together and be made comfortable with their own social beliefs in racial and gender bigotry.

Across the country there were thousands of places just like it, places that were not only isolated but insulated, places that had gone through the growing pains of America without anyone paying attention, places that existed as islands unto themselves with no link to the great cities except that they all sang the same national anthem to the same flag at sporting events. They were the kind of places that you saw from a plane on a clear night if you happened to look out the window, a concentration of little beaded dots breaking up the empty landscape with several veins leading in and out, and then bleak emptiness once again.

It was a view that every traveler had seen a million times before, and maybe if you were a passenger on a plane bisecting the night, you looked down and saw those lights and wondered what it would be like to live in an Odessa, to inhabit one of those infinitesimal dots, to be in a place that seemed so painfully far away from everything, so completely out of the mainstream of life. Perhaps you wondered what values people held on to in a place like that, what they cared about. Or perhaps you went back to your book, eager to get as far away as possible from that yawning maw that seemed so unimaginable, so utterly unimportant.

In the absence of a shimmering skyline, the Odessas of the country had all found something similar in which to place their faith. In Indiana, it was the plink-plink-plink of a ball on a parquet floor. In Minnesota, it was the swoosh of skates on the ice. In Ohio and Pennsylvania and Alabama and Georgia and Texas and dozens of other states, it was the weekly event simply known as Friday Night.

From the twenties through the eighties, whatever else there hadn't been in Odessa, there had always been high school football.

In 1927, as story after story in the *Odessa News* heralded new strikes in the oil field, the only non-oil-related activity that made the front page was the exploits of the Odessa High Yellowjackets. In 1946, when the population of Ector County was about thirty thousand, old Fly Field was routinely crammed with thirteen thousand five hundred fans, many of whom saw nothing odd about waiting in line all night to get tickets. Odessa High won the state championship that year, which became one of those events that was remembered in the psyche of the town forever, as indelible as Neil Armstrong landing on the moon. Where were you the moment the Bronchos won the championship? Everyone knew.

In the sixties and seventies and eighties, when the legacy of high school football in Odessa transferred from Odessa High to Permian High, instead of just waiting all night for tickets, people sometimes waited two days. Gaines and the other Permian coaches were all too aware of the role that high school football occupied in Odessa, how it had become central to the psyche of thousands who lived there. Expectations were high every year and in 1988, if it was possible, they were even higher than usual. The team had an incredible array of talent, the devout boosters whispered, the best of any Permian team in a decade. *Winchell back at quarterback . . . Miles back at fullback . . . Chavez back at tight end . . . Brown back at flanker . . . Hill back at split end . . .* They listed off the names as if they were talking about the star-studded cast of a movie spectacular, and they frankly didn't see how Permian could miss a trip to State this season.

They weren't the only ones to think so. The Associated Press, making its predictions for the season, had picked Permian to win it all. "Although Aldine, Sugar Land Willowridge, Hurst Bell, San Antonio Clark, and Houston Yates are gaining big support, the guess here [is] that there will be a big surprise from out west," the article said. "Remember Odessa Permian? The Panthers and their legendary 'Mojo Magic' always contend for the title."

To the boosters, that story was music to their ears, further confirmation that when the middle of December rolled around they would be on their way to Texas Stadium for the state

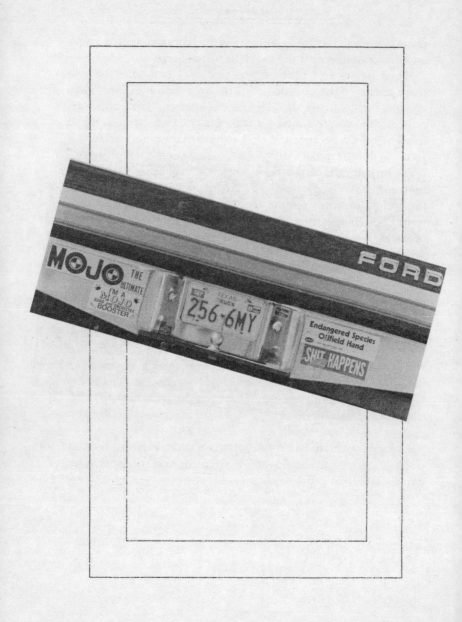

championship. To Gaines, it only created more room for anger and disappointment if the team didn't get there.

When he spoke to the players that very first time, he told them to ignore the outside pressure that would inevitably swirl around them during the thick of the season. "I'm gonna get criticism and you're gonna get criticism," he said. "It don't mean a hill of beans, because the only people that matter are in this room. It doesn't make a difference, except for the people here."

In the solitude of the field house on that beautiful August morning, it was hard to believe that anyone else did matter. But the feeling was only temporary. In just about a week the team would be officially unveiled to the public. And from that moment on, it would become the property of those so desperately devoted to it.

There were certain events in Odessa that had become time-honored traditions, essential elements in the biological clock of the town. There was the annual downtown Christmas tree—lighting ceremony sponsored by one of the banks, when people gathered on bleachers in front of the city hall and sipped free hot chocolate while waiting for Santa to arrive on a flatbed truck. There was the biennial Oil Show, which out-of-town hookers always marked on their calendars in red because of the tantalizing possibility of having thousands of out-of-towners stuck in Odessa for what might possibly be the three longest days of their lives.

And, of course, in late August, there was the Permian booster club's Watermelon Feed, when excitement and madness went quickly into high gear.

CHAPTER 2

The
Watermelon
Feed

THE FAITHFUL SAT ON LITTLE STOOLS OF ORANGE AND BLUE under the merciless lights of the high school cafeteria, but the Spartan setting didn't bother them a bit. Had the Watermelon Feed been held inside the county jail, or on a sinking ship, or on the side of a craggy mountain, they would still have flocked to attend.

Outside, the August night was sweetly cool and serene with just a wisp of West Texas wind. Inside there was a teeming sense of excitement, and also relief, for the waiting was basically over; there would be no more sighs of longing, no more awkward groping to fill up the empty spaces of time with golf games and thoroughly unsatisfying talk about baseball. Tonight, as in a beauty contest, the boys of Permian would come before the crowd one by one so they could be checked out and introduced. And after that, in less than two weeks, would come the glorious start of the season on the first Friday night in September.

Each of those little stools in each of those rows, about four hundred seats in all, was taken well before the scheduled starting time of seven-thirty. It didn't take long before the open area at the back of the room had filled up with several hundred other people who hardly minded standing as long as they were inside. Finally it got so crowded that those who came didn't even bother to try to get in, but stayed in the hallway and watched with their faces pressed up against a long window, like

38

out-of-luck shoppers peering into the bedlam of a once-in-a-lifetime sale.

A concession stand in the corner did a brisk business in hats and T-shirts and jackets and flags. Another one sold decals and little good-luck charms. And each devotee, as he or she walked in, carried a special program about as thick as a city phone book.

Many had their kids with them, for it was clear they thought it was important for children to see this spectacle at a young age so they could begin to understand what it all meant. A little boy wore a T-shirt that said HOLD ON, MOJO, I'M A COMIN'. And another had a towel and a flag emblazoned with the MOJO rallying cry.

People had come dressed up for the event. They weren't in black tie or anything outlandish like that, but just in black—black caps, black shirts, black pants, black jackets. Many others went a step further. They had black key chains and black checkbook covers. If you went to their homes you might find black toilet seats, or black seat cushions, or black phone book covers, or black paper plates, or black clocks, or black felt on their pool tables. To get to and from those homes, they might drive cars with brake lights in the back windows that lit up with the word MOJO every time they touched the pedals. And next to them in those cars might be handmade black purses in the shape of a football with the word MOJO inscribed on them in white. Or the less lavish MOJO handbags, sold exclusively at J. C. Penney ("Our Permian Panther leather, two-toned bag has an understated designer look" extolled the newspaper advertisement), which were regularly $24.99, but were sometimes on sale for $8.99.

There were about eight hundred persons crammed into the Permian High School cafeteria by the time the Watermelon Feed began. Almost all of those in the crowd were white, and their faces had a certain flattened, nonfrilled look, like the land in which they lived. The women tended to be more handsome than pretty with high, articulated cheekbones. The men tended to be taut and well built regardless of age, dressed in beige or gray pants the color of the plains and cowboy boots that were worn for function.

The starkness of the room seemed to heighten the natural warmth of the occasion. About the only items on the white walls were two announcements for Permian students on long strips of computer paper that had nothing to do with the Watermelon Feed, but still embodied the intrinsic spirit of the event.

The one on top read YOU MUST HAVE A STUDENT I.D. TO BE ADMITTED TO FOOTBALL GAMES WITH STUDENT TICKETS. The one underneath it read YOU MUST HAVE A STUDENT I.D. CARD TO CHECK OUT A LIBRARY BOOK.

The fans clutched in their hands the 1988 Permian football yearbook, published annually by the booster club to help generate funds for the program. It ran 224 pages, had 513 individual advertisements, and raised $20,000. Virtually every lawyer, doctor, insurance firm, car dealer, restaurant, and oil field supply business in town had taken out an ad, both as a show of support for Permian football and, perhaps, as a form of protection. The Ector County sheriff had taken out an ad. So had the Ector County Democratic party, just in case there were a few closet Democrats who, under conditions similar to those offered a Mafia informant in the witness protection program, might be willing to divulge their political persuasion.

The grand dukes of Permian, men in their fifties and sixties who had become as dependent on the Panthers as they were on their jobs and children and wives and treated the memory of each game as a crystal prism that looked more beautiful and intricate every time it was lifted to the light, were there in full force, of course.

Friday nights under a full moon that filled the black satin sky with a light as soft and delicate as the flickering of a candle. The road trips to Irving and Abilene and San Angelo in that endless caravan of RVs and Suburbans and plain old sedans rising forth so proudly from the bowels of West Texas. The family reunion atmosphere of each practice where they knew everyone and everyone knew them. They could hardly wait.

"I have to have something to look forward to, or life is just a blah" was the way Jim Lewallen, a retired grocery chain supervisor, had put it earlier in the month as he sipped on an iced tea over at Grandy's and counted off the days until the beginning of practice. "That football is just something that keeps me goin'. You know the kids' moves, you know 'em personally. It's just like your own kids," said Lewallen, built solidly with a fine shock of gray hair, who didn't look right unless he had a thick wad of tobacco chew nestled inside the deepness of his cheeks as sweetly as a squirrel burrows a nut away in its mouth. "Mojo football, it helps you survive all this sand, the wind, the heat. I wouldn't live any other place."

Bob Rutherford, who was sitting next to him in the booth and spent his days in the herculean task of trying to sell real estate in Odessa, felt the same stirrings. "It's just a part of our lives. It's just something that you're involved in. It's just like going to church or something like that. It's just what you do."

They wouldn't have missed the Watermelon Feed for the world. Neither would Ken Scates, a gentle man with a soft sliver of a voice who had been to the very first Permian practice in the fall of 1959, when the school opened. Since that time he had missed few practices, and it went without saying that he hadn't missed any games, except for the time he had heart by-pass surgery in Houston. But even then he had done what he could to keep informed. After his surgery, he had resisted taking painkillers so he would be conscious for the phone calls from his son-in-law updating him every quarter on the score of the Permian–Midland Lee game. When he learned that Permian had the game safely in hand, he then took his medicine.

More toward the back of the room was Brad Allen, president of the Permian booster club in the early eighties when billionaire businessman H. Ross Perot had made his pitch for educational reform in the state. Perot had routinely rubbed shoulders with the most powerful men in the world—presidents, senators, heads of state, chief executive officers of Fortune 500 companies. But the machinations behind building up multi-million-dollar companies or working up a deal to get the hostages out of Iran proved to be mere trifles in comparison to what happened when Perot threatened the sanctity of football in Odessa.

The dominance of football in Texas high schools had become the focus of raging debate all over the state in 1983. The governor of Texas, Mark White, appointed Perot to head a committee on educational reform. In pointing to school systems he thought were skewed in favor of extracurricular activities, Perot took particular aim at Odessa.

On ABC's "Nightline," he called Permian fans "football crazy," and during the show it was pointed out that a $5.6 million high school football stadium had been built in Odessa in 1982. The stadium included a sunken artificial-surface field eighteen feet below ground level, a two-story press box with VIP seating for school board members and other dignitaries, poured concrete seating for 19,032, and a full-time caretaker who lived in a house on the premises.

"He made it look like we were a bunch of West Texas hicks, fanatics," said Allen of Perot. The stadium "was something the community took a lot of pride in and he went on television and said you're a bunch of idiots for building it." Most of the money for the stadium had come from a voter-approved bond issue.

The war against Perot escalated quickly. The booster club geared up a letter-writing campaign to him, state legislators, and the governor. Nearly a thousand letters were sent in protest of Perot's condemnation of Odessa. Some of the ones to him were addressed "Dear Idiot" or something worse than that, and they not so gently told him to mind his own damn business and not disturb a way of life that had worked and thrived for years and brought the town a joy it could never have experienced anywhere else.

"It's our money," said Allen of the funds that were used to build the stadium. "If we choose to put it into a football program, and the graduates from our high schools are at or above the state level of standards, then screw you, leave us alone." At one point Perot, believing his motives had been misinterpreted and hoping to convince people that improving education in Texas was not a mortal sin, contemplated coming to Odessa to speak. But he decided against it, to the relief of some who thought he might be physically harmed if he did.

"There are so few other things we can look at with pride," said Allen. "We don't have a large university that has thirty or forty thousand students in it. We don't have the art museum that some communities have and are world-renowned. When somebody talks about West Texas, they talk about football.

"There is nothing to replace it. It's an integral part of what made the community strong. You take it away and it's almost like you strip the identity of the people."

The pull of it seemed irresistible. Allen's stepson, Phillip, had been a fullback on the 1980 Permian team that won the state championship. Allen readily admitted that Phillip was not a gifted athlete, but he had the fire and desire that came innately in a town that drank as deeply from the chalice of high school football as Odessa.

Allen knew Phillip was something special in eighth grade, when he had broken his arm during the first defensive series of a game. Rather than come out, he managed to set it in the defensive huddle and played both ways the entire first half. By that time the arm had swelled up considerably, to the point that the forearm pads he wore had to be cut off, and unwillingly he went to the hospital. Allen said he was not proud of the incident, but he told the story freely, for it showed that his son had the ingredients to wear the black and white.

And certainly he wasn't the only one to have learned the much-admired lesson of no pain, no gain. In seasons past playing for Permian had involved other sacrifices. It had meant the loss of a testicle to a sophomore player when no one bothered to make sure he was thoroughly examined after he had injured his groin several hours earlier during an away game. Subsequently the testicle swelled up to the size of a grapefruit, and by the time the doctor saw him it was too late; it had to be removed. His mother was livid at what had happened, but the player pleaded with her not to push it because he feared it might interfere with his career at Permian and be held against him. He lost the testicle but he did make All-State.

In seasons past, playing for Permian had meant routinely vomiting during the grueling off-season workouts inside the hot and sweaty weight room. It had meant playing with a broken ankle that wasn't x-rayed because, if it had been known that it was broken, the player would have had to sit out the next game. It had meant playing with broken hands. It had meant a shot of novocaine during halftime to mask the pain of a deep ankle sprain or a hip pointer. It had meant popping painkillers and getting shots of Valium.

But few in the community blanched at any of these things or even questioned them. Because of such an attitude, Permian had established itself as perhaps the most successful football dynasty in the country—pro, college, or high school. Few brands of sport were more competitive than Class AAAAA Texas high school football, the division for the biggest schools in the state.

Odessa was hardly the only town that nurtured football and cherished it and went crazy over it. But no one came close to matching the performance of Permian. Since 1964 it had won four state championships, been to the state finals a record eight times, and made the playoffs fifteen times. Its worst record in any season over that time span had been seven and two, and its winning percentage overall, .825, was by far the best of any team in the entire state in the modern era of the game dating back to 1951.

All this wasn't accomplished with kids who weighed 250 pounds and were automatic major-college prospects, but with kids who often weighed 160 or 170 or even less. They had no special athletic prowess. They weren't especially fast or especially strong. But they were fearless and relentlessly coached and from the time they were able to walk they had only one certain goal in their lives in Odessa, Texas. Whatever it took, they would play for Permian.

Behind the rows of stools stood the stars of the show, the members of the 1988 Permian Panther high school football team. Dressed in their black game jerseys, they laughed and teased one another like privileged children of royalty.

Directly in front of them, dressed in white jerseys and forming a little protective phalanx, were the Pepettes, a select group of senior girls who made up the school spirit squad. The Pepettes supported all teams, but it was the football team they supported most. The number on the white jersey each girl wore corresponded to that of the player she had been assigned for the football season. With that assignment came various time-honored responsibilities.

As part of the tradition, each Pepette brought some type of sweet for her player every week before the game. She didn't necessarily have to make something from scratch, but there was indirect pressure to because of not-so-private grousing from players who tired quickly of bags of candy and not so discreetly let it be known that they much preferred something fresh-baked. If she had to buy something store-bought, it might as well be beer, and at least one player was able to negotiate such an arrangement with his Pepette during the season. Instead of getting a bag of cookies, he got a six-pack of beer.

In addition, each Pepette also had to make a large sign for her player that went in his front yard and stayed there the entire season as a notice to the community that he played football for Permian. Previously the making of these yard signs, which looked like miniature Broadway marquees, had become quite competitive. Some of the Pepettes spent as much as $100 of their own money to make an individual sign, decorating it with twinkling lights and other attention-getting devices. It became a rather serious game of can-you-top-this, and finally a dictum was handed down that all the signs must be made the same way, without any neon.

A Pepette also had responsibility for making smaller posters, which went up in the school halls at the beginning of each week and were transferred to the gym for the mandatory Friday morning pep rally. The making of these signs could be quite laborious as well, and one Pepette during the season broke down in tears because she had had to stay up until the wee hours of the morning trying to keep up with the other Pepettes and make a fancy hall sign that her player never even thanked her for.

These were the basic Pepette requirements, but some girls went beyond in their show of spirit.

They might embroider the map of Texas on towels and then spell out MOJO in the borders. Or they might make MOJO pillowcases that the players could take with them during road trips. Or they might place their fresh-baked cookies in tins elaborately decorated in the Permian colors of black and white. In previous years Pepettes had made scrapbooks for their players, including one with the cover made of lacquered wood and modeled on Disney's *Jungle Book*. The book had clippings, cut out in ninety-degree angles as square and true as in an architectural rendering, of every story written about the Permian team that year. It also had beautiful illustrations and captions that tried to capture what it meant to be a Pepette.

"The countryside was filled with loyal and happy subjects serving their chosen panther," said a caption in a chapter entitled "Joy," and next to it was a picture of a little girl with flowers in her hand going up to a panther, the Permian mascot, roaring under a tree.

The Watermelon Feed began with a prayer by one of the pastors at Temple Baptist Church, the biggest church in Odessa. The sign in front of the church in previous years had con-

tained such inspirational messages as HOW DO YOU SPELL DE-
FENSE? MOJO.

"We thank you for the joy the athletes bring to our hearts
and lives," the pastor said.

Following the prayer, a video was shown of highlights from
the past season in 1987. Since the team had gone to the semifinals of the state playoffs before losing to the eventual champion, Plano, it had been considered not a great year but at least
a pretty good one.

There were sporadic yells of MOJO! but the crowd in the cafeteria didn't become animated until the screen showed running
back Shawn Crow breaking tackle after tackle in the quarterfinal playoff game against Arlington.

At one point Permian trailed in the game 28–7. But then the
team put on a miraculous comeback, rallying around the example of one player who got in his stance, vomited through his
helmet because he had just taken a hit in the stomach, and then
took his defender down with a crushing block. The performance of Crow was also inspiring. Late in the fourth quarter
he scored his fourth touchdown of the game to make it 35–33,
and then he scored the two-point conversion to tie it up even
though everyone in the stadium knew he was going to get the
ball. The game ultimately ended in a 35–35 tie, and Permian
advanced to the semifinals of the playoffs based on a tiebreaker
rule that provided that the team with more first downs advance
to the next round.

Everyone seemed mesmerized as they watched Crow on
a small screen in the front of the cafeteria, the memories of
it, the absolute magic of it, suddenly flooding back. The oil
economy could go to hell. The country could go to hell. But,
thanks to Shawn Crow, never, ever Permian football.

It would be hard anywhere in sports to find athletic feats
more courageous than his. On play after play, each like a dizzying rerun, he had headed down the sidelines, running so low
to the ground that it sometimes seemed as if his helmet skidded

the turf, retaining remarkable balance, sending would-be tacklers flying and dragging others for four or five yards before finally going down. It was the kind of performance that only occurred in high school, for no adult would have had the willingness to sacrifice his body as Shawn Crow had done that night, for his family and his team and his town. It was also a moment, a time in his life, that seemed impossible to repeat.

"If that won't get you excited, I can't believe you *can* get excited," said booster club president Doug Hendrick.

When the highlight film showed Crow scoring the two-point conversion, the crowd rose to its feet and gave the former hero a standing ovation. He was in the audience and gave no reaction, as if he was slightly embarrassed and wished he were someplace else.

He was supposed to have been at Texas Christian University in Fort Worth, the only Division I school that had actively recruited him after a senior season in which he gained 2,288 yards and made first team All-State. But during the high school all-star football game in July at the Astrodome between players from the north regions of Texas and ones from the south, he had felt an intense pain in his back.

No one thought it was serious, particularly since he had a reputation for whimpering, and one coach at Permian who knew Crow well said that the best way to "shut him up" was just to give him the ball. "I can't run, man," he told Tim O'Connell, the Permian trainer who was nicknamed "Trapper" and was the trainer [for the north] during the all-star game. Crow's voice, high-pitched and laced with pain, made him sound almost scared.

"Why don't you just try," said Trapper, who examined him and could find no discernible injury.

Crow continued to play in the game, biting down on his mouthpiece as hard as he could on each play to fight through the pain. After the game it turned out that Crow had not been whimpering. He was diagnosed with a herniated disc, and the TCU coaches told him not to come to school until January, after he had had a chance to rehabilitate. There was no point in coming to school just to go to class.

Injuries were nothing new to Crow. In seventh grade he had broken his leg in practice. In eighth grade he had torn ligaments in his thumb. In ninth grade his arm, already injured from an incident involving an all-terrain vehicle, had been shattered when he tried to throw a block. Off the field he was an endearing, friendly kid, quiet and shy and respectful. On the field, his toughness was almost incomprehensible; his head, as one teammate put it, seemed to be "made of steel." But it was hard not to wonder if his body could endure the physical punishment of the game.

The standing ovation that he received at the Watermelon Feed wasn't particularly surprising. Just as he was used to football injuries, he was also used to lavish attention, as was every former Permian player who had once been ordained a star. So many people had come up to him when he was a senior that he couldn't keep track of their names, and it seemed weird how much they knew about him when he knew absolutely nothing about them. During the playoffs, when he had suffered a bruise on his thigh that looked as if it might keep him out of the game the following week, a hundred people called the trainer's office to ask about his condition. It got to the point that Trapper, half-joking, half-serious, posted updates on Crow outside the trainer's office.

To treat the injury he had spent almost three straight days in the trainer's office and didn't have to go to class. The excuses from class surprised Crow, who would ultimately have to take the SAT college entrance exam four times to get over the 700-point combined score that the NCAA required of a would-be college player to qualify for an athletic scholarship without any eligibility restrictions. On the other hand, the courses he was taking were not very difficult; so that academics would create as little interference as possible during the football season, he had taken English and government during summer school.

"The teachers understood what they were doing. They respect football," Crow said. "My photography teacher loved Permian football. He said it was okay [to miss classes]. The other two didn't want me in class because they knew I would be dripping water from the ice [being applied to his thigh]." The following week in a playoff game against Denton, Crow had gained 119 yards and scored a touchdown as Permian won 16–3 and advanced to the quarterfinals.

After the season he had spoken to a group of elementary school kids over at Dowling. He read them an Amelia Bedelia children's book. A short time later he received letters from little boys asking for his autograph and from little girls asking him for dates.

"I'm sorry I kept staring at you. I just couldn't help myself you are so fine!" said Kaci.

"Even though you have trouble reading, I think you read good. I hope that some day you will become a professional football player," said Shauna.

"I really enjoyed your reading. It was really interesting when you told everybody how many touchdowns you made," said James.

The next burst of applause at the Watermelon Feed came when it was time to introduce the members of the Permian football team individually.

When their names were called they walked down a narrow aisle separating the cafeteria in half. Ivory Christian acted like a bride at the wedding, each step slow and measured, luxuriating in the applause and the hundreds of eyes beckoning to him. He could have spent hours moving down that thirty-foot aisle, for this was the part of the game he truly did love, the attention, the adulation, as far removed as possible from the grit and relentless routine of the practice field.

Not everyone was so eager. Mike Winchell walked with his head cocked toward the floor, those furtive, brooding eyes burning holes somewhere, wishing he could be anyplace but

50

here, in the midst of all this outlandish noise and attention. More than anything in life, he hated crowds, and his dream was to live by himself near the red-rocked canyons of the wild Devil's River.

And then there was Boobie.

As Gaines told the crowd that Boobie would be the one to fill the shoes of Shawn Crow this year, Boobie himself felt a certain nervousness and excitement. Boobie was never one to praise others, particularly other running backs, but Crow had earned the ultimate compliment from him. "Tell the truth, he's the first white boy I've ever seen run like that," Boobie said in his sing-song cadence that sounded like the ruminations of a rap song. "Pretty bad white boy. White that can run like that? Not like Crow. He can run."

But Boobie wasn't worried about stepping into the role. He knew he could do it, get that ball, tuck it under his arm, and do with a football what Michael Jordan did with a basketball, make heads turn with a certain cut so pure, so instinctive, only God could have given it to him. "He can fly and dunk all special ways. I can run and fake all special ways," said Boobie.

He had hardly been a slouch his junior year, scoring fifteen touchdowns in addition to gaining over a thousand yards rushing. But Boobie had very much played under the shadow of Crow and spent much of his junior year blocking for him. But no more.

He acknowledged the loud applause of the crowd like a prom queen or an Academy Award winner having the first of what would undoubtedly be a lifetime of moments such as these. Exuberant chants of "Boobie!" echoed through the room, and the world belonged to him. It also belonged to his uncle L.V., who sat on one of the little cafeteria stools toward the back wearing a cap that had Boobie's number, 35, proudly affixed to the side.

When he thought about the two of them, what they had gone through to get here, it was hard not to feel that some miracle had taken place. "We come a long way" was how L.V. said it with that soft laugh of his. "I guarantee you. We come a long way." But now, at last, came the payoff.

And on this night of the Watermelon Feed, his nephew walked down the aisle with the flushed, irrepressible confidence of someone absolutely sure of his destiny, the smile wonderful and wide, the gait easy and sweet. Call it cockiness, call it a horrendous case of the big head, but there was no one else like him.

"Why are the scores of Permian games so lopsided?" Boobie himself had posed the question one day. "Because they only have one Boobie."

He was right. They only had one Boobie.

And in two days, when Permian went up north to Amarillo for a pre-season scrimmage against the Palo Duro Dons, people would get their first real taste of what he was going to do this season when he, and he alone, was the shining star of the Permian Panthers.

CHAPTER 3

Boobie

——— I ———

THE PRE-SEASON SCRIMMAGE IN THE LATE AUGUST TWILIGHT
had barely started when Boobie peeled off a run that gave
glimpses of why the college recruiters were after him, why
Texas A & M and Nebraska and Houston and all the others
routinely crammed his mailbox with heady testimonials to his
magnificence.

> *You have been recommended to us as an outstanding prospective
> major college student-athlete.*

> *You had an outstanding junior year at Permian and I am sure
> your senior year will be even better. You are in a situation that many
> young athletes dream about.*

> *The entire Houston Cougar football staff has been in the process of
> putting together the top list of high school senior football players in
> Texas. . . . Booby, we feel that you are one of these few select players.*

> *James—we are in New York preparing for the kickoff classic and
> enjoying the sights. Good luck in your first game. Looking forward to
> watching you play later this season.*

They weren't interested in him just because he was big and
looked imposing in a football uniform. There were a thousand
kids in Texas who fit that description. It was something else,

more than just strength or speed, a kind of invincible fire that burned within him, an unquenchable feeling that no one on that field, *no one*, was as good as he was. "Miles had the *attitude*," said former teammate Art Wagner with admiration. "He thought he was the *best*."

He had played his junior year with a kind of seething emotion that sometimes dissolved into quick frustration and discouragement. He easily got rattled, particularly when things weren't going well, and there were times on the field when he seemed as frazzled as a child. But there were other times when that emotion made him spellbinding and untouchable.

It had been there during the Abilene High game when he gained 232 yards on eight carries and scored touchdowns of 62 yards, 80 yards, and 67 yards. His father, who lived in Houston, had been in the stands that night. They had been separated for some time, and it was the first time James senior had ever seen his son play football at Permian. He was almost unprepared for what it felt like to watch his own flesh and blood out there on that field. "Oh, man," he remembered. "The first I seen him carry that ball, he busted that line for eighty yards. Do you know how you feel when you see your son doin' good, doin' somethin' special? It kind of put a lump in your throat. Man, that boy ran that ball that night!"

The fire had been there during the Arlington game in the playoffs, after he had come off the field with tears in his eyes because one of the opposing players had called him a nigger. Gaines tried to comfort him and told him the other team only wanted to get him worked up so he would get himself kicked out of the game. And then he saw a change come over Boobie as if something had snapped, the hurt and humiliation giving way to a raging anger. He only carried the ball twelve times that day for forty-eight yards, but it was his savage blocking that made the recruiters up in the stands take notice, the way he went after the Arlington defenders with uncontrolled vengeance, the way he flattened a linebacker and rendered him semi-unconscious. It proved to them that Boobie had more than just the requisite size and speed to play big-time college ball. He had the rawness, the abandon, the unbridled meanness.

"He's strong as snot," Mike Winchell said of him.

"He's the best football player I've ever seen," said Jerrod McDougal.

Boobie himself was well aware that all eyes were poised on him this season, and while he luxuriated in it, he seemed almost carefree about it. Holding court in the trainer's room shortly after the practices had begun in the August heat, he bantered with the nine-year-old son of one of the coaches as if they were best pals in grade school together, calling him "waterbug head," asking him if he had a girlfriend, grabbing his head and giving him a noogie, telling him that when it came to "the shoe," Adidas would never hold a nickel next to the almighty Nike. He lay on one of the brown trainer's tables, but it was impossible for him to keep still. With his head hanging over the table, he ran his fingers along one of the crevices in the wall and started to do a rap tune.

He asked one of the student trainers to dial the phone for him and call his girlfriend. The student held the phone out as Boobie, shaking with laughter, yelled from across the room, "What's the deal, what's the holdup on comin' to the house?" When Trapper walked in, Boobie called him "cuz" and "catdaddy." A few minutes later he was handed a list of defensive plays to study. He looked at it for several seconds, the droning terminology of numbers and letters as appealing as Morse Code, and started to read it aloud in rap to give it a little flavor, a little extra pizzazz.

He continued to play with the wall and then turned onto his stomach before flipping over again on his back. He spoke in little snatches.

"My last year . . . I want to win State. You get your picture took and a lot of college people look at you.

"When you get old, you say, you know, I went to State in nineteen eighty-eight."

He dreamed of making it to the pros, just as long as it wasn't the New York Jets because he didn't like the color green. And as he flipped onto his stomach one more time, he said he couldn't ever, ever imagine a life without football because it would be "a big zero, 'cause, I don't know, it's just the way I feel. If I had a good job and stuff, I still wouldn't be happy. I want to go pro. That's my dream . . . be rookie of the year or somethin' like that."

He moved off the line against the Palo Duro Dons and everything was in pulsating motion, the legs thrust high, the hips swiveling, the arms pumping, the shoulder pads clapping wildly up and down like the incessant beat of a calypso drum.

He went for fifteen yards and it was only a scrimmage but he wanted more, he always wanted more when he had the ball. Near the sidelines he planted his left leg to stiff-arm a tackler. But the leg got caught in the artificial turf and then someone fell on the side of it and when he got up he was limping and could barely put any pressure on it at all.

The team doctor, Weldon Butler, ran his fingers up and down the leg, feeling for broken bones. Then he moved to the knee.

Boobie watched the trail of those fingers, his eyes ablaze and his mouth slightly open. With the tiny voice of a child, he asked Butler how serious it was, how long he would be out.

Butler just kept staring at his knee.

"You might be out six, eight weeks," he said quietly, almost in a whisper.

Boobie jolted upright, as if he was wincing from the force of a shock.

"Oh fuck, man!"

"We won't know until we x-ray it. It may be worse if you don't stop moving that leg."

"You can't be serious, man! You got to be full of shit, man!"

Butler said nothing.

"Man, I know you're not talking about any six to eight weeks."

Boobie was placed on the red players' bench behind the side-line and his black high tops were slowly untied. The leg was placed in a black bag filled with ice to help stop the swelling. He turned to Trapper.

"Is it gonna fuck up my season, man?' he asked in a terrified whisper.

"I sure hope not," said Trapper.

But privately, Trapper's assessment was different. As a trainer he dealt with knee injuries all the time. His gut told him it was something serious, an injury that might prevent Boobie from ever playing football again the way he once had.

Boobie lay down and several student managers took off his pads. In his uniform, with all the different pads he fancied, he looked a little like Robo Cop. But stripped of all the accoutrements, reduced to a gray shirt soaked with sweat, he had lost his persona. He looked like what he was—an eighteen-year-old kid who was scared to death.

"I won't be able to play college football, man," said Boobie in a whisper as the sounds of the game in the gauzy light—the hits, the whistles of the officials, the yells of the coaches—floated over him, had no effect on him anymore. "It's real important. It's all I ever wanted to do. I want to make it in the pros.

"All I wanted to do," he repeated again. "Make it to the pros."

When the injury occurred, L.V. could only watch with silent horror. He had stayed frozen in the stands, not wanting to accept it or confront it, hoping that it would go away after a few nervous moments. But there were too many people around Boobie, looking at his knee as if it were a priceless vase with a suddenly discovered crack that had just made it worthless.

He had always feared that Boobie would be seriously injured one day, but not like this, not in a scrimmage that didn't count for a single statistic, not when he was about to have it all.

He had pushed Boobie in football and prodded him and refused to let him quit. He did it because he loved him. And he also did it because he saw in his nephew the hopes, the possibilities, the dreams that he had never had in his own life when he had been a boy growing up in West Texas, back in a tiny town that looked like all the other tiny towns that dotted the plains like little bottlecaps, back in the place the whites liked to call Niggertown.

II

From one perspective, the quickest way to understand Crane, Texas, was by thumbing through the ad section of the high school yearbook. There the glossy white pages featured blurbs for T & P Clothiers (HEADQUARTERS FOR STYLE AND VALUE!), Crane Motor Company (JOY AND JIMMY EXHIBIT THAT HAPPINESS IS OWNING A DODGE CHARGER), Crane Flower Shop (SAY IT WITH FLOWERS. LET IT BE OURS), Southern Union Gas Company (IF YOU WANT THE JOB DONE RIGHT, DO IT WITH GAS), Crane Service Parts (YOUR NAPA JOBBER IS A GOOD MAN TO KNOW) and Gloria's Salon of Beauty (BEAUTY IS OUR BUSINESS).

It was the kind of town where the big hangout was the Dairy Mart on Sixth Street because it had curb service, where Saturday afternoons meant plunking down a quarter for a matinee at the movie theater on Fifth Street and Saturday nights meant either a dance over at the county exhibition hall or a drag or two up and down North Gaston looking for girls and a little beer.

Fathers liked Crane because there was steady work in the oil field. Mothers liked Crane because there were few temptations that could entice their offspring. Children liked Crane because they hadn't been anyplace else, except to Monahans or Marfa or Big Lake for a basketball or football game. For many people, it had all the comfortable fixtures and feelings of a small town.

But not everyone liked it, and L.V. Miles had been one of those. For him, as for a handful of others who had the same skin color, the Crane he grew up in might as well have been on another planet.

His life had been defined by a five-foot-high wall of rock and concrete. It ran along a street and had been built so the whites who lived on the edge of Niggertown would not have to see it. He and the handful of other blacks who lived in this town of thirty-eight hundred people could do whatever they wanted inside that wall; no one really cared. But whenever they ventured outside it, it was without welcome.

He had grown up in a place where the only way he could go into a restaurant, if at all, was through the back; where he wasn't allowed to go to high school football games unless he climbed a light pole or snuck under a fence; where it was perfectly fine to go to the Saturday afternoon matinee as long as he took the stairs to the right and sat in the balcony.

The only time he had ever had contact with whites was during summer league baseball, but otherwise he stayed behind the concrete wall that fenced him and his friends in like cattle. He went to the colored school over on the corner. He swam at the colored swimming pool, not the white one where the teenage lifeguards had been placed on strict orders by a county commissioner to shut it down if any "nigger" tried so much as to stick his big toe into it. He played at the colored park, not too far from the spot where the cross had been burned when he was twelve. He went to the colored youth hall.

At Bethune, the colored high school he went to, all the tenth, eleventh, and twelfth graders—about twenty of them—were housed in the same little room near the entrance. He played basketball in a gymnasium that was tiny and suffocating, and he would never forget the one time he was allowed to play in the gym at the white school, Crane High, and how dazzled he was by the beauty of its backboards, by the sweet rows of bleachers rising above the smooth, glistening floor, as impossibly huge to him as a big-city arena.

When he went back to Crane one day more than twenty years after he had left it, it was easy to pick out the landmarks of his life because most of them were still there—the wall that had crumbled in places but was too well built to have disintegrated; the low-slung red brick of Bethune, with its row of grim windows like expressionless eyes; the red brick of the movie theater on Fifth, where he had had to sit in the balcony; the black cemetery where his mother was buried, an unadorned piece of ground with no trees to shield it from the constant clatter of supply trucks heading to McCamey or Texon or some other oil town outpost, next to a sign advertising the South Forty MX and ATV Track three-quarters of a mile down the road.

As L.V. Miles drove through the streets of Crane, memories of the cross-burning and the colored pool and the wall that the whites built bubbled to the surface. They came out at random, with no special significance attached to one or the other, and he talked about them neither with bitterness nor with self-pity. That was just the way things were back then, and Crane had been no exception.

But there was one memory that did seem to stand out above the rest, that he remembered in more detail than the others. It had to do with the one aspect of life that had kept him going while he lived there, which was sports. In 1961 and 1962 the basketball team at Bethune was the Class B state champion of Texas for "colored" schools, running a fast break so fast and fluid that it had the white folks in town actually setting foot in Niggertown to see it. L.V. had been on that team. He was a nice-sized kid back then, six feet and 230 pounds, and there was one thing he wanted to do more than anything else. He wanted with all his heart to play high school football.

But that was impossible. Bethune didn't have a football program. Only Crane High did, and L.V., who graduated from high school in 1963, wasn't allowed to go there.

Instead the best his younger brother James and he could do was watch the Crane Golden Cranes as they went against Monahans and Marfa and Alpine and Big Lake and other West Texas towns for whom the game of football had become a badge of courage. The two of them snickered as they watched, knowing they could do it much better than the bunch of white kids out there on the field who didn't seem very tough or very fast. But inside they bled, wanting so badly to be a part of it, to hear the swell of an entire town that had turned out on a Friday night to rejoice and agonize with the Golden Cranes, except, of course, for those who lived behind the wall of Niggertown and weren't welcome.

"You'd watch these kids play, and it seem like somethin' burning would be inside of you and want to come out," said James Miles, remembering what it felt like to be deprived of the most important rite of male teenage passage there was in the state of Texas. L.V. felt the same sense of helpless frustration.

"I wanted desperately to play football in high school and I never got the opportunity," he said. But twenty-five years later, about forty miles up the road in Odessa at Permian, there was some consolation.

It came in the form of Boobie.

Some who knew L.V. thought that he had pushed Boobie too much, wasn't living for him as much as he was living through him. Maybe that was true, maybe it wasn't. From afar, it was easy to criticize. But no one except the two of them truly knew what they had been through together, how close Boobie had come to being devoured by the Texas Department of Human Resources and the county welfare agency, to become simply another nameless case number shuttled from one place to another.

Boobie had been placed in a foster home when he was a young boy still living in the Houston area. L.V. had visited him and couldn't get his image out of his mind, that of a seven-year-old kid wearing size nine tennis shoes that turned up at the toes they were so big, his hair mangy and unkempt, a wild child who looked as if he had spent his life in the streets among thieves and beggars and animals. L.V. could have turned his back on him, could have let the image go. After all, Boobie wasn't his child. But he couldn't do it. He just couldn't do it, and he became determined to get him out of there. "I didn't want to see him go anywhere else, get away from the family, and never see him again," said L.V.

He also knew that the longer Boobie stayed in a foster home, the greater the odds were of his ultimately landing in a juvenile detention center, or on the streets, or in prison. There was also something about Boobie that excited him, a certain rawness that if channeled the right way could make him into something that no one ever expected.

There had always been something special about Boobie, even in the way he was born, on April 16, 1970, en route to St. Luke's Hospital in Houston with a police escort. Boobie lived with his parents until he was three, when he went to live with his grandmother.

He had a thick lisp when he was growing up and a craving for honey buns, and his grandmother remembered how much he loved to sing, belting out such songs as "Santa Claus Comes to the Ghetto" with relish.

When he was about five, he went back to live with his father, James senior. His father was working two jobs then, and Boobie remembered spending a lot of time alone. Later his father started seeing a woman whom Boobie did not get along with at all.

He remembered an attempt to tie him to a dresser so he could be beaten with an extension cord. He also remembered getting beaten with an extension cord when he was taking a bath. He went to school one day and officials there, believing he had been victimized, would not let him return home.

Case number 32,101 was heard on October 20, 1977, in Fort Bend County District Court in the Houston suburb of Richmond. Subsequent to that hearing, a court order on December 6, 1977, named the Fort Bend County Child Welfare Unit as Boobie's temporary conservator over the protests of his father, who said there had been no abuse but could not vouch for what happened to his son while he was away at work. Boobie was placed in a foster home, and his father was allowed to visit twice a month. The order also noted that a study of the home of L.V. Miles in Odessa would be arranged to see if it would be a suitable place for Boobie to live.

On August 22, 1978, a legal agreement was reached placing

Boobie in L.V.'s care. Two days later Jamie Kolberg, a social worker with the Department of Human Resources who had followed Boobie's case, wrote L.V. a note: "I hope you all had a good trip home, and that James is getting settled in with your family. I feel confident that his life has taken a turn for the better, and that he has a good chance of being a happier child in the future."

The day L.V. went to the Houston area to get Boobie, he had a beard and was so massively built that he looked ominous. And yet there was something gentle and tender about him, in the way he had his arm around Boobie, who was wearing a red T-shirt and shorts with his shoulder tilting down slightly. They both had thin smiles on their faces and they both looked painfully uncomfortable, as if they were embarking on a strange and potentially explosive experiment for which there were no predicted results.

Their initial time together had not been easy, and L.V. made many trips to the elementary school, where Boobie would get in trouble for fighting or talking back to teachers. He searched for something, an experience they could learn and grow from together, some way to channel all the anger that raged within Boobie. He found it when he asked him if he wanted to play on the Pop Warner football team that L.V. coached called the Vikings. From those underpinnings of football, an enormously strong bond developed between the two. They had something they shared.

"He's cool, I love 'im a lot," said Boobie of his uncle. "If it weren't for him, I wou'n't be here. I'd be here but wou'n't be as good because I wou'n't have nobody to push me like he pushed me."

"Boobie, he's the most complete back that ever went to [Permian]," said L.V. with pride. "He's the only running back I ever saw who could take those two-hundred-pound linebackers out, I mean take 'em out." When he said that, he had been watching the video of the 1987 Plano-Permian state semifinal game inside his living room.

The three-bedroom house was owned by L.V.'s wife, Ruby,

and besides Boobie there were three other children living in it. Ruby worked for a department store in the mall. L.V. was a trucker, but with the oil bust, jobs had become increasingly difficult to find and he barely worked at all. Together, their combined income came to about $1,000 a month.

The house itself sat on a corner lot on Lincoln Avenue in the Southside. The house seemed indistinguishable from others on the Southside—some were smaller and shabbier, some had better paint jobs—except for the shiny yard sign that Boobie's Pepette had made heralding him as a member of the 1988 Permian football team. The gleaming white sign looked misplaced and almost silly in comparison to the ones over on the northeast side of town, which were set out on the expansive lawns of homes as serenely as rafts interspersed on a private sea.

"See that little spin there, we worked on that," said L.V. as he watched Boobie dart free from the grasp of a Plano defender and go for several of the 141 yards he gained that day. He watched silently for a while, and then some aspect of Boobie's play struck him again.

"His blocking and stuff, we worked on that even in Pop Warner.

"The Arlington game, that guy from the University of Texas was very impressed with his blocking. He talked to me for a long time."

A dozen other college recruiters were impressed as well, their interest only increasing when *Texas Football* magazine, the Bible of high school football, named Boobie a "blue chip" recruiting prospect and one of the ten best running backs in the state.

Throughout the spring and summer and early fall recruiters were in contact with Boobie by letter, urging him to give consideration to their schools. L.V. carefully kept the letters for him in a large envelope, as if they were the family jewels. They came from all over the country, from Notre Dame, Nebraska, the University of Houston, Texas A & M, Clemson, Texas Tech, Oklahoma, Oklahoma State, LSU, SMU, UCLA, and Arkansas.

Some of them were more personal than others. Some tried

harder than others (Texas A & M led the way with twenty-three pieces of correspondence, which included a hand-written post-card when it played in the Kickoff Classic at the Meadowlands). Some sent glossy football programs; some, personalized mail-grams. But all of them gushed and fawned over Boobie, and it was impossible not to be blinded by them. They bragged about their facilities and their winning traditions and none of them, of course, made any mention of the academic difficulties he would face in college. All they knew about him was that he was big and strong and fearless, and that was enough reason to cram his head with dreams.

Boobie had been classified as a learning disabled student. Up until he went to Permian, he had been placed mostly in self-contained classes. When he went to Permian in the tenth grade, he was mainstreamed into regular classes but could get extra help when he needed it. His status made him exempt from the state-mandated competency tests that were a requirement for a high school diploma, and he had never taken college boards.

His schedule for the fall semester of his senior year at Permian included algebra I, a course that many Permian students took as freshmen and some took in eighth grade; biology I, a course that most Permian students took as sophomores; and correlated language arts IV, a course for students at least two years behind their grade level in reading and writing skills.

Boobie was on a schedule that would give him the required course credits to graduate from Permian. But there was no way he could fulfill the requirements of the NCAA for the number of courses needed to qualify for a nonrestrictive scholarship. Instead, Boobie was an automatic Proposition 48 case, meaning he could be awarded a scholarship but would have to sit out his freshman year, presumably to improve his academic skills. Be-cause of the loss of a year's eligibility, most major colleges didn't like Prop 48 cases and tried to avoid them, with rare exceptions.

L.V. was aware of Boobie's status, but he didn't think it would stop Boobie from getting a major-college scholarship if he was healthy. When it came to the classroom, he said that Boobie was diligent, studying for tests when he had to and doing home-work. But both he and Ruby sometimes wondered what Boob-ie's grades would be like if he weren't playing football, and they also wondered how hard he was being pushed in the classroom. "Boobie being an athlete, it's hard to tell," said Ruby.

Some teachers worked diligently and patiently with Boobie, aware of how hard it was for him to concentrate. Others just seemed to let him go, doing little more than babysitting this kid who, as one acknowledged, was destined to become the next Great Black Hope of the Permian football team.

On the football field, Boobie was frequently reassured and coddled. He had been kicked off the team sophomore year for missing workouts. But he had been allowed to rejoin after the coaches concluded that the same demands made of other play-ers could not be made of him if he was to stay on the team. It wasn't a selfless decision, because they realized that Boobie had the potential to be a franchise player for Permian.

They tried to induce him to do things in much the same way a parent would coax a recalcitrant child to do something—hop-ing, for example, to get him to play a little defense by bringing him a poster of Lawrence Taylor. "He's got a man's body, but you're dealing with the mentality of a twelve-year-old child" was the way Permian running back coach Mike Belew put it, re-membering the time he had criticized Boobie for something and he "laid down just like a mule."

The preferential treatment Boobie received sometimes caused resentment among the other players. The coaches were aware of the gripes, but the bottom line was that Boobie had the talent and they did not. With his size and his speed and his ability, he was worth the special status at whatever cost and whatever ef-fect it had on the dynamics of the team or his own develop-ment. Like it or not he was the franchise, unless, for some reason, they did not need him anymore.

Most who met Boobie agreed that he was one of those kids for whom the game of football had become as important, as indispensable, as a part of their bodies. Taking it away would be like amputating a leg. Some in town, most of them black, worried about what might happen to him if it somehow didn't work out, what the incredible effect of that absence might be. They saw something potentially dangerous in it all. And some in town, all of them white, gleefully suggested that Boobie Miles, without the ability to carry a football in his hand, might as well get a broom and start preparing for his other destiny in life—learning how to sweep the corners of storerooms.

On other occasions, some whites offered another suggestion for Boobie's life if he no longer had football: just do to him what a trainer did to a horse that had pulled up lame at the track, just take out a gun and shoot him to put him out of the misery of a life that no longer had any value.

"What would Boobie be without football?" echoed a Permian coach when asked the question one day. The answer was obvious, as clear as night and day, black and white in Odessa, Texas, and he responded without the slightest hesitation.

"A big ol' dumb nigger."

III

The scrimmage ended. Under the glow of the stadium lights, Ivory Christian helped Boobie adjust to a pair of crutches that was too small for him. It was a beautiful night in Lubbock, windless, in the seventies. Jones Stadium, home of Texas Tech University, was virtually empty, and there was a mood of serenity and peace. The light, falling on the field accentuated the colors—the green of the artificial turf, the red of the seats like a luscious flowerbed. Everything looked wonderfully vivid and clean as Boobie struggled with the crutches to get off the field.

"Take care of yourself, man, so me and you go to the same college," said Clifton Monroe, a running back from the opposing team.

Boobie smiled that wonderful, glowing smile. He liked hearing that, but an instant later came the fear of not being able to go to college at all.

"That's what I'm afraid of," he said.

Gaines huddled the team around him. He tried to be stoic, giving the familiar speech that no team was ever built around one player. But the thought of a serious injury to Boobie gnawed at him. He had been preparing for this season the moment the last one had ended eight months earlier. He was methodical and meticulous about everything, the kind of coach, the kind of man, who prepared for every possible situation through tireless work. And now came something he had no control over.

Boobie's loss was just the kind of news he did not want to hear, an omen that the season was tailspinning out of control, somehow jinxed. If the knee was wrecked, there went the team's star before a single down had even been played. And who could possibly take his place? Who could match the physical skill of Boobie? On the bus ride home he hardly said a word to anyone, the gray shadows of Brownfield and Seagraves and Seminole and Andrews falling across his face like a fine mist. Instead he leaned against a railing right behind the bus driver, gazing at the highway through the bug-splattered windshield, lost in thought, the tension of a season that hadn't even started yet reducing him to silence.

The next day, Boobie came to the field house with a huge smile creasing his face. A doctor's exam had showed it was more a sprained ligament than anything else. The doctor told him he could play again in ten to fourteen days. Boobie might only miss two or three games of the season.

But then, almost as abruptly, the dream changed again. A second examination by another doctor did reveal damage to the knee. Boobie needed arthroscopic surgery. He would be out at least a month before he could come back, and there were some, like Trapper, who believed the road back might take much longer than that.

"It's not an impossibility that Boobie can come back. Can he mentally overcome the injury to come back? Can he be full speed? You have surgery on your knee, they cut it open, and then they say, 'Fuck, you're okay, go back out there.' It's kind of a gut check. Do you really want to play football? Can you really come back from it?"

It meant adjusting to a knee brace. It meant not flinching an inch when the knee was hit full-speed by a helmet, not succumbing to the perpetual fear of pain, not running with the slightest tentativeness, which was the edge between a great player and a mediocre one. And it meant doing all these things at the age of eighteen.

In the aftermath of that meaningless scrimmage in the summer twilight in Lubbock, Trapper envisioned a definite fate for the Boobie Miles who had been the dazzling jewel of the Watermelon Feed.

"I think he's just gonna drift away."

With the season opener a week away, the pressure now intensified on everyone else, on Brian Chavez with his metamorphic ruthlessness and Ivory Christian with his love-hate ambivalence and Jerrod McDougal with his religious zeal. If Permian was to go to State, they would have to perform in ways that no one had ever imagined, rise to heights beyond even the expectations of the fans. But no one would have to have a greater year, be more superb, than Mike Winchell at quarterback.

Now, more than ever, it was up to him.

THE
SEASON

CHAPTER 4

Dreaming
of Heroes

I

WHEN HIS FATHER GAZED AT HIM FROM THE HOSPITAL BED
with those sad eyes that had drawn so narrow from the drinking and the smoking and the endless heartache, Mike Winchell
had been thirteen years old. He knew something was wrong
because of the way his father acted with him, peaceful in the
knowledge he didn't have to put up a fight anymore. Mike tried
to joke with him as he always had, but Billy Winchell didn't have
time for playful banter. He was serious now, and he wanted
Mike to listen.

He brought up Little League and warned Mike that the
pitchers were going to get better now and the home runs
wouldn't come as easily as they once had. He told him he had
to go to college, there could be no two ways about it. He let him
know it was okay to have a little beer every now and then because the Winchells were, after all, German, and Germans
loved their beer, but he admonished him to never, ever try
drugs. And he told his son he loved him.

He didn't say much more after that, the arthritis eating into
his hips and the agony of the oil field accident that had cost him
his leg too much for him now. In the early morning silence of
that hospital room in Odessa, he let go.

Mike ran out of the room when it happened, wanting to be
by himself, to get as far away as he possibly could, and his older
brother, Joe Bill, made no attempt to stop him. He knew Mike

would be back because he had always been that kind of kid, quiet, loyal, unfailingly steady. Mike didn't go very far. He stopped in front of the fountain at the hospital entrance and sat by himself. It was one in the morning and hardly anything stirred in those wide downtown streets. He cried a little but he knew he would be all right because, ever since the split-up of his parents when he was five, he had pretty much raised himself. Typically, he didn't worry about himself. He worried about his grandmother.

But he didn't want to stay in Odessa anymore. It was too ugly for him and the land itself bore no secrets nor ever inspired the imagination, so damn flat, as he later put it, that a car ran down the highway and never disappeared. He longed for lakes and trees and hills, for serene places where he could take walks by himself.

Mike came back to the hospital after about half an hour. "You were the most special thing in his life," his brother told him. "It's a hard pill to swallow, but you're gonna have to make him proud of you." As for leaving Odessa to come live with him, Joe Bill gently talked Mike out of it. He used the most powerful pull there was for a thirteen-year-old boy living in Odessa, really the only one that gave a kid something to dream about— the power of Permian football.

He talked about how Mike had always wanted to wear the black and white and how much he would regret it if he didn't because there were so few places that could offer the same sense of allegiance and tradition. Mike knew that Joe Bill was right. He had already carried that dream for a long time, and despite what he thought of Odessa, it was impossible to let it go.

He stayed in Odessa and sometimes, when he went over to his grandmother's house and talked about his father, it helped him through the pain of knowing that Billy was gone forever. "His daddy worshiped him," said Julia Winchell. "He sure loved that little boy." And Mike returned that love.

"When he died, I just thought that the best person in the world had just died."

74

Billy and Mike.

There was Mike, smiling, curly-haired, looking into his dad's face at Christmastime. And there was Billy, thin and wizened and slightly hunched, like a walking stick that had warped in the rain. There was Mike at the flea markets they went to together on Saturdays and Sundays over on University, helping his father lift the boxes from the car and set them in the little booth. There was Billy following him to a chair so he could sit and rest. There they were together on those hot afternoons that Mike hated so much but never complained about, selling the cheap tools and knives and toys and Spanish Bibles that had been found in catalogues or on trips to Mexico.

There was Mike playing Little League baseball with that go-to-hell stance of his—feet close together, up on the toes, taking as big a stride as he could possibly muster into the ball—jacking one homer after another. And there was Billy, the proud master, watching his gifted disciple from the car, unable to get out because of the pain in his leg and the arthritis.

Under the demanding tutelage of his father, Mike could do no wrong in Little League. He became the stuff of legend, with twenty-seven pitches in a row thrown for strikes, a single season in which he hit thirty home runs. And then somewhere around the time his father started slipping, Mike lost that innate confidence in himself. The gift was always there, but he began to question it, doubt it, brood over it. When he hit three homers in a game once, he didn't go back to the bench feeling exalted. "Why in the hell can I hit these home runs?" he asked himself. "Why could I do it when other kids couldn't?"

There had always been something inward and painfully shy about Mike, but the death of his father forced him to grow up even faster than he already had. He knew Billy was in pain and he also knew that only death could stop it. "It was hurtin' 'im and there was nothin' they could do," he said. "You don't want nobody to die, but you don't want him hurtin' all the time either."

After Billy died, Mike's life didn't get any easier. He had a brother who was sent to prison for stealing. At home he lived with his mother, who worked at a service station convenience store as a clerk. They didn't have much money. His mother was enormously quiet and reserved, almost like a phantom. Coach Gaines, who spent almost as much time dealing with parents as he did with the players, had never met her.

Mike himself almost never talked of his mother, and he was reluctant to let people into his home, apparently because of its condition. "He never wants me to come in," said his girlfriend, DeAnn. "He never wants me to be inside, ever." When they got together it was over at his grandmother's, and that's where his yard sign was, announcing to the world that he was a Permian football player.

"Me and him talked about not havin' a nice home or a nice car and how those things were not important," said Joe Bill. "I told him, you make your grades and stay in sports, you'll one day have those things."

Mike persevered, a coach's dream who worked hard and became a gifted student of the game of football, just as he had in baseball with his father. The one ceaseless complaint was that he thought too much, and he knew that was true, that whenever he threw the ball he didn't just wing it, go with his instincts, but sometimes seemed to agonize over it, a checklist racing through his mind even as he backpedaled—*be careful . . . get the right touch now . . . watch the wrist, watch the wrist! . . . don't over-throw it now, don't throw an interception. . . .*

He started at quarterback his junior year at Permian, but his own obvious lack of confidence caused some of his teammates to lose faith in him in a tight game. When the pressure was off and the score wasn't close, it was hard to find a better quarter-back. When the pressure was on, though, something seemed to unravel inside him. But now he was a senior and had had a whole year to process the incredible feeling of walking into a stadium and seeing twenty thousand fans expecting the world from him. He seemed ready, ready for something truly wonderful to happen to him.

He didn't dwell much on his father's death anymore. It had been four years since it happened and Mike had moved on since then. But he still thought about him from time to time, and he said he had never met anyone more honest, or more clever, or more dependable. He smiled as he talked about what a good "horse trader" Billy was, and how he loved animals, and how he had bought him every piece of sports equipment that had ever been invented. When he had had trouble with his baseball swing, he knew that Billy would have been able to fix it in a second, standing with him, showing him where to place his hands, jiggering his stance just a tad here and a tad there, doing all the things only a dad could do to make a swing level again and keep a baseball flying forever.

And Mike also knew how much Billy Winchell would have cherished seeing him on this September night, dressed in the immaculate black and white of the Permian Panthers, moments away from playing out the dream that had kept him in Odessa. The two-a-days in the August heat were over now. The Watermelon Feed had come and gone, and so had the pre-season scrimmage. Now came the Friday night lights. Now it was show-time and the first game of the season.

Most everyone thought that Billy Winchell had given up on himself by the time he died. But they also knew that if there was anything making him hold on, it was Mike.

Billy and Mike.

"He would have liked to have lived for Mike's sake," said Julia Winchell. "He sure would have been proud of him."

"Some of you haven't played before, been in the spotlight," said assistant coach Tam Hollingshead in those waning hours before Permian would take the field against El Paso Austin. He knew what the jitters of the season opener could do, how the most talented kid could come unglued in the sea of all those lights and those thousands of fans. He offered some succinct advice.

"Have some fun, hustle your ass, and stick the hell out of 'em."

"It's not a party we're goin' to, it's a business trip," Mike Belew told the running backs. "If you get hurt, that's fine, you're hurt. But if you get a lick, and you're gonna lay there and whine about it, you don't belong on the field anyway."

The team left the field house and made its way to the stadium in a caravan of yellow school buses. They went through their pre-game warmups with methodical, meticulous determination. Then they went to the dressing room and sat in silence before Gaines called the team to huddle around him. He didn't say much. He didn't have to.

Everyone knew what was at stake, that if all went without a hitch, this game would be the beginning of a glorious stretch that would not end until the afternoon of December 17 with a state championship trophy. It would be a sixteen-game season, longer than that of any college team in America and as long as most of the pro teams' seasons. Three and a half months of pure devotion to football where nothing else mattered, nothing else made a difference.

"That 1988 season is four and a half minutes away," Gaines said quietly with a little smile still on his lips. "Let's have a great one."

At the very sight of the team at the edge of the stadium, hundreds of elementary school kids started squealing in delight. They wore imitation cheerleading costumes and sweatshirts that said PERMIAN PANTHERS #1. They began yelling the war cry of "MO-JO! MO-JO! MO-JO!" in frantic unison, rocking their arms back and forth. A little girl in glasses put her hand to her mouth, as if she had seen something incredible, and it made her momentarily speechless between screams. As the black wave of the Permian players moved out into the middle of the field, eight thousand other souls who had filled the home side rose to give a standing ovation. This moment, and not January first, was New Year's day.

Brian Johnson opened the season with a fifteen-yard run off the right side through a gaping hole to the Permian 47, lurching forward for every possible extra inch. Two quick passes from Winchell to split end Lloyd Hill gave Permian a first down at the El Paso Austin ten. Winchell looked good, setting up with

poise in the pocket, throwing nicely, no rushed throws skittering off the hand.

Then Don Billingsley, the starting tailback for the Permian
Panthers, got the ball on a pitch. He was a senior, and it was his
debut as a starter.

The roars of the crowd got louder and louder as Don took
the ball and headed for the goal line. A touchdown on the first
drive of the season seemed destined, to the delight of the thousands who were there. And no one wanted it more, no one felt
it more, than Charlie Billingsley.

It was his son Don down there on that field with the ball.
But it was more than the natural swell of parental pride that
stirred inside him.

Twenty years earlier, Charlie Billingsley himself had worn
the black and white of Permian, not as some two-bit supporter
but as a star, a legend. He still had powerful memories of those
days, and as he sat in the stands on this balmy and beautiful
night where the last wisps of clouds ran across the sky like a
residue of ash from a once-brilliant fire, it seemed impossible
not to look down on the field and see his own reflection.

II

There were some kids who came out of Odessa ornery in the
same way that a rodeo bull with a rope wrapped tight around
his balls is ornery, kids who went through life as if they were
perpetually trying to buck someone off their backs to get that
damn rope off their nuts, kids whose idea of a good time was
to look for fights with townies from Andrews or Crane, or do a
little bashing at the local gay bar, or bite into the steaming flesh
of a fresh-killed rabbit, or down a cockroach or two in the
locker room, or go rattlesnake hunting by shining a little mirror
into the crevice of some limestone pit where the only sign of
human life was the shards of broken beer bottles that had been
used for target practice.

They were kids for whom the story of David and Goliath

wasn't some religious parable but the true story of their own lives, kids who were lean and mean and weighed maybe 170 pounds dripping wet but were built like steel beams and had a kind of fearlessness that was admirable and irrational and liked nothing better than to knock some slow, fat-assed lineman up in the air and watch him come falling down like a tire bouncing along the highway.

Charlie Billingsley may not have been the meanest kid ever at Permian, but he was somewhere near the top, and it was hard to forget how that tough son-of-a-bitch had played the game in the late sixties.

His sense of right and wrong had been mounted on a hair trigger. If he thought you were jacking with him, he didn't go grumbling back to the huddle making empty threats about revenge. He just put up his fists right there and if that didn't work, then what the hell, he'd just rear back and kick you smack in the face.

And it wasn't like he left all that anger on the field or anything. He wasn't one of these chameleons, one of these split-personality types. He was as memorable off the field as he was on it, hanging out at Cue Balls or Nicky's or the old A & W over on Eighth Street or wherever he happened to be night after night. He won a lot and lost a few and the coach of Permian then, Gene Mayfield, finally told him that he'd be off the team if there was one more fight. But Charlie Billingsley wasn't about to change his ways. The minute the season was over, he got into a fight and someone broke his jaw. They had to wire it shut and he dropped to 130 pounds but that was okay because Charlie Billingsley got an opportunity for a rematch, which is all he really wanted, and taught the kid who had messed up his jaw a very serious lesson.

If all he had been was a hell-raiser, Charlie Billingsley might have been in some trouble. But he also had the numbers, the kinds of numbers that everyone in Odessa understood and admired: 890 yards rushing to lead the team as a junior, when it went all the way to the state finals before losing to Austin Reagan; 913 yards to lead the team as a senior.

Those were great days back then, great days, and it was safe to say that life was never quite the same afterward. In the succeeding years he had traveled a lot of miles, too many to tell the truth, loaded down with the baggage of too much booze ("I've spilt more whiskey than most people have drunk") and too many wives ("I wouldn't have married a couple of girls I married"), still casting around for the proper fit twenty years out of high school, still trying to find the way home.

He had been recruited by Texas A & M, and as he recalled all the false promises that were cooed into his ear he couldn't help but give a little chuckle. He played for a few years, but one thing led to another, and Charlie Billingsley found out that life in college was a whole lot different from what it was in high school when it came to football: you were a whole lot more expendable in college, a hero one day and a broken-down nobody the next, and if you didn't like it no one really gave a crap because there was always a bunch of guys ready to replace you in a second. He transferred to a small school in Durant, Oklahoma.

"It was the worst mistake I made in my life," said Charlie Billingsley, looking back on it. "Those inbred Okies, they didn't take kindly to the pros from Dover." A friend got shot in a bar one night, and he and some others beat up the assailant.

Charlie Billingsley left school after that. He floated from one job to another, some of them good, some of them not so good. He was in the floor-covering business in Houston, but high interest rates kind of put a damper on that. And then he sold casing pipe during the boom, and that worked out pretty great for a while. He made $40,000 the first year out when Houston back in those days "was blowin' gold." But then the bust set in after a couple of years and Charlie moved back to Odessa. He helped start up a new bar in town that featured bull riding on Sunday afternoons—there was a ring in back—and kick-ass rock 'n' roll acts, but a falling-out with one of the partners put an end to Charlie's involvement in that. He started running another bar-restaurant in town where, as he gently put it, "it was hard to deal with drunks sober." He had also been through two marriages at that point, one to a girl from Odessa, the other to a girl from Houston, and then an unexpected element entered his life: his son Don.

Don had been living up in Blanchard in Oklahoma with his mother. It was a quiet, sedate kind of place and he was a star there, a starter on the varsity football team as a freshman. But Don, who spent part of every summer with Charlie, knew of Permian and of his dad's exploits there. He knew that every year the team had a chance of going to State and had won the whole shooting match four times since 1964. The more he heard, the more he realized how badly he wanted a piece of it.

Right before his sophomore year, he informed his mother that he wasn't coming back to Blanchard; he was going to stay with his father in Odessa so he could play for Permian, even though he had little chance of starting there until his senior year. He didn't want her to take his decision personally be- cause it had nothing to do with his loving one parent more than the other, it just had to do with playing football for Permian High School. Don remembered his mother's being "kind of pissed off" about his decision. But since she herself had been a Permian Pepette during Charlie's senior year, she also understood.

Don had been three when his parents had split up, and his coming back into Charlie's life on a permanent basis wasn't the simplest of moves. Living with Charlie was sometimes more like living with an older brother or a roommate than with a father. There were times when Don stayed up almost all night, regaled by his father's stories of how to live the world and how not to live it. Don treasured those sessions and learned from them. But when Don came home one night with a black eye, Charlie's idea of advice was to tell him to "stop leading with his face."

Charlie's drinking didn't go away. He would go on binges, three- or four-day hauls that were tough for everybody to handle. "I'd get pretty hairy at the end of one of 'em. Those three or four days, they were eventful" was how Charlie Billings- ley said it, giving a hoarse laugh that made you realize that at the age of thirty-seven he had been through one hell of a lot in his life since his playing days for Permian.

During the spring of his junior year, Don moved in with one of his grandparents while Charlie Billingsley went to a clinic for alcohol rehabilitation. Don went to visit him a couple of times. It was difficult to watch his dad try to pull himself through, and Don was glad he had football. The locker room became his home, the one place where he always felt he belonged.

Whether he knew it or not, Don had become the spitting image of his dad, Charlie Billingsley reborn seventeen years later. The physical resemblance they bore to one another was striking—the same thin, power-packed frames coiled and ready to strike if the wrong button got grazed, the insouciant swagger, the same shark's-tooth smile that could be both charming and threatening, the same friendly way of speaking, the words falling casually out of the side of the mouth like cards being slowly flipped over during a poker game.

Like his father, Don was a fighter who didn't think there was anything irrational about mixing it up with kids who were a whole lot bigger than he was. His reputation was established sophomore year when he told Boobie one day after practice to take the stocking cap off his head. Boobie told Don to go ahead and make him, but Don wasn't intimidated. "Those niggers, they talk a lot," he later said, describing how he had eagerly taken up Boobie's challenge. Although he gave up about five inches and forty pounds to Boobie, he took him down easily and earned the admiration of many who had always thought Boobie was too damn cocky for his own good. When Don had a few pops in him, which was frequently, he felt the urge to fight even more.

He had taken his first drink in fifth grade, and by the time he was a senior had built up quite a reputation for drinking. There was nothing exceptional about that in Odessa, where kids drank freely, often with the tacit blessing of their parents, who saw it as part of the macho mentality of the place. When Don went home from school for lunch, he sometimes raided the liquor cabinet. As a sophomore at Permian he was found wandering around the field house parking lot one day drunk. Customers at the various bars his father worked in were quick to buy him beer.

Like his father, Don was also the starting tailback for Permian. Charlie Billingsley had been the most valuable offensive player in the district when he had played that position his senior year. He had left his mark on the program, even though it sometimes seemed he used his fists as much as his legs. But he had been one hell of a runner, tough as leather, hard-nosed, and people around town still remembered him for that as if it had happened yesterday. They always would.

Until he went into the rehabilitation clinic, he admitted, he had been right on the edge, making things tough not only for himself but for Don. Their relationship, he knew, had been at the point of fracturing. But he was more in control now. He had settled down, and he had his son's football season to look forward to. As Charlie Billingsley said, "I got him to live through, and that's something pretty special."

After all, football was what had brought the two of them together in the first place, and it seemed destined to keep them together. At least for as long as the season lasted.

III

With all those eyes focused on him, the ball popped loose from Don's hands without anyone's touching him. He went after it on his hands and knees, desperately trying to recover it and redeem himself, but he couldn't get to it. A groan went up from the crowd as El Paso Austin came up with the ball.

He came off the field, his eyes downcast and brooding, his eagerness to do well in this first game and live up to the legend of Charlie putting his whole body out of sync. "God Almighty," he said to no one in particular on the sideline. "I can't believe that."

El Paso Austin was held to six yards in three plays, the hapless Austin running backs suffocating under a pile of five or six raging dogs in black shirts. *Swarm the ball!* That's what the coaches had told the Permian players time after time after time. *Never let up! Swarm the ball every play!*

Permian took over after a punt. With a first down inside El Paso territory at the 47, Winchell dropped back to pass. He saw flanker Robert Brown open, but the touch was too soft and the ball fluttered, a high fly up for grabs, the kind of pass that had become a Winchell trademark the year before, etched with hesitation. It was destined for an interception, but the El Paso defensive back mistimed. The ball plopped into Brown's hands, a gift, an absolute gift, and he had a clear path down the left sideline. He scored, and the ice was broken.

Winchell, coming back to the sideline, almost, but not quite, looked pleased with himself, a tiny look of relief, perhaps even the glimmer of a smile. "What do you think?" he said, motioning to the crowd, to the stadium, to the starry beauty of it all. "You ain't seen nothin' yet. Wait till Midland Lee."

Permian scored twice more in the first half to go ahead 21–0. Winchell threw a five-yard touchdown pass to Hill and then made it three when he hooked up with Brown for a sixty-one-yard bomb with twenty-four seconds left. In the locker room at halftime he seemed as if he was walking on air. Three touchdown passes in the first half. *Three!* Last season it had taken him his first four games to get three touchdown passes, and he only had eleven the entire season in fifteen games.

As for Billingsley, his debut as a starter had become further mired after that first nervous fumble. Regaining his composure, he had peeled off a nice thirty-four-yard run on a sweep. But then, with time running out in the half, he had fumbled again, as if the ghost of Charlie caused the football to go bouncing along the turf like a basketball. The mixture of excitement and anticipation had him in knots, his legs working so hard he looked like a cartoon character going at fast-forward speed.

The coaches, who had always harbored concerns about Billingsley because of his life-style, were not terribly surprised. They knew of his drinking and partying and the fact that he and his father moved around a lot. "I think we got a big-assed choke dog on our hands," said one at halftime.

Gaines called Billingsley into the little coaches' room and threw him a football. "Hold on to it," he said.

Then Belew took him aside. "Just put that behind you. If you worry about it, it's gonna screw you up. It's history."

The locker room was hot and steamy, and Gaines and his four assistants were hardly euphoric. The Panthers were dominating every facet of the game, but fumbles and penalties had kept Permian from leading 35–0 at the half.

"We should have had two more [touchdowns]," said defensive coordinator Hollingshead. "Don laid it on the ground."

Billingsley continued to drown deeper and deeper the second half. After Permian took over on downs on its 41, he took the hand-off and had clear sailing on the right flank. But his feet were still moving too fast for him and he slipped, adding to the rumbles that Charlie Billingsley's boy sure as hell wasn't going to follow in his father's footsteps, at least not on the football field.

"God damn!" said Hollingshead derisively.

If Billingsley could do nothing right, Winchell could do nothing wrong. Three plays later he threw his fourth touchdown pass of the night, tying a Permian record for most touchdown passes in a game.

The game ended with Permian beating El Paso Austin 49–0. El Paso Austin had been a helpless opponent but even so, the performance of Winchell had been wonderful. He had had the best game of his life—seven for nine passing for 194 yards and four touchdowns. His performance proved how high he could soar when he could unleash himself from the constant self-doubt that had entrapped him after the death of Billy.

Billingsley's starting debut had been just the opposite; it was hardly the kind of game that would make him a legend alongside Charlie, or anyone else for that matter. And now there was something else to contend with, something that to Don's way of thinking was disappointing but somehow inevitable.

It began at halftime when Gaines said he was going to let an untested junior named Chris Comer play the entire second half at fullback. It was Comer's first game ever on the Permian varsity, and it was only because of the injury to Boobie that he was there at all—otherwise he would have been back on the junior varsity. He had talent, but the coaches were wary of him. The previous school year he had been ineligible for spring practice because of academic problems, which put him way down in the doghouse. The coaches questioned his work habits and desire, and they were hardly inspired by his background— from the Southside, living not with his parents but with his grandmother.

But these concerns began to lessen when Comer took the ball early in the third quarter at the 50, lingered behind the line for a split second until a tiny alleyway developed, turned the corner, broke past two defenders with an acceleration of speed, and dashed down the sideline for a touchdown. The run had been so stunning that it was hard to know what to make of it. Had it been a fluke? Or, in the aftermath of Boobie's knee problems, had he just become the new star running back of Permian High School?

When he did it again, this time on a twenty-seven-yard touch-down where he just bullied his way past several tacklers, the answer became obvious.

Belew, who had spent most of the game in the press box re-laying offensive signals to Gaines over the headset, moved down to the sidelines in the waning moments of the game, clearly beside himself. He started to gush about Comer, and then he eyed Boobie, who had had knee surgery the day be-fore. He obviously did not want to hurt Boobie's feelings by raving in front of him about someone else. He moved until Boobie was out of earshot. Then he opened up like an excited child. "Did you see that?" said Belew of Comer's performance, 116 yards and two touchdowns. "Comer's a motherfucker!"

87

With the injury to Boobie, Billingsley had thought he might get the ball more often. But if Comer continued to run as he had tonight, Billingsley could pretty much forget about that. The ball would go to Comer on the pitches and the sweeps and he would lead the noble but anonymous charge trying to take out the defensive ends and the linebackers. Comer would get all the touchdowns, all the attention, all the glory, and Billingsley would get the aches and pains of being a blocking back.

That sure as hell wasn't why he had given up so much to come to Permian, to have a black kid come in and steal away his chance at glory. It was something his father had never had to contend with. There wasn't one black around when Charlie played. Back then they all went to high school on the Southside, had their own stadium, and as long as they stayed put there was no problem. But things were different now.

Don knew they had talent. It was just the way some of them kind of swaggered around that bothered him, how some of them seemed to do whatever they wanted in practice and the coaches let them get away with it. It seemed obvious to him that the Permian system was prejudiced against him—it had rules for blacks and then rules for everybody else. "In practice, the niggers, they do what they want to do, and they still start Friday night," he said. "There are different rules for black and white at Permian."

So the injury to Boobie hadn't made a damn bit of difference. As he later looked back on it, it seemed that the minute one black player got hurt there was another to take over.

"I didn't get to carry the ball" was how Don Billingsley sized it up. "They moved up another nigger to carry the ball."

CHAPTER 5

Black and White

I

*N*IGGER.

The word poured out in Odessa as easily as the torrents of rain that ran down the streets after an occasional storm, as common a part of the vernacular as "ol' boy" or "bless his 'ittl' biddy heart" or "awl bidness" or "I sure did enjoy visitin' with you" or "God dang."

Dumb ol' nigger. Cocky nigger. New Jersey nigger. Smart-aleck nigger. Talk nigger. Blame it on the niggers. Afraid of the niggers. Nigger lady. Let the nigger girl do it. Nigger ball. Run, you nigger.

Like household cleanser, the term had a dozen different uses in Odessa. People said it in casual conversation. They also said it publicly, as just another descriptive adjective. Some people looked tall, some looked short, and some looked nigger.

An elderly man making a complaint to the city council one day in September said he had given documents to a city employee to copy for presentation to the council. He didn't remember the name of the person. But he did recall what she looked like. "The nigger lady," he said at the podium. That's who he had given the papers to. The Nigger Lady.

Certain members of the council raised their eyebrows. Some looked to the side a little as if embarrassed. But that was the extent of the protest. The man continued prattling on, and he was treated with the utmost respect. After all, he was a taxpayer.

People who used the word didn't seem troubled by it. They didn't whisper it, or look chagrined after they said it. In their minds it didn't imply anything, didn't indicate they were racist, didn't necessarily mean that they disliked blacks at all. Instead, as several in Odessa explained it, there were actually two races of blacks. There were the hardworking ones who were easy to get along with and didn't try to cut corners and melded in quite nicely. They deserved the title *black*. They deserved the respect of fellow whites.

And then there were the loud ones, the lazy ones, the ones who stole or lived off welfare or spent their whole lives trying to get by without a lick of work, who every time they were challenged to do something claimed they were the helpless victims of white racism. They didn't deserve to be called black, because they weren't.

To the Reverend J. W. Hanson, a black minister who was the pastor of the Rose of Sharon Missionary Baptist Church on the Southside, the easiest way for blacks to get along with whites in Odessa was by being nonthreatening and obediently towing the line. "If you're the type of leader that as the establishment says can 'handle your folk,' you'll be all right," said Hanson. "As long as you don't rock the boat, then they think you're a pretty good ol' fella."

There were some whites in town who found the use of the word *nigger* offensive, but they were so far removed from the mainstream that no one took them very seriously. With her background as an active Democrat, a Unitarian, an ex-hippie, and a Dukakis supporter, it sometimes seemed surprising that Lanita Akins wasn't forced to walk around town with a shaved head and wearing a pair of striped pajamas like the French collaborators of World War II. The only thing that made her at all typical of Odessa was her passionate devotion to Permian football. "It's the one thing I do that they think is normal."

She loved her hometown, because of what it represented and

despite what it represented. She loved the friendliness of it and the small-town feel of it, the way she knew everyone out at the country club or at the store, the way the gossip made an easy circle. She relished the physical rawness of it, the feeling of the wind across her face and the gorgeous lightning storms during the summer when the sky, as she described it, just seemed to open up and dance. She knew the place was as immutable to the changes of time as an iceberg, but there was something reassuring about that. People stood up for one another. They cared about one another. They held old-fashioned values.

But she also knew that Odessa's values were old-fashioned as well when it came to race, still rooted in the days when the line between white and black was bluntly defined by the American version of the Berlin Wall—the railroad tracks that inevitably ran through the heart of town.

Back in the forties and fifties and sixties, the areas of occupation had been clearly understood. There was the ordinance on the city books making it illegal for any "white person and any Negro to have sexual intercourse with each other within the corporate limits of the city." (The term *Negro* was carefully defined to "include a mulatto, or colored person or any other person of mixed blood having one-eighth or more Negro blood.") There was the public policy of the city planning and zoning commission, which warned that the city's "Negro" population should never be given any opportunity to "invade the white residential areas."

There were the familiar redline laws that made it impossible for blacks to obtain mortgages or home improvement loans. There were deed restrictions preventing whites from selling their houses to blacks. There was a policy at the county medical center consigning all black patients to the basement, which meant that women giving birth were sometimes put next to patients with infectious diseases. There was the basic system of apartheid in which blacks had their own library, their own clubs, their own schools, their own stadium, their own football team, their own carefully delineated areas where they could

91

walk freely and other places where they walked only at their own risk. They were the same laws, the same policies that applied to blacks all over Texas and all over the South.

Some of these laws and policies had given way over time, but the change was slow and excruciating. No black family lived above the tracks until 1968, and it took two painful years of searching to find someone willing to sell the first black family a home. School desegregation, imposed by a federal court over bitter protests, did not take place until 1982.

As a result of that ruling, blacks could move about more freely now in Odessa. They could go to schools in the rich part of town. They could live pretty much where they wanted—assuming they could afford it, which most of them could not. They were still concentrated below the railroad tracks, below where the whites lived. Symbolically and physically, the tracks were still a barrier and still defined an attitude.

"The most amazing thing to me is the shock on people's faces that I'm offended by the word *nigger*," said Lanita Akins. "They are truly shocked that not only am I shocked, but I have friends who are black."

Out where she worked as a secretary for a petrochemical plant, many of the blue-collar workers used the word all the time. She didn't know how to get them to stop so she hit them back where it hurt, saying "Goddamn Jesus Christ!" with the same bitter snap in the voice. It bothered them, and they frankly didn't know how a decent person could say a thing such as that, show such utter disrespect for the Lord. But *nigger*?

What was wrong with the use of that word? Wasn't that what they were? Wasn't that what they always had been? Let a judge shove school desegregation down their throats. Let the federal government have all the free hand-out programs it wanted. It wasn't going to change the way they felt.

Look at how they lived down there on the Southside, in those shitty little shacks where the only thing that was missing was pig slop. Look at how you turned on the national news and saw another bunch of 'em being arrested for raping an innocent white girl in Central Park or running a crack house or blowing each other up in some gang dispute because one of them was wearing his hat tilted to the left instead of the right. What the hell was racist about calling 'em niggers when they acted like that? It was just the truth.

Dwaine Cox, who owned a restaurant downtown, had been raised in Odessa. He had graduated from Permian in 1962 back in the days when it was an all-white school. That was the way he figured it would be for his son, Michael, until the federal government stuck its fat nose in and started telling everybody what to do whether they liked it or not.

Dwaine was proud of his son, who had started at defensive tackle for Permian in 1987 when the team, the biggest bunch of overachievers ever, had gone all the way to the state semifinals. Michael was tough as nails, pushing his way past offensive linemen who sometimes weighed ninety more pounds than he did. Michael was equally fearless off the field too, getting into frequent fights and once showing up for practice in a shirt covered with blood after an altercation with some kids over at Odessa High. Dwaine wasn't so proud of that. He wasn't sure what the hell motivated Michael to get in trouble all the time, but he suspected that the federal government's desegregation plan had something to do with it. And he, like many others in Odessa, resented the federal government's coming in and telling good, hardworking people how they should live and who their children should go to school with.

Dwaine pegged the start of his son's problems to 1982, when the junior high school he went to got desegregated as a result of the fight that had taken place in the courts. "He would not even go to the bathroom in junior high. He wouldn't even go to the bathroom, because he was afraid of the niggers and the Mexicans. I think he just decided that he wasn't going to put up with that crap," said Dwaine Cox.

"You take these kids out of their schools and put them with blacks from the Southside and Mexicans. . . . They dragged the whole school down. They didn't want to be here anymore than

93

we wanted 'em. It just dragged the whole school down. You don't take kids like that, the way they've been raised, and put 'em with Michael, the way he was raised, he'd never been around 'em. I don't see how it could have gotten anything but worse.

"I live over here because I want my kids to go to school near here and I live here because I want to live with people like me and I don't want kids bused in from the black side of town living in a seven-thousand-dollar home. The majority of people over there, they don't better themselves, they're busy with their food stamps.

"My God, Mexico's nothin' but a big goddamn pigpen," said Dwaine Cox. "Hell, look at Africa. They've been here a lot longer than North America and they could be civilized and they're the same way they were three or four hundred years ago."

Some also blamed desegregation for irrevocably changing the character of Permian football.

Daniel Justis, a dentist in Odessa, had been an All-State running back at Permian on the 1970 team that went to the state finals. He knew all about Mojo pride. He knew all about Mojo tradition. Justis had traveled with the team for a couple of years in the early eighties. To him, enormous changes had taken place since his own playing days. He believed discipline had broken down. He believed the coaches allowed certain players to get away with murder. He believed the very essence of Mojo had changed, and he pinpointed the cause of its destruction.

"I blame it on the niggers' coming to Permian," said Justis. "People say you can't win without the blacks, but we did."

The black population of Odessa was quite small—about 5 percent. Since the majority of blacks still lived below the tracks, it was easy for white adults to go about their daily lives, particularly if they lived on the northeast side of town, and never see a single one, not in the mall anchored by Penney's and Sears, not in the supermarket, not in the video store on a Saturday night. The lack of contact created distrust and fear, and only further reinforced the images whites heard about and read about and had been in the town's psyche since the early days when blacks were run out. They found further justification for these feelings as a result of the activities of several blacks who had gained public positions.

Willie Hammond, Jr., had become the first black city council-man in the history of Odessa in 1972 and later the first black county commissioner in the history of the county. Those who knew him, like Lanita Akins, thought he was a brilliant politi-cian who had provided blacks in Odessa with their first real public voice.

Few then could fathom his arrest and subsequent conviction on arson conspiracy and perjury charges in connection with the burning of a building that had been the tentative site for a new civic center. According to testimony, after the bond issue for the civic center failed, Hammond was in on a scheme to torch the building in order to collect insurance money. Hammond claimed he was innocent, the victim of a political setup. His first trial ended in a hung jury, but in the second one a jury con-victed him.

Akins, who was extremely active in local Democratic politics, would never forget the night she had sat in the Zodiac Club on the Southside with Hammond and his lawyer after it became clear that Hammond's political career in the city was finished. She remembered how horrible she felt, not only for Hammond but for the blacks who had supported him, who had seen him as something of a savior in a city that was dominated at every level by whites. What struck her most was their attitude of fa-talism, as if this was how it always turned out, whatever the initial promise or potential.

"They thought they had one chance in this world and it was Willie, and when he lost they felt terrible about that. And they accepted it. They just accepted that they'd lost somebody else."

Laurence Hurd, a Church of Christ minister, came to Odessa and galvanized the Southside minority community into de-manding a desegregated school system. In 1980, twenty-six years after the Supreme Court decision in *Brown* v. *Board of Education*, sixteen years after passage of the Civil Rights Act, and ten years after a federal suit had been filed against the school district, Odessa's schools weren't remotely close to being integrated. Nor, until Hurd came to town, had any significant public pressure to desegregate the schools been placed on the school board and administration by the minority community.

The very presence of Hurd, the way he spoke with such passion, the way he could zero in on the hypocrisy of whites not with anger but with a biting cynicism, made him a wonderful figure on the Southside—their Martin Luther King, their Jesse Jackson. How could those who had been there forget the night at the school auditorium on the Southside when he had stared those whites dead in the eye and exposed them for using the cloak of Christianity, and the issue of busing, to justify that it was all right in Odessa to have two school systems, one for whites and one for blacks and Mexicans? How eloquent he had been that night, how sweet the rhythm of his words as he went to the very edge of emotional outrage but never crossed over into it, never lost control.

> *I hear people today complaining about the time their children will spend riding the bus, but I remember the time when minorities had to walk fifteen to twenty miles to attend school. Minority parents had to get up before the sunrise to till your land, pick your cotton, clean your house, and get their children ready for school, then walk to work. Tonight you see those who had to walk and get up early and return home late. If we had to sacrifice then, why can't you sacrifice for our children to be a part of quality education through integration now?*
>
> *Why will white churches spend money to bus minorities and teach them that God loves us and all are equal in the eyes of God, then turn around and say God does not want me to go to school with you? How can you, who profess to be Christians, not allow the love for humanity to flow from the walls of your Sunday assembly to the community?*

The applause had been thunderous, the auditorium coming alive with yells of praise and whistles and joyful hoots. Brother Hurd had them going that night. With him heading the charge, they now had the courage to say to those white folks who ran Odessa that they were no longer going to accept the crumbs of their paternalism. Without him, who knows how long it would have taken to force the issue into the federal courts. Who knows how long it would have taken for a federal judge to conclude that the Odessa school board, by clear design, had maintained a segregated school system for close to sixty years.

And where was Laurence Hurd today? What cause was he working on? Where were those spellbinding speaking talents and uncanny political instinct being put to use?

In a prison yard selling pastries to help raise money for a little girl who had donated a kidney. And he had plenty of time for it, since he was serving an eighteen-year sentence for the armed robbery of a bank. Soon after the desegregation battle had ended, he got himself into criminal trouble, reviving a past way of life that he had worked hard to bury. In March 1983, he pled guilty to the burglary of a boot shop in Monahans and served seven months in prison. Less than six months later, he and two others were charged with the robbery of a bank in Hobbs, New Mexico. Hurd claimed he wasn't involved, but an eyewitness identified him as having been near the scene and he was convicted by a jury.

What had happened to Hurd, what had happened to Hammond, seemed symptomatic of a larger problem. When these men faded away, to the snickers of whites who had never trusted them and to the sorrow of blacks who had put their faith in them, no one came to take their place. "I feel we've lost ground," said Gene Collins, the president of the Odessa chapter of the NAACP. "I feel we've lost energy. I don't think we're as determined as we were twenty years ago when King died. We have become less tolerant and less supportive of those who are less fortunate."

When Collins gazed across the racial landscape of the town, he saw a place where there were almost no black role models. He saw a place where the great panacea of school integration had turned into a numbers game in which the blacks and the

Hispanics ended up paying the greater price. It was the minorities who had lost their neighborhood high school, Ector High, not the whites. Other than giving some blacks the opportunity to rub shoulders with some whites for several hours a day, what had integration accomplished? Collins didn't know.

"Integration has torn down some barriers," he said. "There is not as much taboo in whites' attitudes towards blacks. But I think that is all it has done."

Jim Moore, the last principal of Ector High School before it was closed down as a means of achieving desegregation, felt the same way. Moore, who was white, saw no great social motive in the desegregation effort. It had nothing to do with true assimilation of the races and everything to do with percentages—how many whites, how many blacks, how many browns—little numbers that could be written down and submitted to a judge as proof that there was no longer any racism.

"There's no integration," said Moore. "There is desegregation. There is no integration in this community, the same as any community in America."

II

In the sixties and seventies, during the social upheaval of freedom rides and cafeteria sit-ins and boycotts in Birmingham and marches on Selma, Odessa stood locked in time. When sporadic pushes came from the federal government to change the status quo, to break down the boundary of the railroad tracks, they were met with swift and well-organized resistance.

"If there are those who insist on integrated schools, let them," said the *Odessa American* in an editorial in the summer of 1970, shortly after a federal judge had issued a court order mandating the school district to make minor changes to hasten desegregation. (As it turned out, the court order had no effect whatever.) "Those who prefer all-white schools, or all-black schools, likewise should be allowed to exercise their choice. It's the initiated force by government, from the levying of taxes to the compulsory attendance, that is wrong. With such an unholy foundation, the public schools cannot hope to educate or teach morality."

"We lived for too many years with segregation, too many years wrong," said Lucius D. Bunton, who was a partner in the biggest law firm in town and the school board president when the U.S. attorney general's suit against the school district was filed in 1970. "But it was there, and I think we really didn't think much of it, that's just the way it was.

"I'm not real certain we were ready for the kind of desegregation that currently exists. I think it would have caused some bad feelings and potentially would have hurt the school system," said Bunton, who was ultimately appointed a federal judge by President Carter and went on to issue a landmark decision finding the FBI guilty of racial bias in the treatment of its Hispanic agents.

At that time there were three high schools in the town: Ector, which was located on the Southside and 90 percent minority; Odessa High, the town's first high school, which was 93 percent white; and Permian, which served the newer parts of town and was 99 percent white. One obvious way of accomplishing desegregation would have been to shift students among these three schools and change the compositions of their respective enrollments. But in Odessa, the drawback of doing that was obvious.

"That would have destroyed the football program, and that's why we didn't do it," said Bunton.

The issue of race in the schools did not come up again for almost another ten years. The federal government's suit sat untouched in the federal court. Then it came to the forefront again, spearheaded by a total stranger.

III

The minute Laurence Hurd set foot on the Southside of Odessa in the late seventies, he knew he had been there before. He had been there when he grew up in Carlsbad, New Mexico, where it was called New San Jose. He had been there when he lived in Denver, where it was called Five Points. The names were different. The towns were different. But the characteristics were the same, as indistinguishable as one white suburban shopping mall from another.

Hurd knew where he was from the antiquated and dilapidated houses with peeling layers of paint, like a set of yellowing teeth falling from the gums because of rot, exuding the stench of decay. He could tell from the yards, which were infested with weeds and litter and looked like tufts of greasy hair on an old man too weak to comb it. He could tell from the vacant lots and the lack of new businesses. He could tell from the whole feel of the place, which simply seemed to sag, as if all hope had been given up long ago—if there had ever been any to begin with. Yes, he had been there before.

As the new minister at the Church of Christ on Texas and Clements streets on the Southside, he undertook the challenge of desegregating the schools and obliterating the boundary of the railroad tracks. He must have known when he took up the cause that his past would one day float to the surface, that as he became more and more vocal, influential white people in town would raise questions about him, want to know a little more about this stranger who started raising hell the second he got here and probably was some plant by those commies over at the NAACP. He knew it was the kind of town where influential white people could find out anything they wanted.

It was only a matter of time before some of those bitterly opposed to court-mandated desegregation were told by a local official that Hurd had an arrest record as long as a football field. In addition to nearly fifty arrests on everything from theft to suspicion of murder, Hurd had been in prison in Colorado separate times for stealing, possession of narcotics, and a parole violation.

But it didn't matter to him if people knew about his past—his life as a hustler that had evolved after he was discharged from the Marines in the middle fifties and realized that the only job he was deemed suitable for in Denver was as a pantry man at an all-white country club; about his almost constant games of cat and mouse with the Denver police in the sixties. Odessa was it, his last shot to do something worthwhile, to stay off the heroin that had ravaged him and make something of himself, to resist the lure of the streets where he had thrown dice and pickpocketed and pimped with the best of them. His survival back then had been based on a certain creed: "I wasn't no snitch, was polite to prostitutes, and did not take things that weren't mine." Now he wanted to live his life a different way.

He threw himself headlong into the desegregation effort, his rhetoric and speech unlike anything minorities here had ever been exposed to. He became the organizer of a group called CRUCIAL, which ultimately entered the desegregation suit as an intervenor and finally brought it into the courtroom after eleven years. He talked and talked and talked, hopping from one meeting to another. Through the efforts of Hurd and a handful of others, the Southside began to organize and come together. Suddenly, desegregation became an issue that was not going to disappear.

During one incredible week at the end of 1980, everything the town stood for—the barrier of the railroad tracks, the separation of white from black and brown, the religion of Mojo football and who could worship and who could not—came into question with the sudden, uncharacteristic refusal of the minorities to fall obediently in line. At the upper end of Odessa that week were the delirious fans of Permian, virtually all of them white, preparing themselves for that greatest moment of all, a state championship game. At the lower end of town were residents of the Southside, virtually all of them minority, demanding desegregation on their own terms.

On Tuesday of state championship week, the regular meeting of the Permian booster club was interrupted by numerous standing ovations. The first came when Jerry Thorpe and Tommy Mosley of the city's largest and almost exclusively white church, Temple Baptist, presented Coach John Wilkins with a plaque that named him WORLD'S GREATEST COACH. A bonfire was announced for six-thirty the following Thursday evening over at the sheriff's firing range on Yukon. Arrangements were also made for chartered planes and buses to go to the game at Texas Stadium in Irving.

The next night a different type of frenzy swept Odessa in a different part of town. The people at this particular meeting didn't believe in Mojo, for its magic, like everything else in Odessa, had never extended across the railroad tracks. They were not part of the great Mojo myth, which was the virtually exclusive preserve of white fans and white kids. But they did believe in something that had become just as sacred, Ector High School. The school was 99 percent minority, with 298 blacks, 463 Hispanics, and nine whites. Some 85 percent of the blacks who lived in Ector County and attended high school went there, and so did 44 percent of the county's Hispanics.

The minority residents of the Southside who attended the meeting clung to Ector High with all their might in the face of threats that it might be closed under a desegregation plan proposed by the school district. It was as uncharacteristic a display of passion on the Southside as anyone could remember, all of it revolving around a school that they had come to love and treasure, the only institution, outside of the black churches, that was truly theirs. They were in favor of desegregation, but not at the expense of losing their school.

It was the night Laurence Hurd rose up to attack the whites in the audience for their hypocrisy, for using religion as a thin veil for their own racism.

It was the night the Reverend Curtis Norris, pastor of the House of Prayer Baptist Church on the Southside, rose up to tell the school board, "Our last stand that we have as a community is Ector High School."

It was the night Dorothy Jackson, a parent whose children went to school on the Southside, rose up to tell the board: "We would like for you to know that not only can we be good sprinters but we too have the minds to become doctors and lawyers and city officials. Please don't be afraid of us. We're very much like you."

The meeting at Ector received extensive coverage in the

Odessa American. But it was overshadowed by events continuing
to unfold across town during state championship week; a full-
page photo spread was given to the bonfire, a school pep rally,
and a Mojo Christmas tree that had little bulbs with the numbers of the players on them.

That Saturday, roughly ten thousand people were part of the
caravan that made its way from Odessa to Texas Stadium by car
and motor home and bus and chartered plane, a phalanx of
support that was numbing even by Texas standards. Permian
scored three touchdowns in the second half to defeat Port Ar-
thur Jefferson 28–19 and win its third state championship in
one of the great upsets in modern Texas high school history.

"Today Mojo reigns supreme over Texas schoolboy football,"
wrote sports editor Ken Broadnax in a front-page story in the
paper.

> *A team of "Little Big Men" has shown that mind can indeed win out
> over matter.*
> *Those Panthers . . . those itsy, bitsy football players . . . those
> hearty, gutsy guys from the oil fields . . . what about 'em? Yep, it's in-
> credible, amazin' and unbelievable, but the li'l fellers do occasionally
> catch the best end of the stick.*

All the reasons for the phenomenal support of Permian
had been embodied by this 1980 varsity team. They were a classic bunch of overachievers who had become living proof of
all the perceived values of white working-class and middle-class
America—desire, self-sacrifice, pushing oneself beyond the expected limit. They were the kinds of values that the Permian
fans harbored about themselves. What made those boys great
on the football field had made the fans great as well. Just as the
boys had produced against all odds, so they had produced in
the oil field against all odds, not with brains and fancy talk but
with brawn and muscle and endurance and self-sacrifice.

Such symbolism wasn't lost on Laurence Hurd as he continued to fight for school desegregation. It wasn't necessary to live
in Odessa for long to realize that the Permian football team
wasn't just a high school team but a sacrosanct white institution.

"Mojo seemed to have a mystical charm to it," said Hurd. The school itself was 94 percent white in 1980, with 14 blacks and 94 Mexican-Americans out of 2,031 students, and he truly believed there would be "blood in the streets" before Permian supporters would allow their school to be tampered with in any way that might be even remotely perceived as detrimental. Another key figure in the desegregation battle, Vickie Gomez, who in 1976 became the first minority candidate ever elected to the school board, had come to a similar conclusion. "The thing was to preserve Mojo's whiteness," said Gomez. The school board and the administration "were determined that whatever happened, Mojo was not going to suffer in any way."

In the spring of 1982, U.S. district judge Fred Shannon ruled that "the failure of the [school district] to dismantle its formerly dual school system is very clear in this case. The historically black schools have never been desegregated, and since 1954 have remained either all Black or virtually all Black and Mexican-American."

In no less than six different areas, Shannon concluded on the basis of testimony, the school system "not only continued to fail to meet its duty to dismantle its dual school system, but actually increased the segregation in its schools of both Blacks and Mexican-Americans."

It was a moment of euphoria for the minority community, until Shannon strongly hinted at a solution. Opposed to increased busing, Shannon concluded that the quickest, surest way to achieve desegregation was to close Ector High School, since it had a relatively small population. As a result, its students were dispersed across the railroad tracks to the remaining two high schools in town, Permian and Odessa High.

As a school, most whites never had much use for Ector once it had become pegged as the minority school. It was on the Southside, and the less heard about the area the better. "I think the community perceived it as a minority place, a place they wouldn't travel into," said Jim Moore. "I think most of them perceived it as a place to keep 'em over there and let 'em have their school."

But with Ector's closing, members of the white community suddenly began to see enormous value in some of its black students. It had nothing to do with academic potential. It had everything to do with athletic potential.

Once the plan was announced, a hotly debated aspect of it wasn't curriculum, or how minorities would fare in schools that had always been predominantly white. Instead there was remarkable focus on which school, Permian or Odessa High, would ultimately get the greater number of black students, and thereby the greater number of black football players. The answer depended on how the Southside was divvied up between the two schools in the aftermath of the court battle. The curious zigs and zags of the proposed division gave Permian a clear edge over Odessa High in the number of blacks assigned to go there based on where they lived. Gomez said the line was drawn that way not for the cause of desegregation, nor to satisfy any academic purpose, nor even to meet any racial quota, but to ensure Permian a greater number of black running backs down the road than its rival.

"It was gerrymandering over football," said Gomez, who had not been in the least surprised. In the endless deliberations over desegregation, the board spent more time worrying about how the high school athletic programs might be affected than how the curriculum might be affected. "Whatever they did, they did not want to hurt the dynasty that was being established at Permian," she said. "I think it clouded their vision. We spent more time talking about the athletic program than the curriculum."

IV

You could search high and low for a black city councilman in 1988, or a black county commissioner, or a black school board member in Odessa. You wouldn't find one. You could search high and low for a black at the Rotary Club breakfasts over at the Holiday Inn. Or at the luncheon meetings of the Optimist

Club over at the junior college. You wouldn't find one there either, just like in every other community in America. But on Friday nights in Odessa, you could gaze down at the football field and see several black players tearing up the field for Permian.

Thanks to desegregation, football was blacks' claim to fame in Odessa, the thing they were known for, and there was no better proof than the Wall of Fame. Just inside the entrance to the Permian field house, the wall contained the framed pictures of sixty-one players, each of whom had been All-State. To have one's picture hanging there in a little frame with black trim was a cherished honor.

The wall also offered a quick and easy lesson on the history of race relations in Odessa. From 1959, when Permian opened, until 1982, there was only one black face on that wall out of pictures of forty-five players. (The name of the player was Daryl Hunt. He happened to be from the first black family ever to live across the tracks in the northeast part of town. He also happened to be the best football player ever at Permian, becoming an All-American linebacker at Oklahoma University and then a member of the Houston Oilers for six years.) Since the desegregation of the schools, the representation of black players on the Wall of Fame had dramatically increased. Of the sixteen pictures added to the Wall of Fame since 1982, five were of blacks.

Desegregation had not altered the essential character of the Permian program. It was still a white institution. The overwhelming majority of its fans were still white. The overwhelming majority of its players were still white. But those few blacks attending Permian had made enormous contributions, one after another shipped across town to Permian for the mass enjoyment of an appreciative white audience and then shipped right back again across the railroad tracks to the Southside after each game. Boobie Miles came from the Southside. So did his replacement, Chris Comer. So did Ivory Christian. So did Brian Johnson, who started at defensive end.

"We fit as athletes, but we really don't fit as a part of society," said Nate Hearne, the only black coach at Permian in 1988. "We know that we're separate, until we get on the field. We know that we're equal as athletes. But once we get off the field we're not equal. When it comes time to play the game, we are a part of it. But after the game, we are not a part of it."

In the fall of 1988, there were 147 blacks—6 percent of the student body—attending Permian. There were none among the forty-seven students taking honors physics I. There were none among the eight taking honors physics II. There were none among the fifty-two students taking honors biology II. There were three among the sixty-five taking honors chemistry I. There were four among the ninety-three taking honors algebra II. There was one among the eighty-two taking honors pre-calculus. There were none among the thirty-seven taking honors calculus. There were none among the ninety-nine students taking honors English III. There were two among the ninety-one students taking honors English IV. There were none on the student council. There were none who were cheerleaders.

On the Permian team, six of the fifty-five players were black. In the basketball program, fifteen of the thirty-nine players were black. Blacks also made up relatively high percentages in remedial courses.

Numbers aside, their domination of the football team was astounding. Of the six who were with the team at the beginning of practice in August, five were starters and the sixth was hurt. Two of these players started both ways, the only ones on the entire team to do so. On offense black athletes started at flanker, split end, and fullback. On defense they started at middle linebacker, defensive end, safety, and rover.

There was an apocryphal story that football coaches all over the state of Texas had cried when desegregation came to Odessa, because it gave Permian the one thing it had never had before—black running backs. The story may have been apocryphal, but it was also true that Permian football benefited from desegregation. It was clear that the coaches expected black athletes to be better because of a belief that their bodies matured earlier than did those of whites. If a black didn't perform up to expectations, it usually had to do not with ability but work habits. "There will never be a mediocre black athlete to play at Permian," said Hearne.

Because of their skill, blacks were openly coveted in Odessa in the football arena. Some would never accept their presence on the team, but many others did, based on the ability to meet the following special conditions: having a speed of 4.6 or better in the forty, great hands, and the perceived ability to cover twice as much ground from the middle linebacking position as could any white boy. The only way to lose that preferred standing, of course, was by not performing.

"We don't have to deal with blacks here," said Lanita Akins. "We don't have to have any contact with them, except on the Permian football team. It's the only place in Odessa where people interact at all with blacks." As she sat in the stands, Akins watched with fascination how the fans accepted the presence of blacks on the Permian team as if they were for the time being part of a different race altogether, as if something magical happened when those boys donned the black and white.

"Those boys are not niggers to them," said Akins. "They are Mojos."

To Laurence Hurd, there was nothing surprising in that attitude.

He was well aware of the enormous allure of the black athlete and the doors that participation in sports supposedly opened, the barriers that it supposedly broke, the way whites suspended all racist judgments when they sat in the stands and gazed down at a football field or a basketball court or a baseball diamond.

He also knew that many black kids thought their easiest way out of the ghetto, perhaps their only way, was through sports. After all, what universally accepted black role models did these kids really have besides the Three J's—Michael Jordan and Bo

Jackson and Magic Johnson? Where else in the world, particularly the white world, did they see blacks consistently gain such praise and prominence and acceptance? Considering the circumstances of their lives, how could they be expected to accept the harsh reality of studies showing that of the thirty million children taking part in youth sports in the United States, only about two hundred would go on to become professionals in any given year?

Laurence Hurd had an opinion about sports. He firmly believed that football, like other sports, used blacks, exploited them and then spit them out once their talents as running backs or linebackers or wide receivers had been fully exhausted. For a few lucky ones, that moment might not come until they were established in the pros. For others, it might come at the end of college. For most, it would all end in high school.

And what would they have after pouring every hope and dream into sports? Hurd believed he knew the answer: a few memories and an education so inadequate they might have difficulty reading their names in "big boxcar letters."

"Before, it was take the blacks and put 'em in the cotton field. Let 'em do farm work. Let 'em do share crops. In the twentieth century, because of football, the real smart people use these blacks just like they would on the farm. And when it's over, they don't care about them. Some people say in their mind, that's all they were good for anyway.

"Today, instead of the cotton field, it's the sports arena."

They were strong, provocative, important words, the very trademark of Laurence Hurd. But no one was listening.

He wasn't any longer a gifted, powerful minister leading a community in a struggle for social change. Instead he was just another repeat offender in the middle of the desert, in the middle of nowhere, behind rows of razor wire that glinted and gleamed in the sun like jagged teeth.

Some considered his life a poignant tragedy, an impossible battle that he ultimately lost between the two souls that raged within him—the Laurence Hurd capable of doing marvelous good for the community, and the Laurence Hurd who had spent much of his life as a street hustler after finding little appeal in being a pantry man for the rest of his life.

"If only he could have kept that other boy down," sighed the Reverend Hanson. "I don't understand how you can do so much good for people, speak up for them and care about them, and do so much harm to yourself."

Others, not quite so benevolent, believed his actions had let down a community where the role of black leader was a precious, almost sacred commodity. Hurd had had it all in Odessa—recognition, respect, dignity, clout—and then he let it go for reasons that were hard to fathom.

"I guess that's the mystery, I guess that's the mystery that I've never been able to figure out myself," he said in the prison visiting room one day, his voice, turned throaty with age, sounding like the bristles of a broom pushing against a slate floor.

Sometimes when he talked his eyes would close and the fingers of his hands would splay across the table, as if they were trying to touch the very part of him that had caused his life to go so wrong just when it seemed to be going right. But then his eyes opened, eyes that were jaundiced and tired, and he spoke with a melancholy weariness. He was tired of giving explanations, tired of being held up to the light and examined as if he were some rare specimen being taken out of an airtight jar, Laurence Hurd the social activist, Laurence Hurd the bank robber, Laurence Hurd the eloquent spokesman for integration, Laurence Hurd the master of three-card monte, Laurence Hurd the model of black success, Laurence Hurd the model of black failure. There were others like him who had fallen off the path and given in to the old demons. He wasn't the only one.

"I guess sometimes there's some force within me that takes great control of me. Who knows? I can't say. You ask me why there has been such drastic change. I wish I knew."

CHAPTER 6

The Ambivalence of Ivory

I

THERE WERE MOMENTS WHEN IVORY CHRISTIAN LOVED THE game he tried so much to hate.

You could tell by the very way he lined up at the middle linebacker position, up on the balls of his feet in a cocked crouch, fingers slicing slowly through the air as if trying to feel the very flow of the play, elbows tucked and ready to fire off the snap of the ball in a mercuric flash.

He even liked it sometimes during the early morning workouts that were held twice a week before classes started inside the school gymnasium. The players ran at full strength under the angry glaze of the lights, the first-string offense and defense going against so-called scout teams simulating the offense and defense of the coming week's opponent.

No one was supposed to tackle, but every now and then Ivory pounced out of his crouch and drew a bead on some poor junior running back unfortunate enough to have become the focal point of his frustration and the need to unleash it on someone. As the unsuspecting prey went around the end, still adjusting to the slightly surreal notion of practicing football indoors on a basketball court at seven-twenty in the morning, Ivory just smacked him. There was the jarring pop of helmet against helmet, and then the trajectory of the underclassman as he went skittering across the gleaming gym floor like a billiard

111

ball hopping over a pool table after a wild cue shot. Ivory then sauntered back to the huddle as if he were walking down the runway at the Miss America contest, basking in the glow of ultimate victory but careful not to show too wide a smile because he had, after all, a reputation for self-restraint to keep up.

Much of the time Ivory fought to rid football from his life, to call a merciful halt to the practices, the dreaded gassers, the reading of page after page of plays and game plans, the endless demands on his time. He liked the games, there was no denying that, but it was hard not to find the rest of it pointless.

There were other coaches around the league who drooled over Ivory's size and speed (195 pounds and growing with a 4.7 in the forty) and his strength (he could bench-press 275 pounds as a sixteen-year-old). They thought he had major-college talent written all over him, but Ivory didn't. He was so sure of it he wasn't even going to bother to take the SAT or ACT entrance exams, which made it virtually impossible for him to get a major-college scholarship even if anyone was interested.

Maybe it would have been different if the coaches had let him start at middle linebacker his junior year. He had had the talent for it, there was little question about that, but the coaches simply didn't trust Ivory at the show position of the Permian defense. They switched him to offensive guard, and he played it brilliantly.

But something snapped in Ivory after middle linebacker was wrested from him. The common explanation, he wasn't rah-rah enough, didn't make any sense to him, although the coaches were hardly the only ones who found him to be stubborn and headstrong. But the way Ivory saw it, they just wanted to deprive him of glory, of what was rightfully his.

And where was all this rah-rah stuff supposed to come from? Was it simply expected that he would become indoctrinated into the blinding passion of the Mojo mystique just like everyone else? He was aware of it—everybody in town was—but up until the sixth grade Permian was off-limits to him because the school system was segregated.

If you lived on the Southside, as Ivory's family did, there was no way of going there. Instead, the big school in town was Ector, which wasn't too far from his home. Ector didn't have the football tradition that Permian had. But it had won State twice in basketball, residents of the Southside packing the tiny school gym to the rafters with twelve hundred fans while others who couldn't get in climbed the roof and stared in the windows. That was the tradition Ivory had grown up with, not Mojo.

Relegated to the position of guard, he had played football out of a dutiful sense of obligation, because it made his father proud and also because it somehow seemed his destiny to do so, regardless of what he thought about it. After all, if you were a strong, fast black kid in Odessa, what else were you encouraged to do? What other outlet did you possibly have? When you looked around, where else did you see a single black role model, except in church?

He had talked with his father, Ivory senior, about it, and he told him he wasn't sure he wanted to play college ball even if he had the chance. The way the words came out of his mouth, so flat and dispirited, Ivory senior thought his son might be burned out on the whole thing altogether, the rigors of being seriously involved in football since the age of nine finally getting to him. He had been playing the game for eight years, as long as it took to go to medical school, serve an internship, and complete a residency, but what loomed down the road because of it?

Ivory couldn't see a thing.

His father had played football in Odessa in the sixties when there was an all-black high school in town called Blackshear. The team had played in its own stadium on the Southside, with equipment that looked like something used in a junior high, and it played in the high school version of the Negro League, its opponents the all-black schools of Amarillo and Lubbock and Midland. Those were the days of strict segregation, and the idea of playing for Permian was of course almost inconceivable.

Ivory senior took great pride in his son's accomplishments.

In the back of his mind it was probably hard not to think about what football could do for his son and how it could make him the first member of the Christian family ever to go to college. But Ivory senior, who drove a truck for a living, wasn't going to push him. He would abide by his son's decision if Ivory chose not to play football anymore after high school. He also knew his son was a teenager going through changes who had, perhaps for the first time, found there might be something else in life besides football to fill up the empty spaces of Odessa that loomed as large as skyscrapers.

It had come to Ivory in a dream. When he related it to his father he talked about being in a narrow tunnel with a tiny light that he could barely see but he knew he had to find no matter how difficult it was.

To Ivory, the message of the dream was crystal clear. He was living his life wrong, emphasizing all the wrong things, football and hanging out in the streets with his friends and alcohol and marijuana. The day after he had the dream he went to church with a hangover on his breath and Jesus in his heart, as he later described it. He told the pastor at his church, Rose of Sharon Missionary Baptist, about the dream and how he was convinced that it had been a calling to preach and become part of God's ministry.

Pastor Hanson welcomed Ivory's conversion. He knew that Ivory was an influential kid whose actions made a tremendous impression on his peers. But there was something worrisome about it, and he didn't want Ivory moving from one world of isolation into another where the only difference was the level of standards.

Before, Ivory had displayed undisguised contempt for just about everything, an attitude of what Hanson perceived as arrogance. Now he displayed a rigid righteousness that made him almost a kept prisoner. At home he hardly communicated with anyone but went immediately to his tiny room, where he listened to the gospel music of James Cleveland. He went on this way for hours on end, until his mother began to worry and think there was something wrong with him. Why was he so withdrawn, so quiet?

As the result of his conversion, he hated alcohol and had contempt for those who touched it. He also hated swearing, and other players in the locker room figured it was better to abide by his wishes rather than run the risk of messing with him. Before his calling to the ministry he had dated. Now he started grilling girls about their habits to see if their moral standards were high enough for him.

"Not everyone you meet is going to be a jam-up Christian," Hanson told him. "They may drink a beer, they may go to a concert. You can still be Ivory, you can be eighteen years old. You don't have to be forty years old. You don't have to isolate yourself."

But Ivory's metamorphosis was total, a far cry from the days when he had led the chorus of laughter in response to the church teachings about fornication. And rarely had Hanson seen anyone with as instinctive a gift for preaching. He was amazed at Ivory's comprehension and interpretation of the Scripture and his ease in the pulpit, the absolute fearlessness he showed in getting up before the congregation and preaching the word of God with those square shoulders that did make him look as though he was born to be a linebacker.

Wearing a blue suit with a little trim of white handkerchief sticking out of the breast pocket, Ivory made a striking figure, his poise like that of someone thirty years old instead of seventeen. He truly seemed at peace in these moments, able at last to lose himself in something without anguish and ambivalence. He rocked back and forth and nodded his head as Hanson gave the altar prayer one Sunday. Moments later he was introduced as "the Reverend Ivory Christian." The very ring of it sounded stirring and wonderful, and it was amazing to see this teenager who showed almost no enthusiasm about anything, who responded to almost everything with the shrug of an octogenarian ready to die, take the pulpit. He started softly but the exhortations of the congregation—"Talk! Talk!" and "Alright! Alright!" and "Take your time, son! Take your time!"—got him going in a sweet and easy rhythm. He connected with the congregation and they connected with him as he stood beneath a mural of the black Jesus and talked about his conversion:

When you let go of this world, Jesus puts a certain joy in your heart. Do we really love him enough to say no to the world?

Ivory let go of drinking. He let go of hanging out in the streets. He let go of parties. He let go of cussing. He let go of every former vestige in his life, except football. It still lingered as his perpetual, unconquerable nemesis. He tried to let go of that too, and he talked to Hanson about quitting football altogether because he felt it conflicted with his calling, and he didn't want anything to get in the way of that. But Hanson gently coaxed him not to drop football too fast. It was there, and it had a place in Ivory's life whether he liked it or not. "If playing football can get you to college, if playing football can get you an education, then play football," Hanson told him.

And no matter how much Ivory tried to hate it and belittle it and scoff at it, something took hold of him on game day as surely powerful as spreading the word of Jesus. Everyone on the team experienced butterflies, but no one got them as badly as he did.

It hadn't happened in the first game of the season against El Paso Austin, because everyone knew that El Paso Austin was a terrible team. But it did happen in the second game, in a stadium 530 miles east of Odessa in Marshall, Texas.

As assistant coach Randy Mayes went over the list of the myriad responsibilities of the linebackers one final time, the drone of his footballese a numbing wash in the bloated air, Ivory's legs began to shake. He started sweating and his complexion turned wan. The more Mayes read from the piece of paper he had prepared, which was based on hours of review of several Marshall game films where every play was diagrammed and analyzed for type, formation, and hash tendency, the worse Ivory looked, as if he was drowning in the expectations of what he had to do.

The alien atmosphere of everything, the strange space he and his teammates occupied underneath the decrepit flanks of the bleachers with its spotted shadows and jutting angles, the crackling screech of "Anchors Away" over and over again on the ancient loudspeaker system to an absolutely empty stadium, the tortuous buildup of heat and humidity like the cranking of a catapult, only magnified the tension.

"You okay?" Mayes asked him.

"I need to throw up," he said.

"Go throw up."

And off he went, trying to exorcise the demon of football.

Perhaps it was the distance that separated the two schools and the fact that Permian, at a cost of $20,000 to the school district, had chartered a 737 jet to get to Marshall.

Perhaps it was the breakfast at Johnny Cace's Seafood and Steakhouse, where he sat in the corner with the other black players and helped himself to heaping buffet-style portions of scrambled eggs and biscuits and chicken-fried steak.

Perhaps it was how some of the shoe-polish signs on the rear windows of cars in Marshall rhymed MOJO with HOMO, or the way the Marshall Mavericks slumped against the doorway of the locker room in their letter jackets when the Permian players arrived, their arms folded, the looks on their faces smug and sullen and smirking, as if to say, *So this is big, bad Mojo, the pride of West Texas. They look like a bunch of pussies to me.*

But probably it was the thought of O-dell, as he had been called all that week during practice, staring across from him in the Marshall backfield.

Odell Beckham, the stud duck of the Mavericks, number 33, six feet, 194 pounds, 4.5 speed in the forty, punishing, quick, able to take it up and out to the outside, a guaranteed lock for a major-college scholarship. *O-dell.* Everywhere Ivory went, everywhere he looked, that's all he seemed to hear about. *O-dell.*

Watch him do this on the film. *O-dell*. Read about him doing that on the scouting report. *O-dell*. Listen to this publication calling him the third best running back in the state. *O-dell*. Could any player possibly be that good, that awesome, that intimidating? Were the rumors true that he had walked on water against the Nacogdoches Dragons and had simply flown across the field like the Flying Nun against the Texarkana Tigers?

Inside the locker room of the Marshall Mavericks, where a sign in thick red letters on the Coke machine read THERE'S NOTHING THAT COMES EASY THAT'S WORTH A DIME. AS A MATTER OF FACT, I NEVER SAW A FOOTBALL PLAYER MAKE A TACKLE WITH A SMILE ON HIS FACE, Ivory went through his physical upheaval, as far removed from the cocoon of the Rose of Sharon pulpit as he ever could be.

He wasn't preaching now. He was playing football.

II

The Marshall game was only the second of the season, and since it wasn't a league contest it had no effect on whether Permian made the playoffs. But the stakes seemed as great as in a state championship, and the air swirled with the edgy sensation that the two teams on the field wanted nothing more than to bludgeon the bloody bejesus out of one another.

Marshall came into the game ranked third in the state and badly desired a hunk of mighty Mojo's hide to prove the Mavericks were for real. That's why the coach, Dennis Parker, had begged the school principal to schedule the game, the first ever between the two schools, despite the distance between them.

"I told him, we can have ten merit scholars at school. But if we beat Permian, we get more publicity."

Permian came into the game ranked fourth in the state with a reputation of invincibility to uphold. Out on the plains of West Texas everyone knew how the Panthers routinely bludgeoned opponents from El Paso and Abilene and Amarillo. But could they handle the pressure of playing in a hot and hostile

environment where thousands drenched from head to toe in Maverick red would be screaming for their heads? Could Winchell hang in if the game got tight and they had to have it? Could Gaines? Could Ivory Christian?

"They got a sellout in Marshall," Gaines told his players several days before the game. "They'll have eight or nine thousand. A lot of fan interest down there for this game.

"I want you to to keep in mind why we're going. It's not a pleasure trip. It's work. We're going to work."

If Permian could survive here, in this rickety stadium hundreds of miles away from home that felt so much like the scene of some bloody ambush, before the biggest crowd that had ever watched a football game in Marshall, Texas, it could survive anywhere. But if the Panthers lost . . .

Odell off tackle on the first play with thousands screaming. Ivory and outside linebacker Chad Payne in his face to drive him to the ground. A loss of three.

Odell off tackle on the next series. Ivory there again, leading the swarming charge of a defense coming at him like darts shot out of a forty-four magnum. A gain of two.

Odell on a draw. Into the open field. Eludes Ivory. Won't go down as the Permian defensive backs ride his back. Sprawls on the ground for every inch to a delighted, roaring crowd. Gain of thirteen. Welcome to East Texas football, Ivory. Stick it up your ass.

Odell again. Busted by Ivory, a hit that sounds and reverberates. He crumples and loses the ball. Welcome to West Texas football, O-dell. Stick it up your ass.

New series. Odell again on a draw. Carries four tacklers with him for a gain of six. Odell to the right side. Stacked up for a gain of one. Odell on a pitch. Ivory leads the charge for a loss of two.

A scout from a neighboring school that will play Marshall in several weeks has his binoculars trained on the game. He is supposed to be watching Odell, and he knows Odell is great. But his eyes keep sliding off to Ivory. He keeps poking his colleague in the side and saying, "You're not gonna believe this but that number sixty-two has made another tackle."

It may be that Ivory Christian hates football. It may be that he is burned out on it. It may be that he considers it pointless, an eight-year journey to nowhere. But it also may be that under the right circumstances, the demon wins the heart of the most steadfast soul, and the nemesis always becomes a lover.

Permian goes ahead 3–0 in the first quarter on a twenty-five-yard field goal by Alan Wyles, but Marshall, capitalizing on a fumble by Comer, moves deep into Permian territory and then scores on a six-yard lob pass from Benny Valentine to flanker Alfred Jackson. The ravenous Marshall fans go wild at this first indication that Mojo can actually be beaten.

The score remains 7–3 at the end of the first half.

The Permian players head into the locker room, which has the feel of a refugee camp, or of a makeshift hospital ward after a catastrophe. Bodies are strewn everywhere and the air is thick with the pungent smell of grass. Ivory lies on the floor with a towel over his head, utterly exhausted from perhaps the most inspired thirty minutes of his life. Brian Chavez, starting both ways at tight end and defensive end after missing the first game of the season because of an ankle injury, walks through the locker room shirtless, his body drenched with sweat. He goes to the bathroom and vomits and when he comes out he looks yellow. He is tired and wilting in the stuffy heat. Winchell, as usual, is silent and ponderous. So is Gaines, who spends most of halftime staring at his play sheet, knowing that without the sloppiness Permian would have twenty-one points instead of just three. The team outgained Marshall in the half 157 to 113 yards, and the great *O-dell* has been held to a mere thirty-nine yards on fourteen carries, but the Panthers are still losing and seem to be bursting at the seams a bit.

"Our own mistakes are the reason we're behind now," he tells the players in the stuffy, squalid darkness. "Let's toughen up. We knew it was a four-quarter football game when we got on the plane today. We just need to bow up."

The Marshall fans give the Mavericks a standing ovation when they come out for the second half. The Marshall band plays a rousing fight song while the Mavettes, in their sequined costumes and tasseled boots and white cowboy hats and with their lips painted as red as a Texas sunset, move their arms back and forth in a mesmeric cadence.

Even the little group sitting in the wedge of bleachers behind the west end zone seems to be getting into the intoxicating pace of the game. It is a delegation of Russians who spent the previous day at the nearby air force base in Karnack to witness the destruction of Pershing missiles as provided by the recent INF treaty between the United States and the Soviet Union.

Courtesy of the chamber of commerce, the Russians are dressed in gray shirts embossed with the word MAVERICKS in red letters. They have on red-and-white MAVERICK hats. They have red MAVERICK carry-on bags with red MAVERICK footballs inside them. They sit on red MAVERICK seat pads and they are holding special GO! MAVS flyers printed up by the *Marshall Messenger* that have the signatures of every Maverick football player and feature good-luck ads from Jerry's Auto Parts and the East Texas Sports Center and Pump 'N Pantry. They look a little wild in their outfits and they don't understand a lick of football, but by halftime they are fairly adept at making a hook 'em horns sign and in any case their understanding of America by the end of the game will be absolute whether they realize it or not.

Winchell drops back to pass and throws deep. Hill tiptoes against the sideline while stretching his head back to pick up the ball. He makes a remarkable catch, as if he has eyes in his chin. The thirty-six-yard gain sets Permian up for another field goal to cut the Marshall lead to one point.

Marshall fumbles the kickoff and Permian recovers deep inside Maverick territory at the 37. With a second and eight, Winchell throws a little pass in the left flat to Hill, who eludes his defender with ease and is gone for a touchdown.

Permian goes for two points. Winchell fakes the hand-off and goes around the right end on a bootleg, angling for the end zone. A Maverick defender heads for the corner as well, the moment of impact unfolding like a game of chicken on a lonely highway; the whole point is not for the players to avoid each other at the last second but to collide. The crowd waits in breathless anticipation for the inevitable head-on. And then the sound comes of two high school boys smashing into each other, as jarring as a bottle flung full force against a wall or a stick being snapped or a club being taken to a set of bones.

It's no good. Winchell is a foot short.

Permian leads 12–7.

Odell takes the hand-off on a draw at the Permian 30 and cuts to the left side. Cornerback Stan Wilkins has a perfect angle on him to make the tackle, a chance to "hit the snot out of 'im" as the coaches like to call it. Wilkins weighs 136 pounds, and of all the kamikazes who dominate Permian and are eagerly willing to sacrifice their bodies for the great cause of football, he is the most fearless, or foolhardy.

But Odell doesn't have time for such mythic self-sacrifice. He outweighs Wilkins by sixty pounds, and with one hand he casually throws him to the ground. He speeds down the sideline and isn't brought down until the eight. The Mavericks score on the next play. The try for two points fails but they are back in the lead, 13–12.

Permian moves to a fourth and five at the Marshall 28. Winchell drops back to pass, throwing a perfect strike on a timing pattern to reserve split end Johnny Celey on the left sideline. Celey turns around too late to catch it. As he comes to the sidelines Gaines is livid. In an uncharacteristic moment, he loses control. Celey hopes to avoid him but Gaines grabs him by the shirt.

"What you thinkin' about, boy!" he screams at Celey at the top of his lungs. He stares at him with a look that seems almost desperate. Celey, like an embarrassed little boy, refuses to make

122

eye contact. Then Gaines lets go, moving back into his anguished solitude, on the headset once again to Belew in the press box trying to crack the Marshall defense for the go-ahead score. He doesn't want to lose this game. A loss will only fuel the fire of those who think he doesn't have what it takes to win the ones that really count. *Sure, he can get his boys to pummel the El Pasos. Anyone and his mother can do that. But against the big boys he big-time bellies up. . . .*

He doesn't need the pressure of it, because he has been through the misery of it before.

Marshall linebacker Kevin Whitworth tries to get up off the field in the middle of the fourth quarter. There is a sudden interlude in the frenzy of the game as he takes off his helmet and, rises only to his knees. The sun is beating down and the humidity makes every piece of clothing stick to his skin like heated molasses and Permian is knocking on the goddamn door again and it's not the Mavericks he is playing for but the entire town of Marshall and there are eight thousand people screaming like they are all giving birth and it is up to him not to let Permian score even though he is sick to his stomach from exhaustion.

Whitworth begins to vomit on the grass, which stinks in the heat and has been torn to bits by cleats and the crash of helmets and the endless screams of the fans. No one pays attention except for Trapper, the Permian trainer, who starts shouting at him from the sidelines, "Gut check, baby! Gut check!" Yes, it is a gut check, a test of how much Kevin Whitworth wants to play this game.

He's done vomiting. He gets to his feet and stays in for the next play.

Permian's fourth down at the Marshall 20 fails.

With a little over a minute on the clock and no time-outs left, Winchell works the sideline brilliantly, the team as precisioned and disciplined as anything in college. Thirteen yards to Robert

Brown for a first down to the 40. Eighteen yards to Hill for a first down to the Marshall 42. Thirteen yards to Hill for another first down to the 29. Ten more yards and they win the game with a field goal.

First and ten. Thirty-six seconds left. Winchell throws a perfect strike, but the ball is dropped. Second and ten. Thirty-three seconds left. The pass is incomplete. Third and ten. Twenty-nine seconds left. The pass is incomplete. Fourth and ten. Twenty-six seconds left. The pass is incomplete. Marshall is penalized for having too many men on the field. Permian has another down.

Fourth and five. Twenty seconds left.

Winchell drops back to pass, the eleventh play of this drive. He has time. He isn't rushed. . . .

He looks for Hill, who has already caught eight passes for 198 yards and cannot be stopped if he gets anywhere near the ball. All the ingredients are there for another Permian miracle. It has to happen. Each and every fan, those who have willingly traveled the 530 miles, those listening at home over the radio, can feel it in his soul. The ball rises and almost seems to freeze in the exhausted air, spent by so much cheering and hitting and incomprehensible effort. . . .

The Marshall players danced and hugged and flashed the hook 'em horns sign as if it were V-day. They ran to the stands with their bright red shirts sticking out of their grass-stained pants in glorious dishevelment. They bowed to the fans and the fans bowed to them and the Mavettes were everywhere with their twinkling sequins and white cowboy hats slightly askew and their mascara and rouge falling joyfully down their tearstained cheeks. Coach Parker gave massive bear hugs to everyone in sight while the Permian team gathered quietly in the center of the field to pray.

Inside the locker room, Parker accepted congratulation after congratulation. One man lingered to the side, waiting his turn. He finally went up to Parker and quietly told him, his voice sounding as if he was about to cry, "Every Maverick, and every person in Marshall, is proud of you."

Parker walked back outside, and about two hundred supporters were there to cheer him. A fan came up to him, gave him a long hug, and thanked him for a "wonderful, wonderful win." Nobody had any intention of leaving, because they wanted to linger in this moment forever.

In the visitor's locker room, Gaines, his face slacked with sweat and his hair matted, closed the door to parents and fans and drew the players around him. "I lay as much blame on myself as anyone," he told them, looking ghostly. "I did a lousy job of getting you ready to play and I promise, I'll do a better job next week." The loss was Permian's first non-conference loss in nine years. With a record of one and one, it was also the first time in nine years the team had been at .500.

The sporadic grumbles that can suddenly overrun a town like a summer forest fire had been given another excuse to ignite again. Those starting the grousing would tell you that problem wasn't the players. But the coach . . .

After all, who in town could possibly forget the debacle of the 1986 season, Gaines's first, when the team had gone only seven and two and didn't even make the playoffs? Many were ready to give up on Gary Gaines right then, ship him and his family back to Monahans where they came from. As booster Bob Rutherford put it, "We'll just have to get another coach, a coach that can win." The 1987 season, when Permian had gone to the semifinals of the state playoffs, helped to redeem him, but the Marshall loss would inevitably stir up the sparks of dissent that he wasn't tough enough and didn't know how to strike the fear of God into his players as his predecessor so effectively had. He was just too damn nice.

Back in the Permian field house after the flight home, Gaines and the other coaches gathered to watch the film of the game and sort out the paradox of it, the alternation of great plays with sloppiness and mental breakdown—fifteen missed tackles, two fumbles, the inability to punch the ball in inside the twenty-yard line. Over its history, Permian had won an awful lot of games it should have lost. It had almost never lost a game it should have won, but this was one of them.

Was there a fatal flaw? Was there something Gaines couldn't detect? Or was it somehow his own fault, his own inability to motivate the team? In the lights of the coaches' office the agony showed, the handsomeness replaced by a weary sallowness, his eyes drawn tight and puffy from lack of sleep. But the exhaustion didn't matter. The Marshall game was an impetus to work harder than ever before. It was a painful loss, but the season was still only beginning and there were eight games left to determine the team's fate.

"Five hundred yards of offense and can't score but thirteen points," he said wistfully near the stroke of midnight as he and the assistants watched the film in the windowless room, where the gray light filtered from the projector lens like a lonely wisp of moonlight.

The party at the home of one of the players started out as a small affair, but then word about it, like the game of telephone, got out to the drag along Andrews and suddenly the vacant lot next to the house was filled with cars. With the player's parents away and unaware of what was going on, there was no problem of parental interference.

There was a keg and a couple of cases of beer. A fight erupted for entertainment. A girl who everybody agreed was about the toughest shit-kicker in Odessa knocked another girl to the ground with a few punches and then started slamming her head against a stone floor, leaving blood all over the place. No one seemed quite sure about the reason for the fight, but there wasn't much attempt to break it up since the girl who got pummeled was generally thought to be a jerk.

The players were upset over the loss to Marshall. But since it wasn't a league game, they could live with it. They didn't need to dwell on it over and over the way the coaches did and flagellate themselves with it. They knew in their hearts they were still going to State, and they also knew that when they got to school on Monday no one would think of them as losers.

They would still be gladiators, the ones who were envied by everyone else, the ones who knew about the best parties and got the best girls and laughed the loudest and strutted so proudly through the halls of school as if it was their own wonderful, private kingdom.

CHAPTER 7

School Days

THE MAJORETTES, THEIR BLACK-AND-WHITE COSTUMES FALLING just below the buttocks, twirled and beckoned as the band—fifty-four clarinetists, fifty-one flutists, thirty-six cornetists, twenty-six trombonists, twenty-five percussionists, eighteen saxophonists, fourteen French horn players, nine baritone players, and nine tubaists—belted out "Boogie Woogie Bugle Boy." The color guard waved its flags to "Barbara Ann." The master of ceremonies made the introductions with the flare of a circus ringmaster asking the audience to direct its attention please to the center ring. "Ladies and gentlemen, the very best football team in the state of Texas!" From all around came whoops and cheers for the two rows of players at the front in their black jerseys, from the stunningly dressed girls over in the corner with their leather skirts and Vuitton bags and blond hair that rose to a rounded peak and then fell like the fanned plumes of a peacock, from the clean-cut boys in their pleated pants and stone-washed jeans and short haircuts, from the teachers dressed in black, from the parents who brought along toddler sons in black football uniforms and toddler girls in cheerleader outfits, from the rows of Pepettes in their white tea-party gloves. The lights went off for a flashlight show, little rings of light twirling around, once again like something from the circus. There was a skit in which the Panther mascot moved about ripping up paper tombstones symbolizing Permian's fallen op-

ponents. The sports director of one of the local network affiliates came forward to give the Superstar of the Week award to the Permian defense, and twelve of the boys in black jersies coyly swaggered forth out of their metal chairs to accept it to more wild applause and whistles. The lights dimmed and the players went to find their Pepettes so they could put their arms around them for the singing of the Permian alma mater. Up in the bleachers the rest of the students locked hands.

> *All hail to Alma Mater,*
> *We'll always loyal be,*
> *Where'er the future leads,*
> *Our thoughts will return to thee.*
> *On every field of battle*
> *Will our banner ever wave,*
> *There'll be a glorious victory for*
> *Permian High always.*

The lights went back on. A couple of Pepettes stayed around to take down the black and white streamers and black and white balloons arching across one side of the bleachers to the other like a covered bridge and the beautiful hand-crafted posters ringing the walls. It was time to go to school, at least for some students.

Understandably heady from the experience of the Friday morning pep rally, Don Billingsley's focus was on the game ahead, not on school. Not all the weekly pep rallies were as rousing as this one had been, but it was always hard to concentrate after them. "I don't do much on Fridays," he said as he sauntered off to class in his black jersey with the number 26 on it, and even if he had felt otherwise about it, there wasn't a heck of a lot to do anyway. School was just *there* for Don, a couple of classes to fill up time that offered virtually no challenge whatever, and he was the first to admit that if he was learning anything his senior year it was a miracle.

His schedule that day included sociology class, in which he watched a video of a Geraldo Rivera television special succinctly titled "Murder" while munching on fresh-baked cookies that he had been given during the pep rally. As his class instruction that day he listened to an interview with the noted criminal theorist Charles Manson and heard relatives of crime victims make such intellectually stimulating comments as "I would like to see him die in the electric chair. He doesn't deserve to live."

It included photography, with the class spending the period learning how to feel comfortable in front of a television camera. When it was his turn, Don dutifully rose to the challenge by successfully mouthing the scripted words, "This is Don Billingsley. Headline news next . . ."

It included English, where the class spent the first ten minutes going over the homework assignment for Monday and the next forty-five minutes doing the homework assignment for Monday.

It included food science, this particular lesson being on Correct Menu Form and the question of what one should place first on the menu when writing it out, shrimp cocktail or Jell-O salad. "This is what I do all day," said Billingsley as he grappled with the shrimp cocktail versus Jell-O issue, moments before plunging into the far murkier ground of the appropriateness of listing cream of tomato soup and grilled cheese sandwich on the same line. "All I do in class is show up. They should make these classes fifteen minutes long. Last year in English I had to work. This year it's like, teach me *something* before I go to college."

Not all classes were like this, but even in accelerated courses the classroom at Permian was hardly a hotbed of intellectual give-and-take. It was not uncommon for teachers at Permian to teach for only a quarter or a third of the period and then basically let students do whatever they wanted as long as they did it quietly. It was also unusual to find teachers who demanded from students their very best, who refused to succumb to the notion that there was no reason to challenge them because they simply didn't care. When there was a novel approach in the classroom, it was geared for a generation indisputably weaned on the fast foods of television and the VCR, not the written word. To get students to learn history, one teacher played a version of "Jeopardy." Another teacher in an honors English course, instead of having the students read *The Scarlet Letter* one year, showed them a video of it.

Many teachers felt that no matter how creative they were in the classroom, it wouldn't make a difference anyway. They talked about a devastating erosion in standards, how the students of today bore no resemblance to the students of even ten or fifteen years ago, how their preoccupations were with anything but school. It was hard for teachers not to feel depressed by the lack of rudimentary knowledge, like in the history class in which students were asked to name the president after John F. Kennedy. Several students meekly raised their hands and proffered the name of Harry Truman. None gave the correct answer of Lyndon Johnson, who also happened to have been a native Texan. .

In 1975, the average SAT score on the combined math and verbal sections at Permian was 963. For the senior class of 1988–89, the average combined SAT score was 85 points lower, 878. During the seventies, it had been normal for Permian to have seven seniors qualify as National Merit semifinalists. In the 1988–89 school year the number dropped to one, which the superintendent of schools, Hugh Hayes, acknowledged was inexcusable for a school the size of Permian with a student body that was rooted in the middle class. (A year later, with the help of $15,000 in consultant's fees to identify those who might pass the required test, the number went up to five.)

Some teachers ascribed the drop in academic performance to the effects of court-ordered desegregation as well as a rapid increase in the town's Hispanic population. In eight years Permian had gone from being a virtually all-white school to one where the proportion of minorities in the student body was about 30 percent. In hush-hush tones, some teachers blamed the school's woes on the "Mexicans," or on the blacks, even though the school still very much had the look and feel of a white suburban high school, its parking lot filled with new and shiny cars, the majority of its students dressed in striking outfits.

Some teachers blamed the erosion on the effects of the economic downturn in the oil patch, which had dealt Odessa a crippling blow. Some blamed it on the breakdown of the family unit; more and more kids were living with single parents who had to work morning, noon, and night just to make ends meet and didn't have the time or the inclination to promote the virtue of doing well in school. Some blamed it on parents who seemed much less interested in pushing their kids in the classroom than in football or band or choir. Some blamed it on themselves, acknowledging that the passion they had had for teaching twenty years ago had run dry. Some blamed it on recent educational reforms passed in Texas that instead of making the classroom more stimulating, more creative, had done just the opposite by turning the teacher into a glorified clerk forced to follow an endless series of rules and procedures.

Despite the litany of possible reasons, it was hard not to wonder if the fundamental core of education—the ability of teachers to teach and the ability of kids to learn—had gotten lost. Its problems didn't make Permian a bad school at all, just a very typically American one.

"It still amazes me when I give a test in grammar and the kids can do it," said English teacher Elodia Hilliard with more than a touch of sadness in her voice. "It used to be the other way around. I used to be surprised whenever they didn't know it. Now I'm amazed when they do know it." When Hilliard looked around the classroom she saw students with no direction, and she wondered if they saw any point at all in being well read and intelligent. She listened to parents who, rather than promising to try to motivate their children, made excuses for them—the homework was too hard, or the book they had been assigned had too many cuss words in it. Even when she got them to read, the leap to conceptual, creative thinking seemed as far off as a trip to Jupiter. It almost seemed to her and other teachers as if students were scared of it.

There was a time when she had had unflappable faith in her profession, when she had encouraged the best and brightest to follow in her footsteps and spread the gospel of literature and grammar with evangelical zeal. But not anymore. "I really felt we made a difference," she said one day in her classroom, devoid of the usual corner shrine to Mojo but instead decorated with lovely posters illustrating the meanings of *hyperbole*, *oxymoron*, *metonymy*, and *personification*. "Now I'm beginning to wonder. I don't know. I'm really uncertain." She bent over backward not to be negative, but she had a view of students she could not suppress. "They like to have cars. They like stereo speakers that are fancy. They like to go skiing. They like to wear good jewelry." In her mind, students seemed in search of only one thing: "Having fun is what it's all about."

Jane Franks, who had been teaching for thirty-one years and eagerly counted off the days until her retirement at the end of the year, felt the same way. Today's students had become enigmas to her. They weren't disrespectful. They weren't obnoxious. They weren't demanding. It wasn't that they were good kids, or bad kids, or any kind of kid at all. That would have been much better than what they were now, deadened to themselves and to the world around them.

"These kids don't take responsibility, or don't know how," she said. "Kids used to worry about where they were going to fit into the world. Kids today don't seem to worry if they are going to fit in society, because they don't give a hoot.

"Twenty years ago I was working my kids to death, and now I have to remind my seniors to use capital letters and put periods at the end of sentences.

"They don't seem to care about their grades. They don't seem to care about each other. They seem to care about having a good time, but don't know how to define *good*. I don't know what young kids are about. I can't get in their minds. I used to . . ."

Like others, Jane Franks looked around for people and things to blame. But sitting in the teacher's lounge one day, her voice soft and weary, she decided the fault might be with herself. A fundamental change had taken place in the classroom. It wasn't a place to learn anymore, but a way station, and maybe she was responsible for that. "I'm tired. I think I'm tired of being ineffective. I must not be doing it right because I don't have a sense of satisfaction. I don't have the close friendships with the kids I used to.

"I used to encourage my good students to be teachers because it was so rewarding. I don't do that anymore. When I first started teaching I felt, My God, this must be like being a pro ball player, getting paid for something I love. It was where I was supposed to be."

If school was boring, Don Billingsley nevertheless did his best to get through it. When the food science teacher made the fatal mistake of asking the class if it knew the meaning of the word *condiment*, Don immediately answered with "lambskin, sheepskin." All joking aside, Don was becoming something of a food science scholar. He had scored a superb 99 on the fill-in-the-blank worksheet on cakes and frostings, not to mention a 96 on his poultry worksheet. The "preparation and service" worksheet was coming a little more slowly; he had gotten only a 60, but there seemed little doubt that Don would eventually get a handle on it. And, of course, when the occasion arose to write out a menu for a black-tie dinner party in Odessa, he would know exactly what to do.

In English, where one of the blackboard panels had a list of questions about *Macbeth* and another a reminder to bring a flashlight to the pep rally, Don had uncovered one of the great secrets of the class with the discovery that if he angled his chair in a certain way behind the other students, the teacher could not see him fall asleep. "Do you like to sleep? This is where I sleep," he said just before he entered the classroom.

A worksheet was due that day deciphering the meaning of some lines from *Macbeth*, and Don was handed a copy of the homework by someone else so he could copy down the answers. The class time was supposed to be spent doing a little crossword puzzle on the play, but Don didn't do much of it and it didn't seem to matter. The instructor for her part believed that the text the students used, *Adventures in English Literature*, which contained selected works by Shakespeare, Edmund Spenser, and Daniel Defoe among others, was too hard for them. She said also that they absolutely hated any assignment in which they had to interpret what they had read. If they had to think about anything, make critical judgments and deliberations, the cause was hopeless. The best they could be expected to do was regurgitate.

In sociology, Don generously passed around his bag of cookies. He and the other students watched eagerly as accounts of one gruesome murder after another passed over the tiny VCR screen, accompanied by the hushed melodrama of Geraldo Rivera. The teacher gave no instruction the entire period, except to applaud the actions of a man who, in broad daylight at an airport, killed a manacled criminal suspect accused of molesting the man's son.

Don, of course, was a football player, which gave him special status among his peers regardless of how he performed in class. In the hierarchy of the school, where girls and partying and clothes and fancy cars were as important as academics, being a football player opened doors that other students could only dream of. All other achievements seemed to pale in the face of it.

Eddie Driscoll, a wonderfully articulate student ranked number two in the senior class, loved to read and debate and throw out ideas. He stood out in class like a sore thumb. There were some who admired him and others who considered him a pompous windbag. Despite all his academic accomplishments, Eddie himself often wondered what it would be like to sit in those two rows at the front of the pep rally each Friday in a brotherhood as supremely elite as Skull and Bones at Yale or the Porcellian Club at Harvard. Such musings didn't make him resentful of the football players; he liked them. He just felt a little envious. No matter how many books he read, no matter how exquisite his arguments in government class about gun control or the Sandinistas or the death penalty, he never got the latest scoop on who was having the weekend parties. Only the football players were privy to that sacred knowledge.

"The football identity is so glorious," he said. "I always wondered what it would have been like if I had been a football player. I think it would be great to be in the limelight and be part of the team, have a geisha girl bring me candy three times a day."

Roqui Pearce, who had graduated from Permian in 1988 and was going out with starting defensive cornerback Coddi Dean, said there was definitely a mystique in the school about dating a Permian football player. "Everybody's into football. Football is *the* sport. I wouldn't say it's an honor or anything but it's looked up to: 'Wow, you're going out with a football player, a Permian football player.'"

Roqui had been chosen a Pepette her senior year. Lots were drawn to see which player each Pepette would be assigned to for the season. Some of the players were obnoxious and egotistical, but Roqui didn't really mind as long as it was a football player she got and not one of the student trainers. "Nobody wants a trainer. You want a football player."

She had ended up being assigned to Coddi, who was then a junior. At the Watermelon Feed that year, she hadn't worn his number on her jersey, which angered him. But they hit it off well. "I liked him, plus I wanted to be a real good Pepette. I didn't want him to think I was a bad Pepette. I wanted to be a good Pepette." She brought Coddi an ice cream cake in the shape of a football field from Baskin-Robbins. She baked him cakes and brownies. She got him a black trash can and filled it with popcorn balls. She gave him a towel and pillowcase decorated with the insignia of Mojo and Texas. After several months they went on a date and then started going out steadily.

From time to time the role of the Pepette became controversial. A stinging editorial in the school newspaper, the *Permian Press*, applauded a new rule prohibiting Pepettes from placing candy in players' lockers every Friday. "Though losing a tradition, Pepettes have gained much respect," said the editorial. "No longer will a member be the personal Geisha girl of a player. Instead, she can focus more on the organization's original purpose, boosting morale. And in so doing she will carry the image of professionalism she deserves for her work bolstering the famous Mojo spirit." But the Pepettes still spent time baking players cookies and making them signs. Since they could no longer put goodies in the lockers of the players, they just handed the stuff to them instead or dropped it off at their houses.

Their role was symptomatic of the role all girls played at Permian. "You hate to admit it in this day and time, but a lot of girls are conditioned towards liberal arts courses rather than engineering and science," said Callie Tave, who found herself perpetually buried under a blizzard of forms and recommendation requests since she was the only college counselor for the seven-hundred-member senior class.

The attitude that girls at Permian seemed to have about themselves was reflected during an economics class one day when Dorothy Fowler, a spirited and marvelous teacher, tried to wake students up to the realities of the world in West Texas where the days of the fat-paying blue-collar job were over.

"Think about your jobs. Where do you want to be in five years?" asked Fowler of a female student.

"Rich," the student replied.

"How are you going to achieve that?"

"Marry someone."

On the SAT exam, boys who took the test during 1988–89 at

Permian had a combined average score of 915 (433 verbal, 482 mathematical), 19 points below the national average for boys. Girls had a combined score of 840 (404 verbal, 436 mathematical), 75 points below their male counterparts at Permian and 35 points below the national average for girls. Of the 132 girls who took the test during the 1988–89 school year, there wasn't one who got above a 650 in either the math or verbal portions of the exam.

"It's very revered to be a Pepette or a cheerleader," said Julie Gardner, who had come to Odessa from a small college town in Montana as a sophomore. "It's the closest they can get to being a football player." Gardner found the transition to Permian enormously difficult. She was utterly unprepared for her first pep rally, for all those fanatical cheers, all those arms pumping so frantically up and down, and she found the girls cliquey and obsessed with appearance. At first she dressed up like everyone else, but then she began to reject it. And because she was intelligent (she graduated from Permian in 1986 and went on to become an honors English major at Swarthmore College), she also felt ostracized.

"It was very important to have a boyfriend and look a certain way. You couldn't be too smart. You had to act silly or they put you in a category right away. It was the end of your social life if you were an intelligent girl." The pressure to conform was so intense, said Gardner, that she knew girls who privately were quite intelligent and articulate, but were afraid to show it publicly because of the effect it would have on their social lives.

Her father, H. Warren Gardner, vice president of the University of Texas of the Permian Basin, a branch of the University of Texas system located in Odessa, believed the disparities in performance between boys and girls were a result of the social hierarchy of the school. Gardner said it was clear to him that girls had to "dumb down" at Permian or else run the risk of being excluded from dating and parties because the boys considered them too smart. "It's not appropriate [for a girl] to be intelligent," he concluded. "It's not popular to be bright."

And being a Pepette, despite the restriction making candy off-limits to the locker room, still carried status. "I hate football players, especially at Permian," said senior Shauna Moody. "They're the most egotistical . . . they think they're God's gift." But for a girl at Permian, the only thing worse than being a Pepette was not being one. Or as Moody explained her own reasoning for having joined, "Well, *everybody's* a Pepette."

Cheerleading had a special cachet for girls at Permian as well. Just as the football players walked down the school halls in their game jerseys on Fridays, so did the cheerleaders in their uniforms. There were five girls on the cheerleading squad, all of them white, and they had enormous visibility.

The most popular of them was Bridgitte Vandeventer, who had always wanted to be a cheerleader. "Everyone knew who Permian was and who Mojo was, and I thought it would be neat to be a Permian cheerleader," said Bridgitte, who had lived with her grandparents since she was eight.

The most wonderful moment of her life, she said, was being crowned Homecoming Queen, and she had vivid memories of it—changing from her cheerleading uniform into a black velvet dress, wearing a fantastic spread of mums adorned with black and white streamers and trinkets in the shape of little footballs that one of the players had given her, dutifully waiting in line with the other finalists at halftime and then hearing her name called, holding the hand of her best friend as she walked around the oval of the stadium with tears in her eyes, receiving four dozen red roses afterward from admirers. Because of her status at school and her friendliness, she had no lack of them.

For a while she went out with Brian Chavez, and it was hard not to feel proud when she saw him on the football field. "It was neat to say, that's my boyfriend out there, that's who I'm dating. The time Brian scored a touchdown, I was never so excited. . . ."

Brian was Hispanic, but that didn't make her uncomfortable. "My grandmother says, 'whites are for whites, Hispanics are for

Hispanics, blacks are for blacks.' I don't think blacks are for whites, whites for blacks. I think Hispanics are fine because they're as close to whites as you can get."

She had many ambitions for her life. She wanted to go into the medical field. She wanted to be Miss Universe. She wanted to open a dance studio. She wanted to be famous. She wanted to write a book about her life.

But for the immediate future, her plans included going to the junior college in town, Odessa College. A main reason she was going there was her failure to take the college boards, a requirement for admission at most four-year schools. Bridgitte said she had been advised by a teacher at Permian not to take the SAT exam until after the football season because of her myriad duties as a cheerleader. But she didn't seem upset about it, and one thing was obvious—her popularity at school was unrivaled. Not only was she crowned Homecoming Queen, she was also voted Miss PHS by her classmates. Clearly she was a role model.

"I just want to be known," said Bridgitte in summing up her hopes in life. "I want everybody to know me, but not in a bad way. My dream is to be known, to be successful, and to help people. I love to help people.

"I look forward to getting out on my own and tryin' the world. They say it's a real rat race and I hope to win it."

With his dark, pouty looks, it was hard not to think of Don Billingsley as a movie star when he walked down the halls of Permian, gently fending off female admirers in his black football jersey, except for those two or three or four or five who seemed to have a certain special something. The way he talked to them, with his head ducked low and the words coming out in a sweet, playful cadence, suggested a certain self-recognition of his aura. Sophomore girls fantasized over having him in the same class so they could catch a glimpse of his buttocks in a tight-fitting pair of jeans. He received inquiries about his availability for stripteases. The characterization used by girl after girl to describe him was the same, said with the wistfulness of irrepressible infatuation: "He's so fine!"

Aware of his image as the best-looking guy at Permian and fortunate enough not to have school interfere with the responsibilities that came with such a title, much of his day was spent flirting either silently with his eyes or with his benign naughtiness in the classroom. He might not be learning anything, but school was a blast and everywhere he looked he was fending off girls—the one who sat behind him in government and wanted a relationship (Don had to explain to her gently but firmly that he didn't "do" relationships), the one who sat behind him in food science (he went out with her for a while but it wasn't what he was looking for), the one who came up to him in the hallway.

Then there was the girl who had been dubbed the "book bitch." So desperate was she to ingratiate herself with the football players that she bought one of them a brand-new backpack and then offered him fifty dollars to sleep with her. When that didn't work, she offered to bring the books of several of them to class. Dutifully, she waited in the hallway, whereupon Don and some others loaded her down with books so she could trudge off to class with them with a slightly chagrined smile on her face, as if she knew that what she was doing was the price you paid for trying to gain the acceptance of the football players when you had blemishes on your face and didn't look like Farrah Fawcett.

Don was clearly not motivated to be a scholar. His class rank at Permian going into his senior year was the second lowest of any senior on the football team, 480 out of 720. He reveled in playing the Sean Penn role in his own version of *Fast Times at Ridgemont High*, but beneath all that was a witty, personable kid. During the fall he was voted Mr. PHS, an honor that delighted his classmates and stunned the hell out of his teachers and coaches. The nondemanding, lethargic nature of the classes he was in made it difficult to fault his attitude about school. Left to his own devices, he did what any high school senior in America would do: he took advantage of it.

Asked what the purpose of school was at Permian, Don had a simple answer. "Socializing," he said candidly. "That's all senior year is good for." That, and playing football. If there was any angst about school, it was over the number of girls who desired to spend at least some part of their lives with him. They were everywhere. Girls in short leather skirts. Girls in expensive designer jeans. Girls who spent the last five minutes of class carefully applying rouge and lipstick to their faces because the teacher had run out of things to say. The perplexity of it all gnawed at him a great deal more than the meaning of *Macbeth*. Or as he put it in a line probably not inspired by Shakespeare's play, "There's so much skin around, it's hard to pick out one."

There were other football players who had light schedules. One of his teammates, Jerrod McDougal, had taken senior English the previous summer so that he wouldn't have to grapple with it during the football season. There was something wonderfully soulful about Jerrod. He was unusually sensitive and spoke with pained and poignant sorrow about the confusion of growing up in a world, in an America, that seemed so utterly different from the one that had spawned the self-made success of his father. His class rank was in the top third, but because of football Jerrod wanted as little challenge as possible his senior year. With English out of the way, he was taking government and the electives of sociology, computer math, photography, and food science.

"That's why I took all my hard courses my sophomore and junior year, so I wouldn't have to worry about any of that stuff," he said one afternoon after food science, where Billingsley and he had just spent sixty minutes on a worksheet containing 165 fill-in-the-blanks on the uses of a microwave. "Maybe that's a bad deal, I don't know."

Permian's best and brightest, those ranked in the top ten, reported few demands made of them in the classroom as well. Eddie Driscoll, who would end up attending Oberlin College, said he had never been pushed at Permian and generally had half an hour's worth of homework a night. Scott Crutchfield, another gifted student ranked in the top ten who would end up going to Duke, said he had two to three hours of homework a week. "I think I'd probably learn more if I had to do more work. As it is, I still learn a lot, I guess. In general, I don't do a lot."

II

In computer science, Brian Chavez wore faded blue jeans and black Reeboks. The number 85 jersey around his expansive chest nicely matched his earring with the numeral 85 embossed in gold. He had a fleshy face in need of a shave and his hair looked a little like that of the main character in *Eraserhead*, high and square on top like an elevated putting surface. It came as no surprise that he held the Permian record for the bench press with 345 pounds.

The way he looked, five eleven and 215 pounds, the way he loved to hit on a football field, the way the words came so slowly out of his mouth sometimes as if he had a two-by-four stuck in there somewhere, it was hard to think he had any chance of making it past high school unless he got a football scholarship somewhere.

He fit every stereotype of the dumb jock, all of which went to show how absolutely meaningless stereotypes can be. He was a remarkable kid from a remarkable family, inspired by his father, whose own upbringing in the poverty of El Paso couldn't have been more different.

Ranked number one in his class at Permian, he moved effortlessly between the world of the football and the academic elite. On the field he was a demon, with a streak of nastiness that every coach loved to see in a football player. Off the field he was quiet, serene, and smart as a whip, his passivity neatly hiding an astounding determination to succeed. "He's two dif-

143

ferent people," Winchell said of him. "He's got a split person-
ality when he puts on that helmet."

From computer science he made his way to honors calculus,
where a black balloon from the Friday pep rally floated casually
from his knapsack. On the way there he was handed a note by
Bridgitte that read, "Have fun at lunch and I either will see you
before lunch or after lunch. Okay! Smile! Love you!" In calculus class he casually scribbled his answers in a white notebook,
an exercise that seemed as mentally strenuous to him as trying
to see whether he still remembered the alphabet. While others
strained and fretted he just seemed to glide, and inevitably several classmates gathered around him to watch him produce the
right answer. After calculus it was off to honors physics and
then honors English and then honors chemistry. These courses
came easily to him as well. Part of that had to do with what was
asked of him—with the exception of English, he said he had
almost no homework.

If he wasn't a typical brain filled with anguish and neurosis,
he wasn't a typical Permian football player either. He was lucky,
but he always knew in the back of his mind that if he failed in
football it didn't really matter anyway.

He had become as indoctrinated into the cult of football in
Odessa as anyone. After all, it was something he had lived,
eaten, and breathed since seventh grade. But as he headed into
his senior year he also realized that he wanted something more.
No matter how glorious and exciting the season was, he also
knew it would come to an end.

In his own private way, he found far more inspiration in the
classroom than he did on the football field. And nowhere did
he seem more determined than in English class, under the spell
of a special teacher named LaRue Moore.

She saw in him a metamorphosis his senior year, a fascination
with vocabulary and literature and trying to write essays with
perception and clarity. He was striving for something she
hadn't quite seen before, and when he told her he was inter-

ested in going to Harvard she joyously encouraged him as much as she could and agreed to read his application essays.

It was simply part of her style. Whenever she could, she tried to show students the bountiful world that existed past the corporate limits of Odessa and how they should not be intimidated by it but eager and confident to become a part of it. On five different occasions, she and her husband, Jim, the former principal of Ector High School before it closed, had taken students to Europe to let them see other cultures, other lands. What she aspired to as a teacher was embodied by a written description she prepared of her senior honors English class for a group of observers:

> *I work not only for the gathering and assimilation of knowledge, but also to teach the fact that one can be brilliant without being arrogant, that great intellectual capacity brings great responsibility, that the quest for knowledge should never supplant the joy of learning, that one with great capacities must learn to be tolerant and appreciate those with lesser or different absolutes, and that these students can compete with any students at any university anyplace in the world.*

A teacher such as LaRue Moore should have been considered a treasure in any town. Her salary, commensurate with her ability and skill and twenty years' teaching experience, should have been $50,000 a year. Her department, of which she was the chairman, should have gotten anything it wanted. She herself should have been given every possible encouragement to continue what she was doing. But none of that was the case, of course. After all, she was just the head of the English department, a job that in the scheme of natural selection at Permian ranked well behind football coach and band director, among others.

As Moore put it, "The Bible says, where your treasure is, that's where your heart is also." She maintained that the school district budgeted more for medical supplies like athletic tape for athletic programs at Permian than it did for teaching ma-

145

terials for the English department, which covered everything except for required textbooks. Aware of how silly that sounded, she challenged the visitor to look it up.

She was right. The cost for boys' medical supplies at Permian was $6,750. The cost for teaching materials for the English department was $5,040, which Moore said included supplies, maintenance of the copying machine, and any extra books besides the required texts that she thought it might be important for her students to read. The cost of getting rushed film prints of the Permian football games to the coaches, $6,400, was higher as well, not to mention the $20,000 it cost to charter the jet for the Marshall game. (During the 1988 season, roughly $70,000 was spent for chartered jets.)

When it came to the budget, Moore did have reason to rejoice this particular year. The English department had gotten its first computer. It was used by all twenty-five teachers to keep grade records and also to create a test bank of the various exams they gave to students.

The varsity football program, which had already had a computer, got a new one, an Apple IIGS, to provide even more exhaustive analyses of Permian's offensive and defensive plays as well as to keep parents up to date on the progress of the off-season weight-training program. At the end of the year the computer would be used to help compile a rather remarkable eighty-two-page document containing a detailed examination of each of the team's 747 defensive plays. Among other things, the document would reveal that Permian used sixty-six different defensive formations during the year, and that 25.69 percent of the snaps against it were from the middle hash, 67.74 percent of which were runs and 32.26 percent of which were passes.

Moore's salary, with twenty years' experience and a master's degree, was $32,000. By comparison, she noted, the salary of Gary Gaines, who served as both football coach and athletic director for Permian but did not teach any classes, was

$48,000. In addition, he got the free use of a new Taurus sedan each year.

Moore didn't object to what the football program had, nor did she object to Gaines's salary. She knew he put in an enormous number of hours during the football season and that he was under constant pressure to produce a superb football team. If he didn't, he would be fired. She had grown up in West Texas, and it was obvious to her that high school football could galvanize a community and help keep it together. All she wanted was enough emphasis placed on teaching English so that she didn't have to go around pleading with the principal, or someone else, or spend hundreds of dollars out of her own pocket, to buy works of literature she thought would enlighten her students.

"I don't mind that it's emphasized," she said of football. "I just wish our perspective was turned a little bit. I just wish we could emphasize other things. The thing is, I don't think we should have to go to the booster club to get books. I don't think we should have to beg everyone in town for materials."

But that was the reality, and it seemed unlikely to change. The value of high school football was deeply entrenched. It was the way the community had chosen to express itself. The value of high school English was not entrenched. It did not pack the stands with twenty thousand people on a Friday night; it did not evoke any particular feelings of pride one way or another. No one dreamed of being able to write a superb critical analysis of Joyce's *Finnegan's Wake* from the age of four on.

LaRue Moore knew that. So did Dorothy Fowler, who fumed to a visitor one day, "This community doesn't want academic excellence. It wants a gladiatorial spectacle on a Friday night." As she made that comment a history class that met a few yards down the hall did not have a teacher. The instructor was an assistant football coach. He was one of the best teachers in the school, dedicated and lively, but because of the legitimate pressures of preparing for a crucial game, he did not have time to go to class. That wasn't to say, however, that the class did not receive a lesson. They learned about American history that day by watching *Butch Cassidy and the Sundance Kid* on video.

III

When Hugh Hayes became the new superintendent of the Ector County school system in 1986, he had known exactly what he was getting into. When he interviewed for the job and was given a tour of Odessa, one of the very first sights he was shown was the football stadium. He was also given a look at the enormous sign heralding the team's fantastic achievements in the state playoffs. When he took the job, the only piece of advice he was given by the outgoing superintendent was never to promise anyone Permian season tickets.

"I felt like not a lot of attention had been paid to academics," he said. "That's not to say they had an inferior program. I don't think an effort had been made to capitalize on the potential they had in the kids. Whatever you did in academics, you were going to look pretty good, because there wasn't much going on."

With the backing of a school board dedicated to making improvements, Hayes went to work to boost academic performance in Odessa. He pushed to improve test scores. He raised the number of honors courses from five to thirty. He started an advanced placement program and stopped making excuses for poor academic performance on the basis of a child's socio-economic background. A school district this size, with approximately twenty-six thousand students in all grades, should have eight to ten National Merit Scholars a year, not just one, said Hayes.

But he also knew there was only so much he could do. As he put it, "Public schools reflect a community's desires, feelings, dreams," and nowhere did those dreams unfold more powerfully than they did on a football field.

"It has put Odessa on the map. It has given them a sense of pride I'm not sure could be achieved any other way. It has created a sense of expectation for the kids that is admirable. I think it has instilled in these kids that go through Permian a real sense of confidence.

"If that sort of confidence and attitude could be transferred into the academic arena, that would be wonderful. I don't see that transfer."

The effect of creating those values in an academic setting had been well documented. The most famous example had occurred at Garfield High in Los Angeles, where a teacher named Jaime Escalante had astounding success in turning Hispanic students, most of whom had been labeled delinquent dunces, into some of the finest calculus students in the country. Escalante, whose efforts were chronicled in the film *Stand and Deliver*, did it by turning his class into an important symbol of status. He did it by accepting nothing but the best from students, by forcing them to sign contracts and to come early to class. In the classroom he cajoled and badgered and tormented and loved. A mystique built up around his calculus class—if you could make it through there, you had truly accomplished something spectacular, something no one thought you could do—and success bred more success. Soon almost everybody wanted to prove that he or she had the stuff to master calculus with Escalante.

Permian had a program every bit as remarkable, one that tradition and mystique had made an irresistible symbol everyone coveted, one whose demands were ceaseless, one in which the instructors cajoled and badgered and tormented and loved.

It was all a matter of values, of priorities.

At Garfield High the priority was calculus, where a student's mastery could potentially lead to an academic scholarship and a career in computer science or engineering. At Permian the priority was football, which beyond the powerful memories and the wonderful joy it created year after year for the town of Odessa, rarely led to scholarships or careers. In the history of the program, only two players had gone on to extended careers in the pros.

"If we prepared our kids academically as we prepared them for winning the state championship, there is no telling where we would be now," said former school board member Vickie Gomez with typical bluntness. "If we prepared them half as hard academically, there is no telling where we would be." But Gomez didn't foresee any great changes.

"Football reigns, football is king," she said. "In Odessa, it's God, country, and Mojo football."

IV

In his first class of the day, correlated language arts, a class for students at least two years below their grade level in English, Boobie Miles spent the period working on a short research paper that he called "The Wonderful Life of Zebras." He thumbed through various basic encyclopedia entries on the zebra. He ogled at how fast they ran ("Damn, they travel thirty miles") and was so captivated by a picture of a zebra giving birth that he showed it to a classmate ("Want to see it have a baby, man?"). By the end of the class, Boobie produced the following thesis paragraph:

> *Zebras are one of the most unusual animals in the world today. The zebra has many different kind in it nature. The habitat of the zebra is in wide open plain. Many zebras have viris types of relatives.*

He then went on to algebra I, a course that the average college-bound student took in ninth grade and some took in eighth. Because of his status as a special needs student, Boobie hadn't taken the course until his senior year. He was having difficulty with it and his average midway through the fall was 71.

After lunch it was on to creative writing, where Boobie spent a few minutes playing with a purple plastic gargoyle-looking monster. He lifted the fingers of the monster so it could pick its nose, then stuck his own fingers into its mouth. There were five minutes of instruction that day; students spent the remaining fifty-odd minutes working on various stories they were writing. They pretty much could do what they wanted. Boobie wrote a little and also explained to two blond-haired girls what some rap terms meant, that "chillin' to the strength," for example, meant "like cool to the max." Boobie enjoyed this class. It gave him an unfettered opportunity to express himself, and the teacher didn't expect much from him. His whole purpose in life, she felt, was to be a football player. "That's the only thing kids like that have going for them, is that physical strength," she said.

After creative writing it was off to Boobie's favorite class of the day, biology I, where just about everyone else was a sophomore. He took a seat in the back row of the room. Except for Boobie, the students had their notebooks open, while the rip of an envelope and the shuffling of paper floated from his desk. He was busy reading a mailgram from University of Nebraska head coach Tom Osborne wishing him luck on an upcoming game.

"Okay, phenotype and genotype," said the teacher.

There was the sound of another rip as Boobie opened yet another letter from the University of Nebraska.

The teacher lectured for about five minutes, and then it was time to do a worksheet on genetic makeup.

"Where are your notes from yesterday?" she asked Boobie.

"I left 'em," he said with a smile.

"You didn't leave 'em. I watched you. You didn't take any notes." She shrugged. He smiled some more.

While other students casually worked to complete the worksheet, Boobie ate some candy and left blank the entire second page, which asked for definitions of certain genetic terms. He leaned against his book bag and poked his pen into the hair of the girl sitting in front of him. She smiled at him as if he were a badgering but endearing little brother and he laughed. The teacher had the students complete some Punnett squares and then began lecturing again in a straightforward, no-nonsense style. She obviously wanted to teach the kids something. But Boobie seemed uninterested.

After a while he gathered up his things and left class ahead of time. He was being excused a few minutes early so he wouldn't be a second late for football practice. Off he went down the empty hallways of Permian High School, happy and cheerful, the mailgrams from Nebraska tucked safely away in his knapsack.

CHAPTER 8

East Versus
West

I

THE NIGHT BEFORE THE FOURTH GAME OF THE SEASON AGAINST
Odessa High, Gaines locked the doors of the field house for a
team meeting. Private gatherings such as this were not held
very often—only when the idea of defeat became not only unthinkable but intolerable. Losing to the cross-town rival from
the west was one of those situations, a possibility even more
horrid to Permian fans than that of Michael Dukakis becoming
president.

To put the game into perspective and draw the proper par-
allels, Gaines told the players the story of Sam Davis.

Davis had been a Confederate scout during the Civil War
when he came face to face during battle with a scout from the
Union army. With the battle over for the day they sat in the
moonlight and talked, and before they parted the Union scout
revealed secrets about his own army's position. When Davis was
subsequently captured by Union forces, he was told he could
go free if he revealed the name of the person who had given
him the information. But Davis had no interest in such a low-
handed compromise. "I would die a thousand deaths before I
would betray a friend" were his final words.

It was a vignette that was deemed appropriate on the occasion of the Odessa High game, much like the quotation from
H. L. Mencken that had been posted on the field house bulletin
board:

*Every normal man must be tempted, at times, to spit on his hands,
hoist the black flag, and begin slitting throats.*

The boys in front of Gaines, out of uniform and away from
the hue and cry usually sparked by their appearance, looked
strangely vulnerable. Dressed in blue jeans and short-sleeved
shirts and well-shined cowboy boots, their hair neatly combed
and their eyes still capable of expressing admiration for stories
such as this, it was one of those rare moments when it suddenly became apparent that they were nothing more than high
school kids.

"I am sure there are many applications that can be drawn
from that little story," said Gaines of Sam Davis's eager willingness to die. "The main applications I get from it are twofold.
One is friendship, and the second one is loyalty.

"We've got a big challenge ahead of us tomorrow night. I
want us to play like fifty-two brothers. All for one and one for
all. I want us to have that cohesiveness, that unified spirit. Fifty-
two people pulling together is hard to beat, men. Fifty-two
brothers are hard to beat.

"We know that OHS is going to be fired to the hilt and I want
to match them emotion for emotion. . . . It's gonna be a big
crowd. It's an exciting game. I wish everybody that has an opportunity to play the game of football all over the United States
had an opportunity to play in a game like this. You're part of a
select group."

As part of the tradition in these meetings, Gaines and the
other coaches then left the room so the captains could address
the players privately.

"I don't care what they think over there," said Ivory Christian. "We oughta just run over them like sixty-two to nothin' or
somethin'. We oughta blow 'em out. I don't think they can stay
on the field with us, man. We play hard like we always do on
Friday night. . . . We know how they are, the first quarter you
start hittin' 'em a couple of times, get a couple of sticks on 'em,
they want to quit."

The next afternoon, the players filtered into the field house

to get dressed and have final pre-game meetings. "I don't want you gettin' blocked by a finesse block. If you get blocked, it better be by a macho man," Coach Belew told the defensive ends. "I want one hell of a wreck out there. I want that boy to be sorry he's playin'. Run upfield like a scalded dog. Run upfield and contain that sucker."

By game time more than fifteen thousand fans had emptied into Ratliff Stadium, where a full moon, luscious and plump, sweetened the languid desert night and turned the sky an incandescent blue. On one side were the Odessa High fans, dressed in red, ready for this to be the year when the jinx was finally broken, when they joyously shed the yoke of football famine that had caused them so much embarrassment and so many feelings of inferiority. On the other side were the Permian fans, dressed in black, arms folded, looking like high-and-mighty music teachers listening to the annual school recital, so used to superlative achievement from their star pupils that only the most flawless performance would break their cold impassivity.

The game began. The kickoff fluttered in the warm air amid shrieks and screams. Permian's Robert Brown took the ball and barely got to the 15 before he was smothered by a crowd of Odessa High defenders. They slapped each other on the helmet after the tackle and ran off the field with exuberance. Maybe that opening kickoff was an omen. Maybe it meant that parity had been reached, that tonight was the night for the west side of Odessa to reach back into history, to show that it too could excel at what mattered most.

Or maybe it meant nothing at all.

Ducking underneath the offensive line, Winchell took the snap from center and handed the ball to Billingsley on a tackle trap. He saw a hole and went for it.

The game was on. . . .

There was no better metaphor for the town, no better way to understand it—the rapidly changing demographics, the self-perpetuating notions of superiority that spread over one half

155

and inferiority that spread over the other. The Permian–Odessa High game had become a clash of values—between the nouveau riche east side of town and the older, more humble west, between white and Hispanic, between rich and poor, between the suburban-style mall and the decrepit, decaying downtown.

Twenty-three years.

Twenty-three lousy, painful, shitty years without beating Permian, worse than the plague of locusts, worse than rooting for the Cubs, worse than the Dust Bowl droughts.

Although some had seen slight improvement in recent times, there was no love lost between the two sides. Savannah Belcher, who had her own show on cable television here and was the closest thing Odessa had to Hedda Hopper, called the boundary line separating the two schools "the Mason Dixon line of Odessa. They're not really at war, but a lot of those scars haven't quite healed."

Each year there was always the dream that this was finally it, the game where the juggernaut of Permian would somehow self-destruct and the sheer emotion of Odessa High would finally prevail. The possibility of that tantalized everyone, whether they liked football or not.

Vickie Gomez was a perfect example. During her two terms on the school board she had gotten more than her fill of sports, and she wondered what good high school football did for the kids who played it. But even Gomez had intense feelings about the rivalry because of what a win over Permian would accomplish not only for Odessa High fans but the whole west side of town—the side of town that seemed to have all the trailer homes and the apartment courts made of glue and papier-mâché and the junkyards and the sealed-off areas filled with the hulks of oil rigs that no one wanted anymore, the side of town that had become identified with white oil field trash and wetbacks up from the border.

In the forties and fifties, most Hispanics who trickled into Odessa settled on the Southside. In the sixties and seventies and eighties, the influx of Hispanics rapidly increased and many began living not only on the Southside but the west side as well.

Nothing else in town, not even the resurgence of the oil industry in another frenzied boom, could give the west side the same sort of psychological lift as a win over Permian. Even if the feeling was momentary, it would put Odessa High on equal footing with those east-siders who went home victorious time after time after time to those sprawling ranch houses in those sweet little cul-de-sacs with those names like something out of a Gothic romance. But every time the Odessa Bronchos got close something miraculously bad happened—a fumble into the end zone with the winning touchdown and no time left on the clock, an unheard-of snowstorm turning a potent offense into mush.

It truly seemed as if nothing less than fate herself was working against them, somehow had it in for the Bronchos, who simply could not beat Permian no matter how hard they tried.

"I'm just living for the day that Odessa High beats Permian," said Vickie Gomez, the thought bringing a smile to her usually serious lips. "That's the one thing I'm living for. I'm gonna get out of this town, but not before that happens."

II

There had been a time . . .

When Odessa High Broncho fans got to talking their fondest recollections centered on another era, an era when Odessa High was the only high school in town if you didn't count the one the blacks went to, which no one did.

Those had been the days back then in the postwar boom of the forties and fifties. The Permian fans thought they had a lock on football and were the only ones in town who knew anything about it, but that wasn't true. If you wanted to see real football mania, if you wanted to see a group of people who cared about a team and loved them as if they were their own children, go back to the 1946 season, when almost half the town was crammed together on the wooden benches of old Fly Field like pencil points. Go back to the days of Byron "Santone" Townsend, the mere memory of number 27's angular moves in the open field, the way he could tilt and turn his body so that he was nearly parallel to the ground, making grown men almost misty-eyed. "God dog could he run!" was the only way Ken Hankins, an independent oil producer who had been born in Odessa in 1933 and was a die-hard Odessa High booster, could possibly describe it.

Go back to the days when people camped out overnight for tickets with huge smiles on their faces, as if they were performing an important service for their country.

"Odessa is a place you have to see to believe," wrote Irving Farman in the *Fort Worth Star-Telegram* during the 1946 season. "At first I thought I was back in St. Louis before the seventh game of the World Series, instead of on the eve of the Odessa-Sweetwater football classic.

"Chairs in the Elliott Hotel lobby were selling for the price of the diplomatic suite at the Waldorf—and for half price you could sit on someone's lap."

Go back to the 1946 state championship game after the Red Hosses had already smitten down everyone else in their path—the Lubbock Westerners, the El Paso Tigers, the Big Spring Steers, the Abilene Eagles, the Amarillo Golden Sandies, the San Angelo Bobcats, the Sweetwater Mustangs, the Lamesa Tornadoes, the Midland Bulldogs, the Ysleta Indians, the Wichita Falls Coyotes, the Highland Park Scotties.

Some thirty-eight thousand people filled Austin's Memorial Stadium three days after Christmas for that state championship game. Thousands came from Odessa, and from all over, to watch one of the greatest schoolboy duels in the history of the game—Santone Townsend versus San Antonio Jefferson's Kyle Rote.

Rote, who later went on to star at SMU and the New York Giants, scored on a six-yard run. He threw a fifty-six-yard touchdown pass. He punted for a forty-seven-yard average and kicked both extra points. He did everything he was supposed to do, fulfilled every promise. But Townsend rushed for 124 yards, scored a touchdown, and threw for one as well. He led the Bronchos to their first, and only, state championship win over the Mustangs, 21–14.

"Out in the middle of West Texas is an oil town named Odessa—a fast growing city that jumped from some 9,000 souls in 1941 to more than 31,000 in 1946. And all of them are football mad," said the foreword to a special seventy-page booklet commemorating that championship season. "A great football team will live in the minds of sports fans for years to come. If moving pictures were made of the Jeff-Odessa game, those pictures will be used to show future gridders just how great a high school football team can be."

One could just imagine the grainy images flickering on a postage stamp–sized screen of boys with sawed-off names wearing helmets that looked like bathing caps: Jug Taylor at center, Steve Dowden and Wayne Jones at the tackles, Herman Foster and Gorden Headlee at the guards, the Moorman brothers, Billy and Bobby, at the ends, Pug Gabrel and H. L. Holderman the halfbacks, Santone Townsend the fullback, and Hayden Fry the quarterback.

"Whether or not Odessa again will win a state title, we can't say," said the commemorative booklet. "But, whether or not they repeat, the city of Odessa has had its moment of triumph."

That moment of glory was never repeated. Little by little the football teams at Odessa High started changing, and so did the makeup of the student body it served. Odessa was growing, the promise of good work in the oil field an irresistible lure. With that growth came the inevitable pattern of social stratification. In 1959 Permian opened, and it hastened the migration of affluent whites away from the downtown to the northeast part of Odessa. The east side increasingly became the repository for the town's white-collar class. The west side increasingly became the repository for blue-collar workers doing grit labor in the oil field, and for Hispanics drawn to Odessa because of the availability of work and the relative proximity of the town to the Mexican border. "The attitude of success was moving in that direction and the don't-give-a-shit was over here," said Hankins of the transition that took place between east and west.

In 1964, the Bronchos beat Permian 13−0. It was their last victory over their east-side rival, the beginning of a winless drought that showed no signs of stopping.

As Permian began to build a dynasty, Odessa High football faltered. Little by little, support for the town's original high school ebbed away, the fanaticism of the forties and fifties being replaced by bitterness. Some of those who had once been the Bronchos' biggest supporters, who had gone to school at Odessa High and played in Fly Field, fled to the suburbanlike security of Permian. They often said they did so because they were disgusted with what had happened to the football program. But behind that veil, many believed, was often a thinly disguised contempt for the fundamental social changes taking place at the school, and on the west side of town in general.

When a suburban-style shopping mall was built in 1980 at the height of the oil boom, it opened on the east side of town, just a few blocks away from Permian. The mall was the final coup de grâce for the downtown area, taking with it the Sears and the Penney's and leaving behind the dirty bookstores. When the new art museum opened, it was on the east side of town. When the new Hilton Hotel opened, it was on the east side of town. When the new stadium opened, it was on the east side of town.

As one school official put it, Permian and the east side of Odessa offered disenchanted rooters a reminder of what Odessa High used to be like in the old days, that is, the days when it had had almost no Hispanic student population to speak of, the days when its football team had been the only game in town.

In 1960, the Hispanic population of the county had been about 6 percent. By 1985, census data showed that 25 percent of the approximately one hundred thirty thousand people living in the county were Hispanic, and that estimate may have been low since the proportion of Hispanics in the school system was around 40 percent.

At Odessa High the effects of the demographic shift were even more pronounced. In 1969 the school had been 94 percent white and 6 percent Hispanic. In 1983, a year after the implementation of court-ordered desegregation, the proportion of white students was 59 percent and that of Hispanics 36 percent. In 1988, for the first time ever, the proportion of white students dropped below half, to 48 percent. Hispanics made up 47 percent of the student population and blacks and other minorities the remaining 5 percent.

There had been changes in the ethnic makeup of Permian, but they were not nearly as radical. In 1983, as a result of desegregation the proportion of white students at Permian was 76 percent and that of Hispanics 14 percent. In 1988 whites made up 69 percent and Hispanics 23 percent of the student body.

To those who continued to remain loyal to Odessa High, the changed ethnic makeup had made the school almost unrecognizable. The place clearly had a stigma attached to it now, and nowhere was that better embodied than on the football field.

There was Permian, where champion after champion was churned out on the gridiron, often with the help of blacks who went there because of the odd way the boundary lines between the two schools had been drawn. There was Odessa High, which many old-line supporters felt had become a dumping ground for Hispanics who, among other things, couldn't play football worth a lick.

"Some kids don't like to play football and the Spanish-Mexicans are one of them," said Vern Foreman, an electrical contractor and former city councilman who had graduated from Odessa High in 1951. "Look at the enrollment of the school, and damn sure that's what you got. So they need to take up another sport, like beer drinking."

"My house sits on OHS property and I can't sell it because

161

OHS is the Mexican school, unless it's [to] a rich Mexican," said Hankins, who had been president of the Odessa High booster club for two years during the seventies.

It became apparent that the quickest way to achieve better racial balance at the two schools would be to change the boundaries. The school board was clearly reluctant to take up the issue. Changing school boundaries was thorny under any conditions, but any effort to achieve a more balanced composition would inevitably be heightened by the politics of football. Would students living in areas of town that had been the nucleus of Permian talent suddenly find themselves in the Odessa High attendance district? If that happened, everybody agreed that all hell would break loose.

"It would be very nice if we could make a decision irrespective of football," said school board member Lee Buice, "but that may be where the gauntlet is thrown." Raymond Starnes, the principal of Odessa High, agreed, stating that "football is in the eye of the storm in the controversy over boundaries."

Or as Ken Hankins put it, "When they start movin' some boundaries around, you're gonna see some people slingin' snot and start crying."

Aware of Odessa High's frustration on the gridiron and the image problems it caused, the administration had tried to shift the focus of Odessa High away from football into other areas. In the regional academic decathlon, a contest pitting teams of students from various local schools against each other, Odessa High had won four straight times. It was a wonderful accomplishment for a school where the background of many students was far more economically disadvantaged than that of students attending Permian.

During the 1988–89 school year, Odessa High also had a greater percentage of students than Permian pass the state-mandated test in math and English that was required for a diploma. That too was a wonderful accomplishment. But it did not mitigate the feelings of failure on the football field.

Permian's streak over Odessa High had created deep-rooted convictions of inferiority, to the extent that Principal Starnes spent time after each loss telling students and teachers that losing to Permian wasn't a reflection on anything. "I spend a good part of the year after the football season drumming that message into the students and the faculty that we are not second-rate," he admitted. And Buice knew that many Odessa High supporters would give academic achievement up in a second for one victory against Permian, just one.

Aware of the rivalry between the two schools, employers searched for some middle ground of impartiality, fearful that any inadvertent slip might cause a mutiny from one half of the work force or the other. One year, an employer simply split the office into two militarized zones on game day, thereby allowing Permian supporters to decorate their half black and Odessa High supporters their half red. Even bank presidents found themselves acutely aware of the tricky diplomacy of east-west relations in Odessa. When Ron Fancher, president of Texas Commerce Bank, dressed up for work on the annual costume day for employees, he arrived in a shirt that tactfully proclaimed MOJO on the front and BRONCHOS on the back.

But such evenhandedness still didn't work. At every level, Odessa High fans saw a conspiracy against them. They pointed to the settlement of the desegregation suit and the strange zigs and zags of the boundary line that resulted in Permian's getting more blacks than Odessa High.

Painfully detailed letters were sent to members of the school board outlining how Permian boosters had recruited athletes who lived in the Odessa High district to move and play for Mojo with promises of cars and bargain prices on houses. The school board checked into the allegations and found no merit in them, but the investigation did little to lessen the air of suspicion, and animosity, between the two schools.

Most of the time the Odessa High supporters did their grumbling in private, but once a year it all came out in the open. The Permian fans got tired of the incessant whining of the Odessa High fans, of hearing that the Bronchos' ineptitude on the football field was always somebody else's fault. The Odessa High fans got tired of the condescending smirks of the Permian fans. They saw an area of town changing in ways they had never dreamed of, the names Taylor and Townsend and Fry and Gabrel and Moorman on the beloved football field replaced by new names in a new era—Villalobos and Paz and Martinez and Limon.

They wanted to feel the past once again, to bridge the gap to that time forty years earlier when the slithery moves of Santone Townsend had swelled their hearts like nothing else. They wanted revenge. They wanted to feel the superiority and invincibility that had once been theirs, to stake a claim once again to Friday night. "It's kind of scary that it can have that sort of an impact," Superintendent Hayes acknowledged of the rivalry.

But it did, and Coach Belew, who had played in one of those games fifteen years earlier, put it best in the waning moments before game time when he told his defensive ends: "It's a big game. It's gonna be a sellout and Odessa High is gonna be higher than a kite. This is their season. This is their Super Bowl."

III

Permian reduced the game that night to a science—every part in perfect sync with all the other parts, no part greater than the other parts, no part, even for a millisecond, ever not fulfilling its role in the great, grand scheme whatever the differences in intellect, background, style and skill. Every ounce of individuality had been stripped to produce this remarkable feat of football engineering, a machine so marvelously crafted and blended year in and year out that every corporation in America could learn something from the painstaking production.

There wasn't a single detail left out, not even the *P* decals on the helmets. They were peeled off after every game and put in a refrigerator to preserve freshness, then placed back on the night before the next contest.

Permian ran eighteen plays on that first drive out of ten different formations. Comer touched the ball ten times, Billingsley four, Hill three, and Brown one. The offensive line moved off the snap as if it was shackled together. Winchell, his confidence growing, threw three passes, all of them short, incisive strikes to Hill, all of them complete. They moved down the field with maniacal, relentless precision. If the Japanese had invented football, this is how they would have played it.

The touchdown came on a perfect pass from Winchell, who, rolling to his right and under pressure, threw off-balance to the middle of the end zone and hit Hill with a bull's-eye.

After the excitement of the kickoff, the Bronchos seemed stunned and shell-shocked, helpless to stop this machine that could have gone on forever, whether the field was one hundred yards or ten thousand yards long, whether the drive for a touchdown took eight minutes or eight hundred minutes.

Odessa High got the ball and immediately fell apart, and the faces of the fans filled with the all-too-familiar looks of glumness and haggard weariness, like the faces of churchgoers listening to a sermon that was just the same old thing again instead of the one announced on the church sign promising the return of Christ. On their very first offensive play the Bronchos were called for offsides. Three subsequent running plays went for four yards and they punted. It turned out to be their most effective offensive weapon: Permian was called for roughing the kicker and Odessa High got a first down.

The machine got the ball again and scored, this time on a nine-play, seventy-one-yard drive. Billingsley took in the touchdown from nine yards out. He was sprung by a block from Chavez, who hit defenders with such savage impact that he drove them back three or four or five yards and then, as a final humiliation, swatted at them like a bear trying to paw a fish.

"Man, that hole, it was five yards wide!" said Billingsley as he came off to the sideline, his eyes ablaze. "That was bad! That was bad, dude!"

Odessa received the kickoff, moved the ball minus two yards in three plays, and punted again.

The machine got the ball at the Odessa High 40 and scored, this time in two plays when Billingsley took the ball on a pitch and outran everyone down the left sideline for a forty-yard touchdown.

It was clear that he was getting better and better with each succeeding game, his fumbling, bumbling performance in the season opener a laughable memory. Like his father Charlie, he was a good, tough football player. The previous week, in a 35–14 win over Amarillo High, he had had the best performance of his life, gaining 141 yards in ten carries and scoring three touchdowns. But it had been difficult for him to enjoy it. During the week he had had acute asthma, and a shot from the doctor the day of the game didn't make him feel much better.

"I feel sick as shit," he had said at one point on the sidelines in the Amarillo game. "I'm out there blowing snot all over myself." A little later he scored on a fifty-six-yard run, but he hardly seemed elated. "Man, I'm about to die in this fucking snot." He had pulled off his helmet and his neck roll and sat on the bench exhausted and almost stunned, his eyes puffy and nearly closed, as if someone had pummeled him in a fight.

With the game obviously in hand and Permian ahead 28–0, he had seen little reason to play in the second half because of the way he felt. But Trapper had thought he wasn't sick at all, just tired, just trying to wimp out, just trying to pull some typical Billingsley shit and get out of something. At the beginning of the second half he went up to Don and stared him in the face. *Do you want to play in this game?*" he screamed. Don, who moments earlier had vomited in the corner of the locker room because of the mucus flooding his throat, nodded slowly that he wanted to.

"No you don't!" Trapper had barked. "You sit down!"

Don had been sufficiently humiliated. He eventually got up from the bench, ready to go back in even though he still felt lousy. "I couldn't feel my legs on the last touchdown," he had said. "They felt like shit. I can go in there but I can't play worth a shit, and why should I go out there and look bad?" But Trapper had already marched down the sidelines by then.

"I hate it when they're pussies," he said. "That makes me mad."

But tonight against the Bronchos, it was different. He felt fine and he was euphoric.

"Hell, I'm beginning to like this," he said as a sea of black-clad fans cheered wildly behind him. They were getting the kind of superlative performance they had come to expect, and they had come alive.

Odessa High received the ball on the kickoff, gained five yards in three plays, and punted again.

The machine this time moved thirty-eight yards in six plays to score, the touchdown coming on a nine-yard pass from Winchell to Hill.

Odessa High got the ball back on the kickoff with less than a minute left in the half. Patrick Brown, the Bronchos' best player, went around the left end on a pitch and was hit. He went airborne and Wilkins, coming full speed from his corner-back position, lowered his helmet and hit him in the side with a savage crack like the sound of a shot from a revolver. Wilkins came off the field a hero among his teammates.

"Way to go, Stan!"

"Good stick!"

"He stuck his shit!"

Brown lay crumpled on the field, the embodiment of this typically nightmarish game for Odessa High. The initial prognosis was that he had broken some ribs, but he got up after several minutes. The half ended. The Permian players ran to the locker room with whoops and hollers, relieved that their ascendancy was safe for another year. Brown, meanwhile, with a person on either side of him, slowly made his way up the steps to the dressing room before being swallowed up in the darkness.

Permian had scored on all four of its possessions the first half. Odessa High had punted on all of its four. Permian had fifteen first downs, Odessa had the one that had come on a penalty. Permian had 214 total yards, Odessa High eighteen.

"That's the kind of intensity I want," Gaines told the players before the start of the second half. When Permian went ahead 35–0 in the third quarter Gaines started to substitute liberally because he didn't believe in running up the score. He put in the second-team offense and defense, but their hapless playing gnawed at him. The game was a blowout, but his sense of concentration was still riveted, still totally focused, no time for letup, no time for relaxation. "First offense!" he finally yelled, unable to take the lousy play of the second-team offense any longer. "Piss on the twos!"

In contrast, some Broncho supporters let their hair down a bit. The Odessa High drum corps marched around the stadium doing rolls with joyous, gyrating turns. Some of them even wore sunglasses, an act that on the Permian band would have been considered as blasphemous as taking out an American flag during the halftime show and burning it. With a minute left in the game and the score 35–7 in favor of Permian, the Odessa High band broke into a hell-bent rendition of "Gee, Officer Krupke" that they played with reckless glee, the gold glint on their instruments bouncing off wildly into the night. The Bronchettes, no longer duty-bound to cheer and serve up those reedy, screechy screams, started dancing away with abandon, their faces fresh and unvarnished by lipstick or rouge powder.

After the game John Wilkins, a former Permian coach who was now the athletic director for the county school system, came into the Permian locker room. He assessed the game with the kind of razorlike bluntness that had earned him the moniker Darth Vader back in the days he coached:

"Hell, you-all carved 'em up like a butcher knife."

He was right. They had, although the glow of victory remained intact for less then twelve hours. On Saturday morning, the Permian players huddled in the coaches' office for the weekly review of the game on film. To listen to the coaches, it was hard to believe Permian had won the game, much less by a 35–7 score. All their eagle eyes saw on the screen was a hodgepodge of mistakes and inexcusable screw-ups. The coaches were relentless. The season didn't stop with the win over Odessa High. They were three and one and back on the right track after the Marshall loss, but the following week they would face the undefeated Midland High Bulldogs, and the shadow of the Rebels was getting closer and closer. In the darkness, the players spent Saturday morning as punching bags for the coaches' derisive comments.

> *Sanford, this is so poor. You being a senior and blocking like that. Stayin' on the ground and watching the goddamn play.*
> *That's terrible, Davila. No punch at all.*
> *That's terrible. How can somebody be so dumb to do that. . . .*
> *That's terrible, Chris.*
> *Heck of a squib kick, David. Come up here for an hour tomorrow and practice!*
> *That's so poor, Chris. That's so disappointing.*
> *Have you ever seen a tumblebug, you know what they roll in . . . those little turds on the ground.*
> *You gone blind or what?*

Across town on the west side the mood was different. In subsequent weeks even the diehards wondered whether all the forces they saw working against them—socioeconomics, white flight, the psychological devastation of losing this game year after year after year—weren't enough to make them finally throw in the towel. In a town where football mattered most, where it defined the mood and the psyche, who wanted to suffer through a drought that seemed destined to continue into the twenty-first century? Instead of having the two schools fight each other in a cause that seemed basically hopeless for Odessa High, why not combine them? One town, one school, and most attractive of all, one football team.

"Look at how it would pull this community together," reasoned Ken Hankins. "Look at what it would do to real estate values on the west side."

There were some convincing arguments for merging the schools. It would alleviate the perception of Odessa High as the "Mexican school," which was having the inevitable effect of steering middle-class whites away from the west side. It would prevent a federal judge from coming into Odessa, as was his prerogative under the desegregation order, and changing the boundaries. It would put an end to the continual allegations that Permian recruited players who lived in the Odessa High district. It would also give Odessa High fans something to cheer about again, a football team that would undoubtedly be superb.

Whatever the merits of the suggestion, unification of the schools was unlikely to happen. The Mojo mystique was a purely east-side creation, and Permian supporters would almost certainly put up a hellacious fight if they were suddenly told they had to share it with people who didn't act like them or think like them.

There was little doubt that Hispanics in Odessa, with their swelling population, were making inroads. In 1988, there was a Hispanic city councilman in Odessa, a Hispanic county commissioner, and a Hispanic member of the school board. There was also a visible and identifiable Hispanic professional class. As in many communities across the country, Hispanics in Odessa were considered a "sleeping giant," with the potential of awesome political power if they ever started to vote in numbers that reflected their proportion of the population. It seemed inevitable that their political power would continue to grow. It was only a matter of time, many felt, before Hispanics comprised over 50 percent of the county's population, and at least one former elected official predicted that the white professional class would ultimately disappear from Odessa completely and move to Midland.

But for the moment the town was still very much dominated by whites—the mayor was white, the head of the school board was white, the chief of police was white, the superintendent of schools was white—and while Hispanics were accepted as part of the community, there was little evidence of whites openly embracing them beyond the widespread opinion that they generally worked harder than blacks did.

The most telling proof of that attitude was the saga of Vickie Gomez. The first minority candidate ever elected to the board, her tenure had been as stirring as it was controversial. Uninterested in the good ol' boy network that had sustained politics in Odessa for fifty years, every vote seemed to end up six to one, with the other six members voting for and Gomez voting against. She refused to equivocate on the issue of school desegregation, and in the Hispanic community she became an important, heroic voice. In 1988, she ran for reelection to the school board for a third time. In her previous bid she had won a district seat with a nucleus of support from the Southside minority community. But then she moved to the northeast part of town and had to run for reelection at-large.

Gomez herself had known what was coming when she handed out campaign literature one day in the northeast. "I know who you are," a white woman told her, staring her dead in the eye. "You might as well get your junk out of here." With the entire community voting, her repudiation was stunning. Despite twelve years' experience on the school board, she had received only 24 percent of the vote.

"I knew there was a lot of concern in the majority community that 'the Mexicans' were taking over," said Gomez, and she was convinced that she had gone down to defeat because whites viewed her as a threat, an encroachment. "I lost with twelve years' experience," she said. "That tells you something." If the east side of town hadn't embraced Vickie Gomez, it was hard to envision a scenario in which it would embrace a school merger with its west-side brethren.

As a result, Ken Hankins's suffering in the football stands seemed destined to continue. When he had taken his customary seat underneath the press box for the game, he privately believed it would take a miracle for Odessa High to win. As that spellbinding first drive unfolded to give Permian a 7–0 lead, Hankins knew it was over even though there were more than three quarters of football left to play. Clearly, tonight was not the night the Villaboses and the Limons and the Martinezes would create a déjà vu of the Townsends and the Taylors and the Frys. Those days were over and they weren't coming back. As his beloved Bronchos sputtered and fluttered against the endless siege of that black-shirted machine, all he could do was wait for the debacle to be over. Through his lips came a familiar, helpless mutter.

"God dang, this is just typical."

CHAPTER 9

Friday Night
Politics

I

TICKETS FOR THE SHOWDOWN AT MIDLAND HIGH DIDN'T GO ON
sale until Tuesday afternoon, which explained why the first
handful of Permian fans started camping outside the gate of
Ratliff Stadium Sunday night.

About fifty came together in the darkness. Once the gate was
opened, others flooded in and began battening down for the
thirty-six-hour vigil. Since many of them had done it before,
there was no particular trick to it. Some spent the night in
elaborate motor homes as long as railroad cars. Others slept in
sleeping bags in the backs of their Suburbans, and others just
caught a few winks in lawn chairs. During the day they used
umbrellas to shield themselves from the West Texas sun. An
Ector County sheriff's deputy was on hand to make sure no
fights broke out over who was where in line.

By Tuesday afternoon the line snaked almost the length of
the parking lot and 366 fans were in it. One Permian booster,
surveying the happy, bleary-eyed skein of people waiting to buy
tickets for what, on the surface at least, was just a high school
football game, looking out over the parking lot filled on a work-
day afternoon not only with vehicles but with generators to
power television sets and card tables for playing dominoes
during the quiet hours before dawn, came to what seemed to
be an inarguable conclusion: "Aren't Mojo fans crazy sons of
bitches?"

Maybe they were, but the wait paid off. And when Friday night came round on the last day of September, roughly four thousand of them were crammed into the visitor's side for the biggest district showdown of the season.

To those who had fretted after the Marshall game, there was cause to breathe easier now. Mojo was back. The performance the week before against Odessa High, the methodical, relentless carving of Permian's crosstown rival, had proven it. But as soon as the game ended, the not-so-subtle whispers started that the Midland High Bulldogs had the stuff to take Permian.

Usually it was the other team in Midland, those bastard Lee Rebels, that gave Permian fits. But the Bulldogs were undefeated with a four and zero record and had stunned the Rebels the previous week in a 35–21 win. They were on a high, and first place in the district was at stake.

At the end of practice during the middle of the week, as the final shadows of September crossed over the field and a merciful touch of coolness crept into the wind, Gaines gathered his players around him.

"I guarantee you, men, it will be a sick, sick feeling if we go over there and play poorly," he told them. "We're not that talented. If we go over there and play poorly and lose, it's somethin' you'll remember for a long, long time. Till the day you put your body in the ground, you'll remember it."

The Bulldogs were big, with a defensive line that averaged 220 pounds across, including one 263-pound defensive tackle whom the Permian coaches described as a "big ol' humper." On offense they averaged 364 yards a game, and they had the leading rusher in the district in Dwane Roberts.

"I'm pretty scared," said Chavez, and if he was scared, then the Bulldogs must be for real. "They're pretty quick and pretty good. They're pretty fucking big."

During Gaines's speech in the locker room minutes before the game, the obligatory phrases about the kicking game and field position gave way to something more emotional, the treble on his West Texas twang turned up high like the fat wail of a guitar string in a country and western tune. The players knelt before him as willing, eager supplicants, echoing his phrases with their own uncontrolled snatches in the brightly lit room, which was decorated in the Bulldog color of passion purple.

"We gotta have that Permian swarming defense!"

"Let's go, guys!"

"Permian swarming defense!"

"Let's go now!"

"We're gonna match 'em physical for physical!"

"Let's go now!"

"We're gonna be more physical!"

"Yes sir!"

"We're gonna hit 'em longer! We're gonna hit 'em harder!"

"Yes sir!"

"Four full quarters. That's our credo!"

"Let's go!"

"Four full quarters and we're gonna be tougher than they are! They're gonna come out fired up and we're gonna knock hell from 'em!"

"Let's go! Alright!"

Outside the Midland High band, dressed in its purple and gold costumes, played the national anthem. An announcer's voice then came over the public address system, asking the sell-out crowd of eleven thousand to rise for the prayer, which everyone eagerly did. At the kickoff, hundreds of purple and gold balloons dreamily floated into the sweet, gorgeous night.

The two teams traded punts back and forth to begin the game. Comer scored from two yards out to cap a fifty-four-yard drive. Several minutes later Winchell threw a thirty-six-yard touchdown pass to Hill. It was a nice enough throw. But it was his second touchdown pass that lit up the night and stirred wonderful fantasies of what he might be capable of, how the idea of a scholarship to a Southwest Conference school might not be so farfetched after all. Rolling to his left, he lofted a pass forty yards downfield, the spiral true and perfect. The stadium became absolutely quiet as everyone tried to gauge where the

175

ball was going to land. It sailed on an arc right into Hill's hands. He never had to break stride and easily shed cornerback Julius Bowers for a forty-nine-yard score.

Hill and the rest of the Permian offense went off the field exultant while Bowers lay flat on his face on the turf, abject and humiliated in the glare of the stadium lights, as if he had just been run over. Had it been his choice, he probably would have stayed there forever, but then a teammate went over to hoist him up. That made the score 21–0, and the rout was on.

With the score 35–0 by the fourth quarter, the Midland High Bulldogs, sufficiently humbled, might have expected a little letup from Permian, but there was none. Just as it had been at the beginning of the Odessa High game, the team was in that special fifth gear. As Permian drove for its last touchdown of the night, Jerrod McDougal, from his tackle position, hit defensive end Jeff Rashall at the knees. Rashall got up and McDougal hit him again. When he didn't go down, McDougal hit him again. After the play was over Rashall went to punch him, and McDougal responded by saying, "Your mother's a whore." Chavez went at it with one of the Midland High defensive players as well. Every time he made a good block, the defender would line up across from him on the following play and simply say, "Fuck you." Chavez didn't say much in return, just pinned him to his back again with another crushing block and lined up to hear the comforting lilt of another *fuck you.*

From the stands Brian's father, Tony, beamed with pride.

Tony didn't profess to know his son very well. At home Brian was virtually silent, and Tony wasn't sure what had been the catalyst for his keen intellect, or how and from where he had acquired it. But he had great admiration for Brian and when he thought about what his son had done, and what he wanted to do, it seemed like nothing short of a miracle. Not only was he one of the captains of the Permian team, not only was he number one in his class, but now he was thinking of applying to Harvard.

Harvard?

Never in a thousand years could Tony Chavez have imagined it turning out this way. Never in a million.

Not back in South El Paso, where he had first lived in a little apartment above a bar, then in a little adobe house that had a cesspool instead of a sewer. Not when he had grown up with humble, mismatched parents who had come from Mexico, his father a door-to-door insurance salesman who was laid-back and easygoing, his mother a dental assistant who was red-haired and high-strung. Not when he cut class as a sophomore to cross the border to Juarez to shoot pool and drink. Not when he finally found a high school, his fourth, that let him graduate instead of kicking him out for drinking and fighting and chronic truancy.

When Tony was Brian's age the thought of college, any college, was as funny as it was ridiculous. Just getting through high school was miracle enough, and the way Tony and most other kids from South El Paso looked at it, everything after that in life was gravy, a gift.

He entered the army in 1964 when it became clear that if he didn't join the military and get off the streets, something serious was going to happen. Tony was stationed in Germany. He got drunk one night, took a truck without authorization, and hopped from town to town until he wrecked it. He wasn't court-martialed, but he was stripped of his rank and confined to the base for six months.

"It scared the shit out of me," he remembered, and he'd decided he'd better straighten up. He went to various army missile schools and intelligence schools and communications schools. For the first time in his life he realized that he wasn't born to be a delinquent but actually had some smarts, or else the army was filled with exceptionally stupid people. "It was amazing how dumb these motherfuckers were," he remembered. He came out of the army and went back to El Paso without any idea of what he should do. He got a job as an electric meter reader, and then he saw an ad in the newspaper for openings in the El Paso police department.

He became a cop in 1967 at a time when just about everyone in the world hated cops. It was a fascinating, bizarre line of work that he was perfectly suited to because of his street smarts and not so suited to because of his liberal outlook, and he quickly realized that 50 percent of his colleagues "had no business carrying a fucking gun." He worked patrol for five years, then became a detective in vice and narcotics, then made sergeant.

In the meantime he had gotten married, and right after his first child, Adrian, was born, he decided to go to college full-time to get a degree. He worked the late shift as a cop from eleven at night to seven in the morning, showed up for class at the University of Texas–El Paso an hour later, went all day with a full course load, got in a few hours' sleep, and then went back to the late shift. He majored in political science and English and by going year-round he graduated in three years. He never had a weekend off during that period, and looking back on it, he didn't know how he had done it. But something was pushing him. If the opportunity was there to get a college education under the G.I. Bill, he figured he might as well take advantage of it.

He came up for lieutenant, but then he decided to quit the police department altogether and go to law school. He went to Texas Tech University in Lubbock at the age of twenty-nine.

When he graduated from law school in 1978, he had hoped to get a job in neighboring Midland instead of Odessa. On his trips between Lubbock and El Paso he drove through Odessa, down the hodgepodge of Second Street with its junkyards and cheap motels and auto supply stores, across Andrews Highway with its endless row of fast-food restaurants and corrugated warehouses, and he thought the town was dirty and seedy and trashy. But the district attorney's office made him a job offer even though he didn't have his license yet, and he accepted it. He was the first Hispanic lawyer ever to work for the office, and he later found out why the offer had been made so quickly—the office had come under a lot of heat for its investigation of the death of a Hispanic inmate in the county jail. Several witnesses claimed he had been beaten to death. The allegation was never substantiated, but the office needed a token Hispanic fast, and Tony was it. He worked in the district attorney's office for two years and then opened a criminal practice of his own. It became a gold mine. Seventy percent of his clients were Mexican-American, and much of his work was in the lucrative area of drug-related cases. In 1982 he moved his family from an apartment to a house in the most elite section of town, the Country Club Estates.

His law practice thrived and soon Tony Chavez had it all, money, a six-figure income, a fancy house with a pool, fine cars, an American Express Platinum card. When he was growing up he had never once gone out to dinner with his parents or to the movies. He lavished his sons with all those things and much, much more, trips, jewelry, a brand-new RX-7 sports car for Brian that took him less than a week to crack up in a mall parking lot.

His life seemed the embodiment of the American Dream, living proof that anything could happen if a person had enough drive and a willingness to take risks. But Tony had never forgotten where he came from. Beneath the successful lawyer was still a kid on the run in South El Paso—a little boyish, a little roguish, a little unorthodox, a little iconoclastic, and he didn't feel imperial or privileged because of what had happened to him.

He had done well in Odessa. He had come at a time when it was impossible anymore to ignore Hispanics, and he made good from that circumstance. He and his family had assimilated as well as any Hispanic family in town had, but there were still signs of subtle and not-so-subtle racism.

Even now it was still hard for Tony to get used to many of the popular values of the place—the love for Reagan, the rise of the religious right with what he felt to be its thinly disguised hatred for blacks and Hispanics and homosexuals, the hue and cry in favor of the death penalty, the way people had no tolerance for others who were less fortunate.

179

"They treat Reagan like he's a saint," he said. "He never went to church. They look at him like a family man. His family hates him. They think he's a war hero. The only place he was a war hero was in the movies." He sometimes wondered if the country had lost its moral center, its sense of benevolence. He had come to Odessa at the height of the boom. He had seen men with fourth-grade educations who could barely read making money hand over fist, and he saw the place overcome by decadence and greed until the bust.

Because of the success of his son Brian, he had become as faithful a devotee of the Permian football program as anyone. He went to all the games and made all the Tuesday night booster club meetings. He went to the annual steak feed, where the coaches and the booster club board sat at long tables inside a warehouse and ate delicious slabs of rib eye as thick as a Bible. He sat in the stands of Memorial Stadium cheering and clapping and feeling delighted as the Permian Panthers destroyed the vaunted Midland High Bulldogs. He wore the same black garb as everyone else, and he admitted that he was to some extent living vicariously through his son, who was doing something that he had never done in South El Paso.

But despite these common characteristics he was different, very different from those who surrounded him—in background, in what he believed in and what he did not. And despite his own conversion to Mojo he seemed not to understand it all quite, the devotion, the obsession, the way some people clung to it as if there was nothing else in life. But he also knew it had become a kind of sacred value.

"When Permian football goes in Odessa," he said with a laugh late one night, "then everything will go."

Permian scored again to make it 42–0, and some of the starters stood on the benches behind the sidelines, finally able to relax. The win raised their record to four and one overall and a perfect two and zero mark in the district. They were on top now and it didn't seem possible for anyone to catch them. They had

their helmets off and they looked like a row of beauty queens. There was Chad Payne with his hands on his hips and his chiseled California surfer good looks, the hard jaw, the opaque eyes, the blond hair. There was Chavez, who wasn't scared anymore but was laughing uproariously after a wonderful performance. There was Billingsley, who after another good night with ninety-four yards rushing on twelve carries, now had his mind on more important pursuits, like what party to go to and what girl to charm and who might be worth fighting if he got drunk enough. There was Stan Wilkins, who had played a heroic game despite a painful thigh bruise that required a special pad and wasn't helped at all by the medication he had been given because it made him throw up. They smiled and laughed and turned to wave at proud parents and proud fans.

All around them the world seemed to be caving in; the way of life that had existed in Odessa for sixty years was badly shaken. Wherever you looked the economic news for this already hard-strapped area was dismal. Echoes persisted of the 1986 crash, when the area had become a scavenger hunt for repossessed Lear jets, Mercedeses, mobile homes, oil rigs, ranches, and two-bedroom houses with walls so thin they seemed translucent. The very day of the game, oil prices, the bread-and-butter benchmark of everyone who lived here, had skidded to $13.25 a barrel, their lowest level since August 1986 and far from that of the halcyon days of 1981 when $35 a barrel oil had made this part of the country a combination of Plato's Retreat and the Barnum and Bailey Circus.

The same day, federal regulators announced they were spending $2.49 billion to rescue six Texas savings and loan institutions that had finally fallen under the weight of the crash in oil prices, and everyone knew that that was just the tip of the iceberg. On the immediate local front, reports showed that rental rates for apartments in Odessa had dropped 10 percent and occupancy rates 8 percent, boding disaster for a market that was woefully overbuilt from the boom. In addition, a news report showed that over the past six years the number of employed workers in Odessa had dropped by 22,400, from 65,200 to 42,800.

But here in Memorial Stadium in Midland, where a near-sellout crowd had gathered to watch a high school football game, none of that seemed to matter. The joyous swells of the band, with no note ever too loud or too off-key, the unflagging faith of the cheerleaders and all those high-octave cheers served up without a trace of self-consciousness, the frenzied screams of grown men and women as the boys on the field rose to dizzying, unheard-of heights—little was different now from how it had been almost forty years ago when a young businessman had sat in this very stadium.

> It was the most feverish Friday night of the season: Odessa against Midland, the grudge game to settle bragging rights between the two towns for the next twelve months. There was an overflow crowd of twelve thousand–plus fans in the stadium, rattling the stands from the opening kickoff. Our guest put his hands to his ears, then shook his head. [We] could empathize . . . it would take us several seasons, living in both Odessa and Midland, before we understood the game, not as we knew it back east but West Texas–style as a quasi-religious experience.

The man who wrote those words never forgot that moment in the stands. It gave him a valuable insight, one that he would find useful at another point in his life. By conjuring up an image of America as simple and pure as the scene of pomp in Memorial Stadium, by telling people that he was no different from any of them sitting in those packed stands and rooting for the Bulldogs or the Panthers, that he understood exactly how they felt and how they thought, about Friday night football, about life, about religion, about America, he managed to become the president of the United States.

II

A week after the game, Republican presidential candidate George Bush came to the Midland-Odessa area for a campaign appearance. The scene on the tarmac at the airport wasn't as feverish as the one at the parking lot of Ratliff Stadium, where Permian fans had been lined up for two nights to buy tickets. Some things, after all, would always be more important than others. But it did have the aura of a Friday morning pep rally.

Shortly before noon the parking lot outside the south terminal was filled with people carrying cardboard signs that read MIDLAND LOVES BUSH or MOJO LOVES BUSH. There were little boys dressed in white shirts and blue ties, and high school girls wearing lovely red velvet dresses with white shoes. There were baby strollers decorated with American flags. And there was a whole bus full of kids from Midland Baptist Temple School, the girls in red dress uniforms that went to the knee and the boys in blue ties and red cardigan sleeveless sweaters that made them look grandfatherly. There was a smattering of people in cowboy hats, and a man in a PHILLIPS 66 cap, and another man who wore a military-style cap that said BRAZOS VALLEY WAR GAMES. When he took it off during the rally to put on a free one that said BUSH/QUAYLE 88, he didn't look any different.

Cheerleaders from Midland High milled about in their uniforms, which made them look a little like old-fashioned movie ushers, and in the middle of it all sat a red Mercedes convertible with a paper sign taped to the side: LEE HOMECOMING DUCHESSES WELCOME HOME GEORGE AND BARBARA BUSH.

There were almost no blacks or Hispanics in the audience. There were no signs of poverty, no signs of homelessness, no signs of drug abuse, no signs of the social fissures that were tearing apart America's urban centers to the east and west. The country was perfect and unblemished on this day. As the crowd eagerly awaited the arrival of *Air Force II*, it snacked on the free hot dogs and cups of Coke that were neatly laid out on long picnic tables sprinkled with brimming bowls of mustard and onions. Everything was neat and orderly. Everything you could have wanted was there.

As the time drew near, the Midland High and Midland Lee bands moved past a fence onto the runway. The Midland High band played "Deep in the Heart of Texas," then "Come a Little

Bit Closer" to the accompaniment of hundreds of little American flags bobbing up and down. The cheerleaders erupted into a spontaneous little cheer of "Midland High, yeah, Midland High!" and then *Air Force II* came into view.

"There he is, the next president of the United States!" said the emcee of the rally. "Let's go! We want George! We want George!"

"We want George! We want George!"

"Come on, West Texas, louder!"

"We want George! We want George!"

The excitement was in part due to Bush's being something of a native son. After his graduation from Yale he and his wife had moved to Odessa, where Bush worked as a salesman and clerk for an oil field supply company. They lived in Odessa for about a year in a little shotgun house on Seventh Street that was next to a whorehouse. They became quite popular, which could perhaps be attributed to their down-home personalities, or to the fact they had one of the few working indoor toilets on the street. Bush had then moved to Midland, where he got into the independent oil business, and lived there for about ten years.

Many in the audience were there because they considered Bush's visit a kind of proud homecoming, his visit a claim to fame to an area of the country that most people had to look up in an atlas to find out where the hell it was. But beyond all that there was something in the air, an outpouring that seemed unusually powerful, almost desperate.

The Lee and Midland High bands both broke into "Deep in the Heart of Texas." Bush, wearing a blue suit, stepped off the plane onto the gangplank and for the briefest of moments looked like Notre Dame coach Lou Holtz coming home after leading the Irish to a national championship. He started waving. In return, all the little American flags and the handmade signs started bobbing up and down again.

By the standards of the national press, Bush said virtually nothing to those gathered at the airport in Midland, Texas. It was simply another campaign stop, another orchestrated moment; the only difference, as one correspondent wearily put it, was that this particular rally had two high school bands instead of one playing at full throttle. Bush's speech contained nothing newsworthy about drug policy, or Nicaragua, or the Federal Reserve, or balancing the budget, or social ills, or the homeless. But no one cared. They weren't there to listen about problems.

Bush said everything, everything that the people assembled at the airport wanted to hear, so tired had they grown of the litany of how American education was failing, how the Japanese were taking over, how America couldn't compete anymore, couldn't feed its own anymore, wasn't strong anymore, just wasn't any damn good anymore. In his simple remarks he confirmed for them that America was still great, still number one in the weekly top twenty poll, whatever the threat of the Japanese and the Germans and OPEC. He also confirmed for them that what they believed in, what they cared about, was the very essence of what it meant to be an American. It took almost no time for him to get his astonishingly simple message across.

"I believe that I am on the side of the American people and the state of Texas in terms of values!"

The crowd erupted in cheers, and the cheers only intensified as he listed some of those values: prayer in the schools, the right to own a gun, the outrageousness of furloughing dangerous prisoners, particularly dangerous-looking black ones like Willie Horton. He took out the dreaded *L* word and planted it squarely on the forehead of his opponent, Michael Dukakis.

"I am not going to be deterred by one or two liberal columnists or the liberal governor of Massachusetts!"

The word came out with a sneering nastiness, as though he were spitting out a rancid piece of food, and it successfully conveyed the desired effect: being a liberal wasn't just a political state of mind, but was something threatening, something dangerous.

"Texas is on the way back!"

It was an absolutely mystifying statement given the precipitous drop in oil prices at that very moment and news the same week that yet another Texas bank, MCorp, had announced that it could not go on unless it received a billion-dollar bailout from the FDIC. The announcement meant that nine of the state's ten largest banking organizations now needed an aggregate sum of money from public and private sources well into the tens of billions to stay afloat. The problems of MCorp and the other banks were nothing, of course, compared to the S & L crisis, which according to one estimate was going to take $65 billion to solve. But it didn't matter.

People liked hearing that Texas was back, that they were tough and could take it and were up on their feet again. Fact and fiction merged. They liked George Bush in the same way they absolutely worshiped Ronald Reagan, not because of the type of America that Reagan actually created for them but because of the type of America he so vividly imagined. As Tony Chavez pointed out, it was an amazing illusion, as contradictory as Reagan himself becoming the great promoter of the family despite his own life as a divorcé and a father whose children hated him, as contradictory as Bush's passing himself off as a down-to-earth Texan despite an upbringing in the ultra-rich ozone of Greenwich, Connecticut, followed by sojourns at the equally elite Andover and Yale. There were more cheers, more frantic wavings of tiny flags.

"Thank you for the magnificent welcome home. I'm glad to be back. God bless you."

The two bands once again broke into "Deep in the Heart of Texas." The five hundred or so people who had come out for the five-minute speech then left to go home, happy and satisfied. In that brief interplay, it was easy to see why the election was over. Dukakis, with his painfully methodical, low-key approach, didn't have a prayer.

Bush then left to give a speech at the Petroleum Museum to an audience of independent oilmen. He talked about his time in Midland and his wife Barbara's "world record as the mother that watched the most Little League games." He talked about a community pulling together in the fifties when times were not simply tough but "pretty darn tough." Mostly he talked about "values," the most important buzzword to be added to the lexicon of American politics in the 1988 election.

"My values have not changed a bit since I was your neighbor in the fifties. My values are values like everyone here that I think of: faith, family, and freedom, love of country and hope for the future. Texas values. Some just call it just plain common sense.

"I am an optimist and I'd much rather go around the United States of America talking about how things are on the move and that we can do better . . . than in telling everybody how sad everything is because my faith in this country has never varied since I learned from many of you what it is to take a risk and build something and to get out there and do something for the community.

"I've stood shoulder to shoulder with many people here today in starting the first YMCA in Midland, Texas, and then let that liberal governor ridicule me about a thousand points of light but it is neighbor helping neighbor, it is community, and Odessa and Midland stand for community and we are right!"

It was the same thing he had done at the airport. He created an image of a country that was still as good, as fundamentally sound as it had been in the fifties, when Bush and thousands of others had watched the American Dream blossom before their shining, ever-hopeful eyes, days when the United States produced 44 percent of the world's oil, when the most dominant force affecting price was the Texas Railroad Commission and not OPEC since there was no OPEC, days of heaven that no longer existed.

Their belief in him seemed ironic, perhaps even crazy. Far from blossoming, the economy of Midland-Odessa had fallen apart during the Reagan-Bush administration, and it was hard to think of any other single area of the country that had suffered as much. The price of oil had plummeted, and there were theories that this had happened because of an orchestrated maneuver by the Reagan administration, in concert with the

Saudis, to reduce oil prices as a way of stimulating economic growth. If that was true, Bush was part of an administration that, far from protecting the oil industry, had pulled the rug out from under it.

The estimated drop in spot oil prices in 1986, from about $24 a barrel to $8 a barrel, resulted in a savings to consumers nationwide of about $200 million a day. With a 2.5 percent drop in the consumer price index, everyone around the country had a great deal more money to spend, except in Midland-Odessa and other oil-producing regions, where life under the Reagan-Bush administration became as bleak as it had been during the Depression.

The statistics were numbing. In 1986 unemployment in Odessa shot up to 20 percent. The number of bankruptcies filed with the federal court in Midland went up by 65 percent. The price of housing in the Midland-Odessa area fell the most of any area in the nation, 11.4 percent. More gripping than the statistics were the images: hundreds of people waiting outside the Permian Bank in Odessa after it had failed to see if they could get their money out; a row of once-proud oil field workers who never in their lives had dreamed of applying for unemployment stretching down the block like a bread line; an FDIC auction featuring the complete inventory of a failed Toyota dealership—14 mobile homes and more than 150 cars and trucks; a full-page newspaper ad by Fannie Mae advertising great deals on sixty-eight houses that were in foreclosure—not the lavish palaces that everyone associated with the Texas oil boom but starter homes bought by people trying to grab a piece of the dream.

And yet when it came to the election none of the devastation seemed to matter. "The Republicans have done nothing to help the Texas oilman for the last eight years," said Clayton Williams, a Midland oilman. "But when it comes down to voting for a liberal versus a conservative, most oilmen are conservative.

"If other oilmen are like me, they're probably going to bitch and scream and moan. And then go ahead and vote our principles—conservative."

Voting on principles was hardly a new phenomenon, but it seemed to go a step further in 1988. In Odessa and Midland, as in other places, liberalism had come to be perceived not as a political belief but as something unpatriotic and anti-American, something that threatened the very soul of the hardworking whites who had built this country and made it great. And Dukakis, by the very way he looked and acted, embodied every bad stereotype of a liberal—brooding, clenched, frowning, swarthy, hairy, a man who came across as one gigantic, furrowed eyebrow.

As election day neared in Odessa, the antagonism toward Dukakis and all that he represented became more and more venomous. Ever since the college was built for the Pennsylvania Methodists in the 1880s, there had been nothing but distrust for Yankees in Odessa. And Dukakis was as Yankee as they came, from Massachusetts, or Taxachusetts as it was derisively called, with a Harvard background, surrounded by Harvard people who all spoke high-and-mighty Yankee talk and treated simple, earnest people like the citizens of Odessa with as much respect as they did the hind rear of a donkey. The tone of the comments and the campaign literature about him went far beyond simple dislike for a presidential candidate because he was a Democrat. Even the jokes about him seemed bitterly cruel.

> *What do Dukakis and panty hose have in common?*
> *They both irritate Bush.*

> *"What's twelve inches long and hangs in front of an asshole?*
> *Dukakis's necktie.*

During the election season a so-called Michael Dukakis Fact Sheet started making the rounds in Odessa. The pamphlet, drawn up by a group called the League of Prayer in Montgomery, Alabama, and handed out at a local doctor's office, brutally condemned Dukakis as a pro-choice, pro-homosexual advocate of sodomy who was soft on defense and soft on criminals and who sought "to rid America of its Godly heritage." The pamphlet described him as a "card-carrying member of the ACLU," which it said was the equivalent of being "against everything moral, ethical, righteous, holy, Christian, Godly and patriotic." Homosexuals, the pamphlet said, were nothing more than a "minuscule band of sexual perverts."

In the Permian locker room, players old enough to vote for the first time talked about Dukakis as the "homo" president and depicted a world with him as president in which it would no longer be possible to exercise the inalienable right of taking a forty-four magnum to blow the brains out of a criminal robbing or physically assaulting you.

The comments about him depicted a man who would not simply take the country in a different direction but would threaten its very sanctity, its very core. They translated into an almost irrational fear—fear that Dukakis would shut down the military, fear that he would take away the right of people to protect themselves against violent intruders, fear that he would ruin the economy, fear that the only people who would benefit from his administration would be the poor, while they, the hardworking guts of the country, got sold down the river.

"Boy, I think he would be the worst thing that could ever happen to this country," said city councilman Dub Kennedy, who found Dukakis's membership in the ACLU abhorrent.

"I think he's the biggest liberal I know running for president," said Ken Scates, who had lived in West Texas for almost forty years and had built up his own oil field service company from scratch. "All I know is what I have read in *Reader's Digest* and other things. I think he's too liberal. He'd shut the military down. Inflation would be bad. The only person that I see voting for him are other liberals and welfare recipients."

"First of all I'm a gun collector," said former city councilman Vern Foreman. "You tell me I can't have any guns, you're gonna see a helluva fight. I don't see how anybody could vote for Dukakis. The son-of-a-bitch is too damn liberal."

Certainly it would have been hard for Dukakis ever to play well in this part of the country. West Texas had a history of staunch conservatism, not to mention a virulent dislike of government as practiced by Democrats. In the fifties and sixties the John Birch Society had had a significant membership in Odessa. The last time the county had voted for a Democratic presidential candidate was in 1948, when it went for Harry Truman. If the politics was conservative, so obviously were the attitudes.

In 1982, the mayor of Odessa proclaimed Decency Awareness Week and asked citizens "to give appropriate recognition to this week by suitable observances and prayer and supplication to Almighty God to deliver our City, State and Nation from the threat of public decadence and crimes of indecency."

In the early eighties, a group called Odessans for Decency had been formed. The group avowed a four-point platform—stamping out abortion, pornography, and homosexuality, and establishing prayer in the schools. For a time it was quite popular and quite effective. It engineered a successful campaign to force an adult bookstore out of the downtown. It successfully lobbied the city council to block a cable company from offering a sexually explicit program called Escapade. It also led a spirited campaign to prevent Ozzy Osbourne from playing a concert in Odessa in 1983 because of the British rock star's outlandish behavior, which had included biting the head off a bat as well as performing songs that allegedly encouraged Satan worship, but a federal judge ruled that Osbourne had a contractual right to play here.

Joe Seay, one of the founders of Odessans for Decency, said the group then asked its followers, who he said numbered twelve thousand, "to pray that God himself would prevent Ozzy Osbourne from coming to Odessa, Texas." Osbourne ended up canceling because he had the flu.

In 1987 Seay stepped down as president of Odessans for Decency to found a group called the Christian Voting Bloc, an organization aiming to promote political candidates with Christian values. During election time he sent out a list of endorsements to a secret mailing list of twelve hundred registered voters. Influential Democrats in town, much to their chagrin, believed the group had significant influence. The platform of the Christian Voting Bloc was much the same as that of Odessans for Decency—fighting pornography and working to curtail any special rights for homosexuals.

In the latter part of 1988, when a state district judge from Dallas said he gave a murderer a lighter sentence because the two victims were homosexual, Seay was one of the few to support him publicly.

"We'd work to keep him in office," Seay told members of the press. "We need more like him."

When George Bush came to Midland-Odessa he didn't go quite as far, but it was the family and school prayer and allegiance to the flag that he highlighted over and over. As historian Garry Wills pointed out, he seemed as closely linked to Pat Robertson as he did to Ronald Reagan, and it was a strategy that worked brilliantly.

Dukakis forces in Texas had thought they could win the state on the basis of the economy. They thought that the issues of gun control and the Pledge of Allegiance were emotional fads that would quickly die out. They never thought that Bush's rhetoric, a kinder, gentler version of the "Morton Downey Show," would have much lasting effect. They patiently waited for the campaign to get back to the greater good of forging practical solutions to massive problems, but that shift never took place.

Perhaps just once Dukakis should have left the rarefied atmosphere of Boston and Harvard that seemed to entrap him no matter where he was, hopped in a car by himself, and taken a drive down one of those lonely, flat-as-a-pancake roads to the gleaming lights of a Friday night football game. As in ancient Rome, any road he chose would have gotten him there. He could have pulled down his tie and unbuttoned his collar. He could have gone to the concession stand to eat a frito pie and a chili dog and then wash it all down with one of those dill pickles that came carefully wrapped in silver foil. Instead of keeping track of the score, he could have sat in a corner of the stands to listen to the conversations around him as well as take note of the prayers both before the game and after. He could have seen what people were wearing, observed how they interacted with their children, listened to the songs the bands were playing, watched those balloons float into the air like doves of peace, and let the perfume of the Pepettes and the Golden Girls flow sweetly into his nostrils. He could have counted how many blacks were there, and how many Hispanics.

There was a heartbeat in those stands that dotted the Friday nights of Texas and Oklahoma and Ohio and Pennsylvania and Florida and all of America like a galaxy of stars, a giant, lurking heartbeat.

Michael Dukakis never heard that sound, and even if he had he probably would have dismissed it as some silly tribal rite practiced in the American boondocks by people who made no difference. But his opponent didn't make the same mistake. He had been down the lonely road to those games, where the heartbeat had resonated more spectacularly than in the healthiest newborn. He knew it was still as strong as ever. He knew what kind of values these people had.

In his acceptance speech for the Republican nomination for president Bush reminded an entire nation, an entire world, of where he had been and what he believed in, his echo of the past a reaffirmation of the present:

> *Now we moved to West Texas forty years ago, forty years ago this year. And the war was over, and we wanted to get out and make it on our own. Those were exciting days. We lived in a little shotgun house, one room for the three of us, worked in the oil business, and then started my own.*
>
> *And in time, we had six children; moved from the shotgun to a duplex apartment to a house, and lived the dream—high school football on Friday nights. . . .*

193

CHAPTER 10

Boobie Who?

I

WHEN BOOBIE MILES RETURNED TO THE FOOTBALL FIELD, NO one called out his name with those bellowing chants that had rocked the Watermelon Feed in a moment that seemed like a millennium before. There were no bursts of applause, no coach's speech comparing him to the great Permian runners of the past, no take-your-sweet-time walk down the aisle of the crowded high school cafeteria. In the space of five weeks he had become an afterthought whose past performance earned no special privilege and seemed largely forgotten.

Had there been a waiver wire in the world of high school football, a place to dump former stars, he would have been on it, dangled at a bargain-basement price to Andrews or Kermit or Wink or maybe Seminole or any other town that might be willing to take a chance on a once-hot prospect with a bum knee for the stretch run to make the playoffs. Or maybe he could just be traded for a reserve defensive tackle and a player to be named later.

"In a week or two the fans will think he already graduated," said Trapper. "They'll be saying, 'Boobie who?' "

Boobie who?

The only thing to herald his return was the shame and ignominy of a white shirt. There were dozens of other players wearing them as well, and together they blended into the dry heat of the practice field like lingering cattle waiting to be herded in

194

this or that direction. There were a select few who didn't look that way and clearly stood out, but Boobie didn't merit that distinction anymore.

As part of a long-standing tradition, the Permian starters wore black shirts during practice and the subs wore white. In the life of a player few single moments were more stirring than to open up the locker one day and find a black practice jersey hanging there like a gilded, sacred robe in the middle of a foul-smelling pile of pads and pants and shoes and jocks. Conversely, few single moments were more humbling than to have that black shirt taken away and given to someone else.

Boobie had worn a black shirt his junior season. Up until the knee injury, he had worn one his senior year without a remote thought of change. But in his absence Chris Comer had come to own the black shirt at fullback. He had rushed for a hundred yards or more in each of Permian's five games, and it was becoming the general consensus of the coaches that he was better than Boobie ever had been or ever would be. For one thing, he worked harder in the weight room than Boobie and didn't coast on his natural strength. For another, he didn't try all those pretty-boy spin moves all day long like he was some damn ballerina or something but knew that the best way sometimes to get by someone was to lower the shoulder and punish the living shit out of him, use that stupendously strong body of his as the weapon God had clearly intended it to be. Boobie might have been able to run like that, but it was difficult to get him to try it. In the past all that was a necessary part of coaching him. But now it didn't matter nearly so much. If he wanted to show off his fancy spins and jukes, he could do it at home in his backyard in between the broken-down cars and the little pieces of trash that swirled in the wind. He wasn't a black shirt anymore, just another white shirt trying to work his way back into the starting lineup.

When he returned to practice and discovered his reduction in status, he was livid. It wasn't supposed to be this way, not his senior year. "They made me wear a white shirt," he said afterward. "They jacked me. If I don't play, I'm not gonna suit up. You know me. If I suit up, I want to play."

On the field, the coaches were as gentle with him as ever, treating him once again as an explosive time bomb that could be set off by the slightest impulse. When Boobie went up to Coach Belew and asked him if he was going to play that Friday night against Midland High, Belew gently told him that they had to make sure he was ready, make sure his knee could take the stress of a live football game. But off the field in the coaches' office after practice, Belew couldn't believe the nerve of Boobie to ask such a ridiculous question.

"Did you hear what Boobie said to me? He asked me if he was going to play Friday," Belew told the other coaches. "It would be a miracle if he can play this year. It's a tough road to hoe, coming back from knee surgery and playing in the same year. It would be suicide to let 'im play."

It raised the question of why he was out there at all, since it had already been determined that Boobie would need knee surgery after the season. For the team, his return appeared to be a no-risk proposition. If he came back, it was a gift, a pleasant surprise. If he didn't come back that was okay because they had found someone who had not only replaced him but surpassed him.

But for Boobie, the risks were enormous. If he did play well, it might rekindle the interest of recruiters, who had gone on to whore after other tricks. But by playing there was always the risk of further damage to his knee, as well as the psychic damage of having to adjust to being a bit player in an extravaganza that had originally been written for him.

Initially there had been nothing but the blindness of hope, as if a magic wand would appear and make his knee pure again.

"I can't wait to come back," he had said shortly after the arthroscopic surgery that was done at the time of the injury. "Put on that knee brace and fly." He felt certain he would regain his role as starting fullback by the Odessa High game, when the stadium would surely be rockin' 'n' rollin'. But it was a belief only he held.

"He thinks he's gonna be ready for OHS, but he's sadly mistaken," said Trapper. Initially, he had been surprised by the dedication with which Boobie worked toward rehabilitation. But like most everyone else associated with the program, he had little real faith in him. When the reality of the injury set in, when it became apparent to Boobie that there was no magic wand, the grueling regimen of rehabilitation became more frustrating and futile.

"That was out of his nature for him to do that too hard, out of character," said Trapper. "You have to be thinking that he's seen the handwriting on the wall—the team hasn't fallen apart without him."

When the Odessa High game took place, Boobie was still in street clothes. Watching the pre-game warm-ups, he seemed devoid of any emotional connection to the team, his infectious self-confidence dissolving into detached coldness, an observer peering in on something that had no place for him. "Nah, I'm not that excited," he said as the stadium began to fill up, and during the game he said almost nothing but looked on glumly as the team moved effortlessly ahead without him.

He came back to practice the following week to the shame of a white practice jersey, and he had no role in Permian's 42–0 trouncing of Midland High.

During the next week, when it became clear he was going to get a chance to play, his mood alternated. There were glimpses of the old Boobie holding court once again in the locker room, turning to Jerrod McDougal and addressing him with "Hey, Baby Ostrich Head Face." There were also glimpses of his finding the game of football a difficult struggle. During one of the early morning practices in the gymnasium, he was pushed while running with the ball. After the play, he turned around and hurled the football at the offender.

That Friday night against the Abilene High Eagles, he suited up with the familiar paraphernalia: the high-top Nikes, the silver stockings, the white TERMINATOR X towel. He watched from the sidelines as Comer scored the first two touchdowns of the game, one on a three-yard run and the other on an eighty-eight-yard run where he broke up the middle on a trap and just out-ran everyone else to the goal line. Boobie stood behind the other players glassy-eyed, his hands clasped.

He got into the game in the second quarter and gained four yards on his first carry of the season. He got the ball again, spinning for a gain of two yards, and then he blocked from the tailback position as Comer scored his third touchdown of the night to make the score 28–0 at the half. Comer had already gained 125 yards on nine carries. Boobie had gained six yards on two carries.

He carried the ball eight more times in the second half. It was obvious he was tentative, the knee looming as if all the bone and flesh and ligament and cartilage lay there exposed for ev-eryone to take a shot at like some carnival game. "I think he's scared, real scared," said Trapper from the sidelines as he watched Boobie drag his leg a little bit and get up slowly from a pile of tacklers. But Trapper had to admire his gutsiness. "I think he's doing a lot better than I expected."

With a third and two at the Abilene 23, he took the ball on the hand-off and suddenly all the justifications flooded back of why he had once been touted as one of the ten best running backs in the state of Texas. He cut up the middle and broke past several tacklers for an eight-yard gain and a first down. The old fire was there and the indelible image of Boobie tow-ering over hapless tacklers.

Watching him your heart rose and you began to believe that he could do it, get it all back again, have the type of season that he wanted so badly to have. But it was only a flash, a haunting glimmer of what could have been. Several plays later, he left the game limping with a cramp and did not return. In the meantime, Permian scored an easy 49–0 win to improve its rec-ord to five and one and solidify its top-ten ranking in the state-wide polls.

A year before against this same team, Boobie had had the night of his life. He had gained 232 yards on eight carries. He would have easily broken the Permian record for the most yards rushing in a single game if Gaines, deciding the game was a rout, had not taken him out [Gaines said he hadn't known that Boobie was close to the record]. But the performance was still spectacular enough to earn him a mention in *USA Today*. L.V. carefully kept the clipping, just as he carefully kept a pile of other glowing clippings about Boobie from the *Dallas Morning News* and the *Odessa American* his junior year. On this night against the Abilene Eagles, he gained forty-six yards on ten carries, and his return to action earned a single paragraph at the tail end of the *Odessa American* account of the game. There was no reason to give him more mention than that. Compared to Comer, who finished the game with 138 yards, he hadn't done anything.

For L.V., watching Boobie play against Abilene had been harrowing. On every play he couldn't help but worry that his nephew would do further damage to his knee, even though the brace did provide good protection. He saw the emotional effect the injury was having on Boobie—the prolonged periods of depression as one Friday night after another just came and went.

"He wants to have that magic wand and have it be like it was before [his knee] got hurt," L.V. said, but he knew that wasn't possible.

He wondered if he was doing the right thing by letting Boobie play at all. He had always risen to protect Boobie and somehow make life right for him. He had fought for him and with him, and whenever Boobie had veered off course he successfully put him back on it. Early in the season, before everything had turned so hideous, L.V. had stood in the failing afternoon light and silently watched Boobie perform. The other boosters and parents and hangers-on traveled from one end of the practice field to the other in friendly little packs. But L.V. stayed off by himself, as if he felt he didn't quite belong. Instead his eyes just followed as Boobie danced and weaved and did all those things on the beautifully manicured, well-watered fields that L.V. had patiently taught him. He didn't have the look of a proud, gaping parent but the look of someone always there for Boobie, always keeping an eye out for him.

It had seemed so simple then, but now every option was

fraught with painful uncertainty. Should he let Boobie play—even if it meant the risk of further injury—because it was the only way he could still contend for a major-college scholarship? Or should he put the dream in jeopardy and elect to have the surgery done on Boobie now, before it was too late, before there was more physical and psychological damage?

"High school is important, but this is a stepping stone," said L.V. one day, sitting on a bench in the locker room of the field house, surrounded by all the little pictures on the Wall of Fame. "If he gets hurt here . . ." The thought made him shudder. Back home in a worn envelope were the letters from Texas A & M and Nebraska and Oklahoma and all the rest that glowed as powerfully as kryptonite. In his heart, he believed the recruiters wouldn't run from his nephew just because of a knee injury. With a little time, he'd be as good as new.

But the Permian staff said there was no way a major college would touch Boobie now unless he came back and proved that he had recovered. He was damaged goods, like a crate of Florida oranges that had gone rotten in delivery, and the big boys were not going to deal with him unless they had positive proof some sweet juice could still be squeezed out of him, not some mess of pulp and seeds.

Privately the Permian staff, with the exception of Coach Hearne, didn't see any dilemma in Boobie's decision at all. The doctor had cleared him to play, which in the coaches' minds meant he *could* play. And all the things that went along with the injury—the mental aspect of having to adjust to being a white shirt substitute, the necessity of major knee surgery after the season whether he gained one yard or a thousand, the fluid that had to be drawn from it, the fear of getting hit on it—were necessary prices to pay. Others had done it. He wasn't the first. To a large degree, they saw him as selfish and undisciplined and utterly undedicated to the great cause of Mojo.

"Playing to him is not what it's all about," said Trapper. "He just doesn't want to play. Fuckheads can just play. He wants to be number one. He wants to be the one with his name in the paper. He wants to be the leading rusher in District Four Five-A. He wants to be the one they're talking about.

"I think he can come back. It's a mental block. He has blinded himself. His attitude is, 'If I can't be the center of attention, I don't want to be anything at all.' He's not just letting himself down. He's letting the team down, he's letting [Gaines] down, he's letting his uncle down."

"It takes a special kind of kid to overcome an injury like that," said Belew. "I don't think he'll ever do what it takes to be one hundred percent."

Sometimes it sounded as if they were talking about a pro player making a million dollars a year with a contractual obligation to play, not an eighteen-year-old kid playing for his high school team who, to be here at all, had overcome abandonment by his mother and foster homes and learning disabilities.

L.V. understood the team's interest, but he also understood the needs of his nephew as well as himself. They weren't in this so that Boobie could be a dutiful substitute, coming off the bench to give Comer or Billingsley a rest. There was no ticket to the promised land in doing that.

"I'd rather hold him out and let him take his chances in college. If it wasn't the football season, it would be much easier," he said in the silence of the locker room. But L.V. knew how much emotion and energy had been wrapped into Boobie's senior year, how so much of Boobie's life, as well as his own, seemed to hinge on it. How long had they waited?

L.V. gave one of his little laughs and lowered his palm until it was about four feet from the ground. "Ever since he was right there."

He decided to let him continue.

Boobie played sparingly the following week in a 48–2 win over Dallas Jesuit that upped Permian's record to six and one. He ran the ball five times for fourteen yards and seemed even more tentative than he had against Abilene High. He broke to the right on one carry but had no acceleration at all and was easily tackled for no gain. He rumbled for five yards on another play but went down before taking a hit.

The next Friday night, Permian met the Cooper Cougars in Abilene. On the second play of the game, Comer went sixty-four yards for a touchdown, his seventh of the season. Boobie got his first carry of the game on the next series as a substitute and scored his first touchdown of the year on a one-yard dive. He was livid after the play and threw the football at a Cooper player. Boobie said the player had pulled his face mask and punched him in the face.

"You're a senior, you got to be able to handle that," Gaines told him as he came to the sidelines.

"I ain't gonna sit there and let somebody hit me in my damn face," said Boobie as he walked to the players' bench, his voice strained and agitated. Early in the fourth quarter he scored another touchdown to make it 49–14. It was his last carry of the night, giving him forty-nine yards on twelve carries. As at the Abilene High game there were times one could see tiny flashes of the old brilliance, but there were more moments of watching him try to cut upfield into freedom, only to fall helplessly to the ground.

There were also times when his undisciplined running style seemed wilder than ever, as if he was frantically trying, in a single carry, to make up for an entire season that he knew was fleeing from him.

II

There was hope now, and bit by bit, with each game, it had gotten brighter and brighter. It still seemed impossible half the time but it was there, a glowing speck like the last drop of the sun on the horizon. Could he cradle it? Could he catch it?

Was it totally ridiculous to think of this skinny, earnest kid wearing the orange and white of Texas next year? Maybe so. Even Mike Winchell wondered how he could possibly compete

with the studs that he read about over and over in the worn pages of *Texas Football* magazine, guys from Hurst Bell and Denison and Langham Creek who were taller and faster and stronger, guys with discreet half-smiles on their faces who always looked as if there wasn't a thing in the world that could ever get to them or rattle them.

Mike himself had a wonderful smile, but it suggested warmth and innocence, not serene self-confidence in the face of all challenges. "I was kind of an oops," was the way he described his entrance into the world. Sometimes he half-jokingly suggested that he should have gotten out of football back in Pop Warner when he was at the top of his game. And yet, on days when he was feeling good about himself and everything just seemed to click, he knew he threw the ball with a special gift.

The Abilene Cooper game had been like that. It was all so wonderfully, effortlessly easy. He already had had several great games—the opener against El Paso Austin, the one against Midland High—but this was his greatest. Midway in the first quarter, when he had seen the Cooper cornerback go into motion before the play started, he knew they were going to be in man-to-man. He looked for flanker Robert Brown down the right sideline and threw the ball crossfield on a dime about forty yards. Brown caught it in stride for a sixty-two-yard touchdown. In the second quarter, he lined up and saw the Cooper secondary once again out of kilter. They were giving Brown too much cushion, laying off him six or seven yards. Once again he won the chess match and laid the ball in for a nineteen-yard touchdown. Still in the same quarter, he lined up over center and saw Cooper in one-on-one coverage against Lloyd Hill. That was more idiotic than giving Robert Brown a seven-yard cushion. The play immediately formed in his mind. Hill ran a fly pattern and Winchell hit him for a forty-five-yard touchdown. Still in the same quarter, he backpedaled, saw Robert Brown break free, and threw another touchdown pass, this one good for eighteen yards.

By the time the first half ended, Winchell had thrown nine

passes. Five had been incomplete. The other four had been for touchdowns. He didn't throw any more passes that night, but it hardly mattered. Through the first eight games of the season he had thrown for seventeen touchdowns. Assuming Permian got into the playoffs, which seemed automatic at that point, he was destined to break the single-season record for most touchdown passes.

"Michael has had so many strikes against him, and has struggled so hard, you just want to see him succeed," said Deborah Hargis, a social studies and history teacher at Permian. "There just aren't a lot of good kids, and he's a good kid."

Like many who met him, she became both intrigued and enchanted with him. She saw something rare there, and when she thought of him a particular image often came floating back to her.

The year before, when he had been in her history class, they had held a Beautiful Baby contest. Mike brought in a picture of himself, but it wasn't one of those smiling-from-ear-to-ear shots taken at Sears or Penney's. Mike had never lived a life like that. Instead he was holding a piece of gum while a single tear, like the wispy trail of a jet, fell down his cheek. Mike explained that he was crying because he had never seen a camera before and thought it was a gun. Hargis always remembered that picture and the softness of those brown eyes as Mike apparently thought he would be shot the second the shutter button clicked.

She loved the way he was with children, particularly those who worshiped him and came to the school pep rallies wearing a jersey with his number, 20, on it. She loved the relationship he had with his grandmother, how he delighted in her and always watched out for her. She loved the way he was a klutz off the field despite his enormous athletic abilities, how he invariably spilled food on himself when he went out to eat or how when he got up from his desk in class one day he knocked it over.

There were times when a dark cloud descended over him, making him virtually silent. His face became filled with a look of sad, aching brooding, as if he was thinking about something that only he could understand and somehow resolve. But there were other times when he became alive and animated, like a child gingerly touching the edge of the ocean before plunging in, displaying a curiosity unique among kids who lived in Odessa.

New York, Philadelphia, the towering cities of the East beckoned to him with the exoticism of stories by Kipling, and he wanted to know about them, to see if the things he had read in magazines and saw on television were true. Were there muggers on every corner? Was there really a Mafia? The absolute lack of guile in his voice as he wondered about places that seemed to exist in a universe separate from the one he occupied in Odessa, the twinkle of a smile spreading over the flat contours of his face, made it easy to see why his favorite book, outside of the sports autobiographies he had read of Jim McMahon and Ken Stabler and Reggie Jackson, was *Huckleberry Finn*. Floating on a raft down the Mississippi to one mysterious place after another with nothing else around except trees and water, it beckoned to him. "I could stand to do that, go down the river," he said.

As he probed and pawed about worlds so different from his own, something in his own life would suddenly hit him—the time he had gone deer hunting and had one in his sights but couldn't bring himself to shoot it; another time when he had camped out near the Devil's River down around Del Rio; fishing trips on the Pecos, where he and a friend went river rafting on old tables they had found; the road trip with his brother to the state high school football championship between Mart and Shiner. He talked for a minute, or maybe two or maybe even five, as if something inside him had been punctured, had been unleashed and come alive again. And then, abruptly, the torrent stopped and his face once again regained its brooding stare.

Hargis knew there were days when it was best to leave Mike alone, when he seemed impervious to the emotional gestures of anyone. But there were also days when her poking and prodding led to a small foothold inside him, a tiny ray of light inside an intricate cavern with more depth than anyone could possibly have realized.

She desperately wanted him to make it, as did everyone else who had ever met him and become aware of some of the tidbits of his past—the death of Billy, the way he refused to let virtually anyone inside his home, the way he had raised himself.

As Boobie's season became a sad and sour struggle, Mike Winchell's only continued to rise. As Boobie tried to find the natural rhythm of the year before, Mike edged closer and closer to a dream he had quietly harbored for much of his life.

As they headed into the ultimate showdown against Midland Lee, they were two opposites, one plunging so fast he could barely hold on anymore, the other soaring beyond all expectations.

Led by Winchell, Permian trampled the Cooper Cougars 56–14 to push its record to seven and one. Everywhere you looked that night you saw a star—Winchell at quarterback, Comer at fullback, Hill at split end, Brown at flanker, Christian at middle linebacker, Chavez at tight end—a team so damn good it hadn't missed a single beat when Boobie had wrecked his knee and went on without him as if he had never been there. And every fan couldn't help but believe that the following week's game would be little more than a continuation of the Cooper obliteration, only a thousand times more sweet.

It was hard to get too worked up over Abilene and the Cooper Cougars. They didn't look down their noses and act as if Odessa was some sort of primeval desert wilderness with people whose intellectual capacity fell somewhere between that of the Goths and the Visigoths. No, there wasn't any reason in the world to hold a grudge against Abilene.

But the same couldn't be said for Midland, which held a unique place in the hearts of almost every Odessan. Even the most liberal ones who had spent a lifetime fighting racial and social injustice and who cherished the notion of open-minded-ness drew the line at the Midland border.

"Texans everywhere, except Midland, are tolerant of each other," said Odessa attorney Michael McLeaish, still smarting from the time he had gone as a kid to a party in Midland over at the country club and walked around in a bow tie that began to feel as big as a ski jump while everyone else looked so cool and casual. "Midland is a principality. I don't like people from Midland. They don't like us and we don't like them. I just can't stand those bastards and they feel the same way about us."

PUSH FOR
THE
PLAYOFFS

CHAPTER 11

Sisters

I

Logically THEY SHOULD HAVE BEEN UNITED, NOT ONLY BY THE common bond of oil that had kept them in clothes for sixty years, but by the bonds of loneliness. As your car fought its way across West Texas along Interstate 20 in the blistering heat and it felt as though you had been in the state for a week and had another week to go before you saw any sign of human life, they suddenly rose out of the emptiness like territorial forts.

There was Midland with its improbably tall buildings, glassy and shimmering in the sun like misplaced tanning reflectors. Fifteen miles to the west there was Odessa, sprawling and oozing, its most striking feature the fenced-off fields with row after row of oil field equipment that looked like rusting military weapons from a once-great war.

It seemed natural that they needed each other, as all good sister cities should, but instead they had spent most of their histories trying to prove just the opposite.

Midland was the fair-haired, goody-goody one, always doing the right thing, never a spot on that pleated dress, always staying up late to do her homework and prepare for the future. Odessa was the naughty one, the sassy one, the one who didn't stay at home but sat at a bar with a cigarette in one hand and the thin neck of a bottle of Coors in the other humming the tune of some country and western song about why it was silly to worry about tomorrow when you might get flattened by a pickup today, the one who dressed like an unmade bed and could care less about it, the one who liked nothing better than to drag her sanctimonious sister through the mud in a little game of football and then kick her teeth in for good measure.

In 1983, when the editors of *Forbes* compiled their annual list of America's four hundred richest individuals, they had discovered that six people, each worth $200 million or more according to their calculations, lived in Midland. As for plain old millionaires, which in a town like that had become as notable as people saying they were going to church on Sunday or planned to vote Republican (in 1976 Midland County became the first county in Texas where more Republicans voted in a primary than Democrats), various estimates pegged the number at two thousand or so during the height of the boom. If the number was accurate, one out of every forty-five people in the town in the late seventies had reached millionaire status.

Forbes published a glowing nine-page article about Midland. Despite its eye-popping wealth, the article said Midland had still retained all the quaint virtues of a small town. "There are no chained storefronts, traffic jams or pedestrians wandering around wearing Walkman headsets. The Texas League baseball park still has billboards on the outfield fence." There were a few blemishes, according to the magazine, but they came from Odessa.

"Why, I can pick out Odessa guys on sight," said a high school student. "The guys are big, muscular, wear gaudy jewelry and belt buckles big enough to eat their lunch off of."

At virtually the same time, Odessa found its way into the national press as well.

"For Murder Capital U.S.A., it isn't much—just a depressed oil town in an arid stretch of West Texas," wrote *Newsweek*. "But last week little Odessa, with 29.8 homicides per 100,000 residents, gunned its way past Miami to take dubious honors as the most perilous city in the nation this year. . . ."

It was easy to see why the two towns hated each other.

When oil started booming in the late forties the availability of office space had made Midland a corporate center. As the grunts of the oil business flocked to Odessa to work and service the fields, the majors and colonels and generals came to Midland to control those grunts who worked the fields. They were a different breed, with eastern roots that often included four years at St. Paul's or Choate or Lawrenceville or Andover, followed by four years at Yale or Harvard or Princeton or M.I.T. They were men with the hearts of pioneers and teeth sharpened to razor points by years spent dutifully at the knee of their good daddy capitalists back east. Although he turned out to be the most famous among them, George Bush was just one among friends. In 1951, shortly after Bush had moved to Midland, the *New York Times* described it as a "modern" city whose twenty-three thousand inhabitants could raise $200 million in capital with little effort.

As the years passed the place became ever more exclusive. Residents named streets Harvard and Princeton. They played at the Polo Club, which had been started by a graduate of St. Paul's and Princeton whose father had been an executive at U.S. Steel. They sang high praises of a black waiter named Max because of his flawless performance at formal dinner parties at their homes. They clearly saw their town as the one exception in an area of the country once described as having enough ignorance to support not simply a four-year university but an eight-year one.

People in Odessa, watching what was going on over in Midland, could only shake their heads amid the smoke in the bar and wonder why God, of the millions of damn places in the world he could have put them next to, had chosen one as strange as Midland. The Ivy League didn't cut much muster in Odessa, unless "Yalie" meant the same thing as "Okie," and Odessans didn't seem bothered one bit by the oft-repeated slogan that people went to Midland to raise a family and to Odessa to raise hell. There was no dispute that Odessa had its share of one-word bars and prostitutes and sometimes the only way to win an argument was to shoot the guy, but it was free and fun-loving and a man was measured by who he was, not by how well he concealed the size of his income.

Beyond oil, the two towns had nothing in common, not in outlook, not in the style of the clothes they wore (Odessans dressed free and casual, whereas it could be presumed that Midlanders wore Polo Shop pajamas to bed), not even in the quality of excess that marked these towns during nine very remarkable years from 1973 through 1981.

II

There were some nice stories about the boom that came out of Odessa. There was the one about Jerry Thorpe, pastor of the Temple Baptist Church, going with a parishioner down to Vegas by private jet to watch the Holmes-Cooney fight and being given a $10,000 watch by him as a token of appreciation for all those inspiring sermons.

There were several wonderful stories about the legendary Ron Wells, who, according to his banker, had started his oil field supply business with about $10,000 and suddenly found himself with monthly cash flows into the hundreds of thousands. There was the one about how he invited his banker out to the warehouse under the guise of discussing business and they sat around drinking champagne instead and then hopped over to the airport to pick up the Lear jet that Ron had just given himself for his thirtieth birthday, and since it was kind of stupid to let the plane just sit there and the day was pretty much shot anyway, they flew to Vegas and gambled all night.

There was another one about the huge party Ron threw for his customers out at the warehouse, where huge cattle tanks were iced high with beer, and how he got up toward the end to thank everyone for coming and then mentioned something about his air force, and how his two planes (by that time he had a sixteen-seater Gulfstream I prop as well as the Lear) flew low overhead with the symmetry of the Blue Angels and how some of those in attendance were pretty impressed by the sheer balls of it all and how one guy immediately whispered to his partner that from now on he wanted ol' Ronnie to pay for his supplies in cash so they wouldn't get stuck with a huge unpaid bill down the road when the upkeep of the air force and all the other toys got too expensive.

There were stories of welders who had trouble getting through the alphabet without taking a break making between $80,000 and $90,000 a year, and were so flushed with money that when the state Highway Patrol picked them up for drunken driving in West Odessa they often had $8,000 or $9,000 in cash on them. There were stories of them marching into Gibson's, the big discount chain that eventually went belly up like everything else, and plunking down $2,000 or $3,000 to redecorate their mobile homes from head to toe. There were stories of big, burly men coming into town in Rolls Royces to sell as many Rolex watches as they could dish out.

There were stories of competition in the oil patch turning into a Mafia turf war. Companies arranged kickbacks for buying certain products, and a black market in stolen equipment thrived. There were stories of men who suddenly realized that they were born to be oil operators, not the doctors and lawyers and shoe salesmen they had been before their conversion, men who, as independent oilman Ken Hankins put it, "wouldn't know a drilling rig if they walked up on one."

There were the usual hair-raising statistics, how, over a ten-year period through 1979, total construction in Odessa rose 520 percent and population 31 percent and bank deposits 294 percent and retail sales 276 percent and divorces 28 percent.

They were all nice stories, until you compared them to what was going on in Midland. Then they seemed like the kind of stories passed around an Amish quilt circle. Greed, delusional visions of grandeur, the mercenary mercilessness that made every relationship expendable—Midland perfected all these long before they became the standard of the eighties around the rest of the country.

III

Of all the deals that Aaron Giebel had made from his base of operations in Midland during the boom, the hardest part, by his own account, was figuring out which one was the worst.

Had the five planes, and the three full-time pilots to fly them, really been necessary? Should he have bought the Brangus bull for $1 million? Should he have paid cash for the thousand head of hybrid cattle? Did he think it through as carefully as he should have when he took a multi-million-dollar position on a method of breeding "super cattle" by hormone injection and embryonic implant? Had it been reason enough to pay $17.5 million for the seven-thousand-acre ranch in El Indio with the palm trees that had been flown in and the private runway and the breathtaking view of Mexico when he used it largely for entertaining and hunting? Should he have planted the twenty-eight thousand pecan trees when the only thing he knew about pecans was that "they're all named after Indians?" Had it been such a wise thing to go into the home construction business with his former son-in-law and end up with a loss of $1.2 million? Had he really needed the trucking business that cost him $4 million to move drilling rigs in and out of the oil field? Had he been slightly impulsive when he decided to open five additional offices in San Antonio, Oklahoma City, Denver, Calgary, and Lafayette, Louisiana? Had the revolving $24 million line of credit over at the First National Bank of Midland truly been a good thing after all? Was it possible to have built a new house that wasn't thirteen thousand square feet?

It was all so hard to know.

By the time you added it up, Aaron Giebel's losses from boom to bust totaled somewhere around $55 milion.

He had filed for bankruptcy, and by 1988 he was back on his feet again, in the oil business, although on a far reduced basis. He still had his wife and he had his health, which was more than he could say for a lot of his friends, who lost both when the absence of money for impulse trips to Paris suddenly made them seem a lot less attractive. He was the first to admit there was no justification for what he had done, except that he had gone literally mad in Midland. But he spoke about it with candor, as if he saw a danger in what had happened that needed to be exposed, materialism and a desire for money and wheeling and dealing that became as impossible to resist as any addiction.

"There was a euphoria round here that was almost like an opiate," said Giebel. "It *was* an opiate. And I succumbed to it. And I don't know a guy who did not.

"You just get caught up. You get caught up in the euphoria, like you're sitting down at the gambling table."

For a period of time Giebel had actually resisted it. By nature he was a careful man. He had a round, soft face with eyes that seemed incapable of anger, and there wasn't anything remotely swaggering about him. He spoke softly, without the twang that in some seemed to reverberate from one end of the state to the other. Born in Fort Worth, he had moved to Midland after college and ultimately became the chairman and chief executive officer of the MGF Oil Corporation. The company grew enormously during the boom, and when Giebel resigned in 1979 he did so with millions of dollars' worth of stock. He had resolved not to build another oil company, but he did, A. F. Giebel Petroleum Consultants. With the price of oil skyrocketing, Giebel found himself worth $100 million. He still restrained himself from other investments, but as he saw friends everywhere expanding, he wondered if he was not crazy to do the same. "I felt that I was behind the progress curve. I was demeaned by my peers—'Giebel, you rich dog, what are you gonna do, eat it?' "

That got to him. In Texas, no man was more of a coward than the one who was chicken shit with his money.

So he had jumped, thoroughly convinced that all the odds were in his favor. And how could he lose? Not when the price kept going up and up, not when just about every banking and investment institution in the country said oil was going to go to $65 a barrel, not when Giebel Petroleum had drilled 195 wells with a fantastic 55 percent success ratio. He had the Midas touch. The moment was suddenly at hand not only to make ungodly sums of money but to build an empire, a lasting monument. "I made fast decisions. I just got to wheeling and dealing. . . . 'I'll have a dozen of these and a half dozen of these.' I got in on so many deals. . . .

"It changed me, because I was one heck of a businessman," said Giebel. "I became a fast-moving promoter type." And so it went, from oil exploration, which he knew a great deal about, to loyally following the creed of Texas entrepreneurship during the boom: the less a man knew about something, the more money he was obligated to sink into it.

In 1981, with oil hovering around $40 a barrel, any idiot could have made money from it. But hitting big off something you didn't know the first thing about had special meaning. Brangus bulls, pecan trees, trucking, home construction—they all became shiny new toys in Aaron Giebel's ever-widening collection. Just hearing him talk about the technique to breed super cattle was enough to make the hairs on the back of the neck stand up and wonder how this man, with dual degrees in geology and petroleum engineering from Texas A & M, could have spent vast sums on a scheme that sounded as if it had been borrowed from one of those comic books about the possibilities of life in the twenty-first century. Giebel wondered that himself.

He had gotten into it through a "veterinarian friend." The way it worked was that he bought "super cows" that cost $17,000 apiece. These super cows were injected with hormones to increase ovulation drastically and cause the production of multiple embryos. The embryos were removed and placed in common cows, who would then produce super calves. Every time his veterinarian friend came back and said he needed just a little more money before these Frankensteins dominated the cattle world, Giebel dutifully anted up.

He lost $7 million on the deal.

"We're talking failure to the square root," was the way he bluntly described it.

Giebel had also got caught in the classic Texas trap of who could be the most flamboyant and outrageous, flipping a coin once with a fellow oilman to see who would get the drilling rights to a tract near San Antonio. Giebel won. Frankly, it was hard to see how this method of investment differed from how he approached all the other ones he was making. If anything, it may have been a little less impulsive. If Giebel had been the only person acting out of character in the quest for crazy-quilt expansion, it would have been more difficult to excuse or explain his actions. But he wasn't.

From 1973 through 1981, when the price of oil went up more than 800 percent, he and thousands of others made the fatal error of forgetting that every ounce of their success was due to the geopolitics of the Arab oil embargo and the Carter energy policy and the Iranian Revolution. They had actually thought that they themselves had something to do with what was happening and were somehow in control of their own destinies. Over at the country club, or in enormous corner offices with picture windows that seemed to deserve something more than wide-angle views of scrub brush and mesquite, they confused luck with business acumen. Instead of understanding that they were the beneficiaries of history, they began to believe they were the creators of it.

In Odessa, it had been a matter of riding the boom to the hilt and just trying to keep up with it. In Midland, it had been a matter of the town's becoming even more improbably tall than it already was, the Brasilia of the United States with the linear coldness of Gotham, a town where all human scale was rendered insignificant by the sheer magnificence of achievement. Of all the places that got caught up in the frenzy of the oil boom in those days, Midland may well have been the most incredible.

There had been many indications that things were getting out of hand, but the one that confirmed it was the opening of a new business east of the airport. If you had something to sell, odds were you could do it in Midland or Odessa; at the height of the boom Odessa ranked second in the country in retail spending per capita and Midland fourth. After all, this was an area where people had developed an insatiable craving for boats, big, big boats, even though the nearest water was a hundred miles away. But it was still hard to predict the success or failure of the new Rolls Royce dealership. The country was in the midst of a recession in the summer of 1980 and interest rates were close to 20 percent. But that didn't matter. Even before the dealership opened, it had made about seventeen sales for its line of cars, which ranged in price from $85,000 to $200,000.

A year and a half later, the Rolls Royce dealership was barely noticed. "We're experiencing a transition—from a town to a city," said I. David Porras, a developer who tooled around in a Lear jet with red leather seats and painted black on the outside. Porras announced plans for a fifty-four-story office building. The First National Bank of Midland announced plans for two forty-story-plus bank towers. MGF Oil Corporation also announced that it was entering into a venture to build a forty-story-plus world-class luxury hotel to be designed by I. M. Pei.

In 1982, according to one report, the value of nonresidential construction that had been legally permitted in Midland led the state of Texas, even ahead of Dallas and Houston, both of which were undergoing incredible booms of their own. The 3.2 million square feet of office space actually under construction in Midland was equivalent to the amount in San Antonio, Fort Worth, and Austin combined. The population of these towns was twenty-two times that of Midland.

As real estate was booming, so was banking. The First National Bank of Midland, the great financial and moral beacon of the town for over ninety years, its $1 million corporate art collection with works by Thomas Moran and Norman Rockwell the essence of conservative good taste, had suddenly become a casino ten times grander than anything in Atlantic City or Vegas. Junior officers were making loans of up to $1 million without any review. Careful checks of collateral became almost laughable and utterly contrary to the ultracompetitive, machismo attitude that pervaded the banking industry in Texas. One of First National's highest-ranking officers wasn't above taking undisclosed interests in some of the ventures in which the bank lent money. As it turned out, the reckless, freewheeling ways of the First National Bank of Midland made it a trendsetter in the American banking industry during the eighties.

In 1980 and 1981, the assets of the bank had more than doubled in size, to $1.6 billion, and loans tripled as well, to $1.1 billion. The bank, the 205th largest in the country in 1976, was the 115th largest by the middle of 1982 and the largest independent bank in the state of Texas.

In February 1982, the bank's economic research arm estimated a 13 percent increase in the number of oil rigs and concluded, based on careful consultation with the country's leading economic experts, that the price of oil would increase at least as fast, if not faster, than general U.S. inflation for the next ten years.

It was around this time that Aaron Giebel had begun work on his house—although calling it a house was the same as describing the Statue of Liberty as a figurine. It really wasn't a house at all but a private kingdom. Initially his wife was against building it, but Giebel pushed it because it was a wonderful symbol in a part of the country where subtlety was owning an eight-seater prop instead of a Lear. It was, as he said, "a salute to our success." The thirteen-thousand square-foot house had a pool, a tennis court, a gazebo, two jacuzzis, a workout room, ten bathrooms, and a special wing with a video room for his seven grandchildren. It cost $2.4 million.

Along with the other things going on in Midland—the trip

to Palm Beach that one oilman had sponsored for himself and several hundred of his friends in a chartered 747, the announcement that the Rolls Royce dealership had received a Silver Lady award for being one of the three top Rolls dealers in the United States—Giebel fitted comfortably into the rhythm of things.

And then it had ended. Just like that. Not with a warning, not in a way so that those who got caught had only themselves to blame. One day the lights were on; the next day they were off. Demand for oil began to slacken significantly in 1982, and the result was a glut. "[The price] just dropped, like off the side of a building," said Giebel. "We were like children. I said, 'Oh, my God, it can't stay like this. It can't really be happening, the situation will rectify itself.'"

Almost as soon as Aaron Giebel had finished his house, he knew he was going to have to sell it to meet cash flow problems. And it was hard to remember a worse day in his life than the one when he turned to his wife and simply said, "This thing's got to go." He sold it without ever moving into it, at a loss of $700,000. In a year, from the end of 1981 to the end of 1982, his empire was in ruins. Thousands of other empires were in tatters also, including that of the seemingly untouchable bank that had financed him.

At the end of 1981, a record 4,530 drilling rigs were running in the United States. Ten months later that number had dropped to 2,379.

The First National Bank, which had dished out loans as freely as a doctor gives out lollipops, was in grave trouble. In July and August 1982 alone, deposits had dropped $150 million. An examination was quietly begun by the Office of the Comptroller of the Currency off the bank premises to preclude local panic. Every day, credit files were flown from Midland to Dallas, where examiners pored over the loans. The examination, done in the summer and fall of 1982, turned up startling news: $108 million in loans—8 percent of the total—was overdue; $357 million in loans—26 percent of the total—did not have sufficient documentation. To the examiners, the situation was crystal clear: the bank had become a running crap game.

The bank, which on its seventy-fifth anniversary had received a resolution from the Texas State Senate congratulating it for its "active, aggressive and effective" role in the community, became an example of all that had gone terribly wrong. The town's mightiest symbol suddenly found itself on its knees because of the blindness of its greed and its utter lack of caution.

In the bank's dire need for cash to keep it afloat, everyone became a potential pawn, even its best, most loyal customers. They trusted the bank blindly—stupidly, as it turned out. When asked to jeopardize millions of dollars of their own money to keep the bank going, they did so, still rooted in the ethos of the fifties, when you just gave help with no conditions attached when a friend asked for it. But this was the eighties, when nothing was sacred—except, of course, the making of money and the protection of glass-house empires at all expense.

At the end of 1982 the bank, desperate to show a profit, proposed a whirlwind deal to sell its headquarters to a partnership of seven customers for $75 million. These men, either personally or through their companies, had over $200 million in loans from the bank. The way the deal was structured they would be able to do it without putting up any significant amount of cash, and there might also be some nice tax advantages in it. Beyond that, all of them felt a certain amount of moral indebtedness to the bank since it had helped them make their fortunes. Several of those who signed promissory notes did so without reading the paperwork.

"Come on, you know me better than that," oilman Tom Brown, who had $160 million in loans from the bank through his company and had executed three promissory notes for $6.25 million, told a lawyer in subsequent court testimony. "I did not read any papers. I wanted to get back home, for one reason. . . . It was New Year's Eve."

The bank used the alleged profits from the sale to show a profit in 1982 of $11.9 million instead of a loss. The Securities and Exchange Commission later said that those figures were "false and misleading," in part because the sale price for the headquarters had been overvalued by as much as $40 million. But for the time being, the First National Bank was still afloat. In June, however, the results of another examination by the Office of the Comptroller of the Currency showed that 39 percent of all of First National Bank's loans were in trouble.

The bank was dying, but still the people of Midland, and even Odessa, refused to believe it. There was an air of unreality to it all, as if the situation would somehow, someway, magically fix itself.

In the backs of people's minds there had to have been days during the boom when they looked out at their world, a world so drenched in materialism that even Ronald Reagan might have gasped, and wondered when, like a stage set, it was all going to disappear, when the Lears and the Rolls Royces and the eighteenth-century antique desks would eventually have to go back into their boxes. But never in a thousand years did anyone in Midland, in Odessa, in all of West Texas, ever think that the bank would crumble. Sure, it would take a few hits, just like everyone else did. But if anything could withstand the bust, it was be the First National Bank, the institution that had made Midland unique and had set its course from the very beginning.

"It was more important than the Father, Son, and the Holy Ghost," said attorney Warren Burnett. "They truly thought it was untouchable." But as for many other institutions in the eighties, greed overcame history. On Friday evening, October 14, 1983, at 6:13 P.M., the First National Bank was declared insolvent by the Comptroller of the Currency. In terms of the size of assets, the bank's failure was second largest in U.S. history.

When the First National Bank of Midland went down, it certified not only that the boom had ended, but that a way of life had ended. Its failure was a precursor to the falls that would later inevitably take place all over the country, on Wall Street in New York and State Street in Boston. "It was like dropping an atomic bomb on a town," said former mayor Hank Avery, and the explosion was felt in Odessa. For perhaps the first time ever, there was no gloating over the misfortunes of Midland.

"It was frightening," said Lanita Akins. "It brought you back to reality and made you realize that the boom was over and that it wasn't going to turn around the next day. I remember gasping for breath."

But Aaron Giebel, who had been forced to file for corporate bankruptcy when the bank had foreclosed on several of his oil properties, had a different view of it, a view colored by his own experiences, but also by the craziness of the times that he had lived in. "There is no question the banks were tantamount to prostitutes during the boom," he said, recalling how representatives of banks all over the country had called up begging to do business with him.

Several years later federal judge Lucius Bunton compared the First National Bank to the *Titanic*. "The First National Bank, like the vessel, was a magnificent, extravagant, enviable Camelot," he wrote in an opinion in a case involving the bank. "It was regarded as unsinkable, said to be designed and engineered to withstand the formidable forces of natural laws. The bank, like the liner, was doubly-supported, tightly-compartmental. If one of its parts were weakened or damaged, the other sections were designed to keep it afloat."

It was a wonderful analogy, not only for the bank but for all of Midland. For eight years the whole area had been like the *Titanic*, a raucous, crazy ship equipped with every possible amenity, towering atop the nubby, gnarled brown sea of West Texas, its passengers dining every night at the fabulous first-class restaurant where between bottles of $150 wine they pulled out their wallets to show off laminated pictures of their jets and rigs and Brangus bulls, so caught up in the revelry and the merriment that they forgot it was still a dangerous, unpredictable world out there over which they had no control. Did

Aaron Giebel see the iceberg looming as he built his San Simeon and dreamed his dream of cows strong enough to pull buildings? Did Tom Brown, as he took out $160 million in loans and signed promissory notes for $6.25 million without reading the paperwork? Did any of the hundreds of others who had expanded beyond all imagination? Of course not. Should they have?

Maybe it wasn't the *Titanic* at all, but just a Ship of Fools turned mad by money and greed.

If Aaron Giebel was thankful for anything, it was that his son Mark had been there to witness the terrifying things that oil and money could to do a man. "I thank God that my son has been in here," said Giebel. "He has seen all this, and thank God, he is not going to succumb to it."

IV

In the fall of 1988, Midland and Odessa were still in the doldrums of the bust. Nothing quite as dramatic as the sinking of the First National Bank of Midland had taken place for some time, but by then people had become immune to catastrophe anyway. In July 1986, the nation's rig count hit an all-time low of 663, some 85 percent fewer than the high it had hit less than five years earlier. At the same time the wellhead price of U.S. oil dropped to $9.25 a barrel. There was some slight improvement afterward, but not enough to make a difference. The oil production industry in West Texas had collapsed.

People had been drilling for oil in the Permian Basin for over sixty years. They had punched thousands of holes into the scrubby earth, and some believed it was only a matter of time before the place got tapped out. Unlike the Middle East, where oil almost literally flowed out of a spigot, finding it here was getting harder and more expensive. The days of the great gushers had been gone for years. It took extensive drilling to find what was there, and the yields were not enormous. When the price of oil had been high in 1980 and 1981, it was worth the cost. But when the price dropped, the frantic search for oil in the Permian Basin, and all of Texas, quickly became much less attractive. In 1987, the amount of oil produced in North America had actually been the same as the amount of oil produced in the Middle East, about 12.5 million barrels a day. But it took nearly six hundred seventy-five thousand wells to produce that amount in North America. In the Middle East, it took about forty-five hundred.

The bust had extracted a terrible toll, and the list of people and institutions that had been destroyed read like a horrible casualty list. Six banks had failed; ten bankers had been convicted of criminal activities ranging from embezzlement to fraud and received prison sentences as high as twenty-four years; hundreds, big and small, had filed for bankruptcy, and many more were still trying to extract themselves from the rubble of houses they couldn't sell and creditors they were trying to pay off. All around were signs of what was and now wasn't—office buildings of darkened glass in downtown Midland and Odessa that were virtually empty and had the scent of unopened boxes, streets where three-quarters of the houses were for sale, warehouse lots filled with beautiful new rigs that had never been touched.

There may not have been a more awesome graveyard in the country than the old MGF lot off Highway 80—thirty acres filled with equipment that had cost $200 million and in the fall of 1988 might have fetched $10 million—with three hundred thousand feet of new and used drill pipe up on metal stilts like pixie sticks, four hundred drill collars, and the guts of nineteen rigs.

In its heyday MGF Drilling had had about twelve hundred people working for it and about fifty-five rigs. Then the bust came and MGF, bloated with $121 million in loans from the First National Bank, was finished. It had filed for bankruptcy and was bought out by another company, Parker & Parsley, for virtually nothing.

The man in charge of the yard, Don Phillips, pointed to Rig 79, a twenty-five-thousand-foot beauty that was built for $9.5 million in 1982 and had never been used. It seemed like a steal at $2.5 million, but with the glut of rigs on the domestic market there weren't any takers.

"We're asking two and a half and we ain't sold it," Phillips said.

He drove through the yard pointing here and gesturing there, giving the history of this one and that one, as if the gigantic metal shapes in front of him were ancient artifacts that had come from a fantastic archaeological dig and were waiting to go off to a museum somewhere, the symbols of a fallen empire.

"That one right there is a fourteen-thousand-foot rig.

"The brown one right there, that's a twenty-four- to twenty-five-thousand-foot rig.

"That rig right there was a seventeen-thousand-foot rig. It did one well. Cost $3.5 million brand-new. If I was gonna sell it, I'd try to get $400,000."

On and on the lot went, with gigantic pieces of equipment lying in the gravel as far as the eye could see, as forlorn as bloodied elephant tusks: Rig 201 with its 144-foot pyramid and five-hundred-ton hook; Rig 202, powered by three GE Custom 8000 generators that kicked in at seven-hundred kilowatts apiece; Rig 10, Rig 11, Rig 23, Rig 203; even Rig 1, which had first been used in the fifties. It was appraised for over $400,000, but Phillips knew he would be lucky to get $40,000 for it.

Phillips drove to the last rig MGF Drilling had had running before it crashed, HCW no. 2. He climbed up the metal steps to the top of the substructure, an elevated base upon which sat the draw works and the doghouse for the roustabouts and the tool pushers. The rig was perfectly assembled, but sitting in the middle of a warehouse yard, it looked as if someone had put it together to use as a toy.

The view from the substructure was stagnant—the drab warehouses along Highway 80 with parking lots that were either empty or filled with jaunty-colored trucks that never went into the oil field anymore, the pockets of brick houses on crescent-shaped streets in half-finished subdivisions, the clump of rust-colored freight cars sitting along the railroad tracks, the ribbon of the interstate with the tiny silhouettes of trucks making their way across the country in the shimmer of the heat.

"There's days I sit here and look and I wish all of these rigs were working," said Phillips. "You can stand up here and see a lot of equipment. The worst part about it is, you look at good equipment.

"When I was in business, it was a dream to have a yard like this and equipment like this. Now it's a nightmare."

As for the boom, it had become a faraway blur, a kind of confused, powerful, contradictory dream that made some people chuckle and others wince in the retelling of it. Many said they were glad the boom was over, that it had been too wild and both Midland and Odessa had suffered for it. But others were more honest.

Leaning back in the soft chairs of their offices with plenty of time on their hands to talk and reflect, they said they had come to grips with the hard reality of the world. They loved their President Reagan and they would no doubt love their President Bush, but they knew these men didn't make a damn bit of difference anymore. They knew their economic livelihoods were completely at the mercy of OPEC and that it was all but impossible to have much say in the matter when the average American well produced 13 barrels of oil a day while the average one in Saudi Arabia produced 6,881 barrels a day and the average one in Iran 27,233 barrels. The Saudis, the Iranians, the Iraqis, they called the shots, they were the ones with the vast stockpiles of oil, not the Americans, where the holes were running dry. They set the price of oil, and that felt funny as hell. But things could always happen over there—it wasn't the most stable place in the world, after all—and then a little devilish smile came to their lips. You could see the light go on as they visualized the days when all those beautiful rigs crippled on their sides over at MGF would be up and running once again and the whole place would be gloriously, sweetly mad and out of the lips of everyone would come that beautiful rallying cry: *The boom is on!*

It could happen. Anything could happen in America.

"After all," one oilman reasoned, "we're just another Middle East war away from another boom."

About the only thing in the two towns that had maintained its frenzied tempo was the rivalry between Permian and Midland Lee. In 1983, when the two teams met each other in the quarterfinals of the state playoffs in Lubbock, thirty-two thousand five hundred people were in the stands. In 1985, the second game of the National League playoffs between the St. Louis Cardinals and the Los Angeles Dodgers was preempted by the local NBC affiliate for a live broadcast of the Permian-Lee game.

Forty years earlier, playwright and author Larry L. King, who had grown up in Midland back when each town had only one high school, had had the misfortune of being a member of the Midland Bulldogs when it came time to play the Odessa Bronchos.

"Their savagery was intimidating: we sissybritches Head-quarters-City-of-the-Vast-Permian-Basin-Empire boys lost to Sintown by 20 to 7 and 48 to 0 in my time," wrote King in *Texas Monthly*. "Only by joining the Army before my senior season did I avoid the record 55–0 plastering of 1946. High school football was, I think, a legitimate cultural and psychological measuring stick of that time and that place: many of us concluded that Odessa was, indeed, the rawer and tougher community."

Little had changed since then, except in one fundamental respect.

The sissybritches, maybe because they weren't thinking about building fifty-story office buildings anymore, had learned how to play football.

Never in his entire life had Mike Winchell felt more embarrassed than he had his junior year. The Rebels scored more points against Permian in a 42–21 win than any team had scored against them in twenty-three years, and Winchell's own performance had been abysmal. With twenty thousand fans filling Ratliff Stadium that night, he had been nervous, almost scared, and had thrown three interceptions. Boobie, under the glare of all those screaming, raging, madcap fans, had trouble holding on to the ball. Jerrod McDougal remembered the taunting of the Lee players, their gleeful finger-pointing and gloating, the way they just loved letting Odessa know that its pride and joy wasn't so fucking tough anymore and that Permian had become the new sissybritches. Even Brian Chavez, who usually maintained some perspective, had cried after the game.

But this year it would be different. Permian was rated a twenty-one-point favorite over the Rebels, and now would be the time for sweet redemption, to drive them, and everything they stood for, straight into the snot-assed ground from which they came.

The night before the game at the private team meeting behind locked doors, Gaines told the story of a swimmer named Steve Genter, who had been set to go to the Munich Olympics in 1972 in the two-hundred-meter freestyle when his lung collapsed. He was cut open to repair the lung and then sewn back up. Doctors said there was no way Genter could swim unless he took painkillers, the use of which was illegal under Olympic rules. But Genter, who had dreamed of going to the Olympics since the age of nine, decided to swim anyway—without medication. In the silent locker room, Gaines told what happened next, for he clearly saw a message in Genter's actions.

"His face was ashen-white because the pain was so excruciating. He hits the water, he makes the first lap, does a spin turn at the other end and pushes off, and comes up for air and lets out a blood-curdling scream. Because the pain is so intense, the sound just echoes off the walls of the swimming arena. He makes a split turn at the end of the second lap, pushes off, and he breaks his stitches, his stitches split apart and he starts bleeding. They said he lost a pint and a half of blood over the course of the next two laps.

"I guarantee you, I'd want him in my corner," said Gaines of

Genter, who ended up losing the gold medal to Mark Spitz by the length of a finger. "When the chips were down, I'd want a guy with that kind of character in my corner, I promise you, 'cause he's a fighter."

Steve Genter had come too far to let it all go, and Gaines saw an obvious parallel. "You guys are not that much different than he was, because many of you in this room right now, when you were eight, nine, ten years old, were dreamin' about sittin' in this locker room and wearin' the black and white of Permian High School.

"You guys are fighters and you have proved it. And we're gonna have another chance to prove it tomorrow night. We're playin' for somethin' very important, everybody knows what's at stake. Everybody knows what's ridin' on it."

Gaines and the assistant coaches then left the locker room to let the captains address the team.

"I don't know about y'all, I've been waiting for this game all year ever since last year when we lost," said Brian Chavez. "After that loss I just wanted to kill 'em so bad, I was just so pissed off. Last year they were the bad-asses. They came over to Ratliff and they kicked the shit out of us. This year we're the bad-asses and we're gonna kick the shit out of them. I'm not talking five or ten points, I just want to fuckin' maul 'em, thirty, forty points.

"Right here, tomorrow night, that's what we've worked for for a whole year, off-season, all the gassers, all of their bullshit, everything, man, tomorrow night."

Brian felt supremely confident until right before the game, when he glanced over at Coach Gaines. In the team meeting Gaines had told the players to ignore the pressure, to put out of their minds how much was at stake and how much the game meant to the people of Odessa. But as Brian stared at Gaines for those few seconds, he didn't see someone who had blocked out those enormous pressures at all.

He saw a man who looked as ashen-white as Steve Genter.

CHAPTER 12

Civil War

I

EVENTUALLY THE SOBS CAME TO AN END. SO DID THE EMBRACES that under the gray glow of the moonlight seemed as lingering as a slow dance with someone you suddenly knew you no longer loved. One by one the members of the crowd, usually so buoyant, so unshakably optimistic, quietly tiptoed into the night.

Once they were gone, Sharon Gaines entered through the double doors of the field house with some medication for her husband. The place was empty. All those little pictures on the Wall of Fame with those square jaws and steely-eyed gazes, all those heart-shaped plaques with the inscribed, once-glittering names of this player or that one who had been the very best at running back or linebacker or lineman, all those typewritten phrases of inspiration on the bulletin board painfully culled from such sources as H. L. Mencken and AC/DC now looked like decorations for an elaborate wedding that had suddenly been canceled without warning.

In the aftermath of a win there was no place more giddy than the locker room, the players whooping and hollering, readying themselves for the spoils of victory with strokes of the comb as meticulous as brushstrokes by Michelangelo and gobs of Lagerfeld aftershave as pungent as the smell of ripened Juicy Fruit. They would leave the field house and waiting outside for them would be a haze of boosters and parents and Pepettes and cheerleaders. The faces of the parents and boosters would be etched with the same stunning kind of pride you might see in a hospital delivery room, eyes shining and brimming and filled with love at the joy of their creation. The cheerleaders and the Pepettes would be coy and coquettish and adoring, their blond hair falling down in wonderful piles as high and soft as down pillows, dressed in letter jackets from their boyfriends that fell to the knees and had white patches on the back as bountiful as uncontrolled clusters of daisies. For the players it was impossible, whether you were a starter or a fourth-string substitute, not to feel as though you owned the world at that very moment, that everything you had ever dreamed of, imagined, prayed for had somehow come true before you were even twenty. But in the aftermath of a loss the field house emptied quietly and quickly, as if the place was cursed and it was somehow shameful to be there at all.

And no loss had been worse than this one, by a single point to the Lee Rebels.

Winchell asked someone to walk out of the field house with him and act as if the two of them were deeply engrossed in conversation so he wouldn't have to face anyone and hear all those people tell him how sorry they were. He knew they meant well, but he couldn't stand scenes like this. McDougal's eyes were red when he left the field house: he had sobbed in the stadium dressing room immediately after the game; he had sobbed on the way to the bus when he and his mother, who was sobbing also, had clutched fingers through the tiny holes of the fence separating them; he had sobbed in the locker room of the field house when he sank his head into the arms of a male cheerleader. Billingsley's eyes were red also, but as girl after girl came up to him to give him a long hug, he realized there were possibilities in the situation he had not yet considered. "This is better than winning," he whispered to someone with that wonderful shark's grin.

Chavez, his hands in the pockets of his gray-and-black letter jacket, had a little smirk on his face, as if he knew who exactly who was going to shoulder the blame for the whole disaster.

Boobie Miles left the scene almost immediately, convinced that the coaches had deceived him into letting him think he was going to get into the game, consumed with the rage of having to melt away on the bench in front of thousands. "I'm not going to play anymore," was all he said when L.V. picked him up. Ivory Christian, filled with so many tortured feelings about the whole thing, didn't show any emotion one way or another. They had lost to the Rebels and instead of winning the district championship and guaranteeing themselves a trip to the playoffs, there might be only one game left in the season. But Ivory didn't know whether that was bad. Or maybe good.

Sharon Gaines met her husband in his office, which was filled with the usual stock-in-trade of a football coach: a helmet mounted on a pedestal, pictures of his two children, several footballs etched with fading script to commemorate wonderful wins, a map with a huge arrow pointing to MOJOLAND, smiling portraits of him and his assistants in better days before the season had ever started, a little plaque commemorating Permian as the team with the best winning percentage in all of Texas in the decade of the seventies. He had spent so much time in the lousy light of a film projector in that office, watching play after play in the creep of slow motion for a secret, a clue—a raised shoulder, an extra sliver of space between the guard and the tackle—focusing on the seemingly imperceptible details of those grainy images as intently as a scholar pores over a rare manuscript. The time he spent coaching seemed unimaginable. Like a soldier of fortune, he kissed his wife and children goodbye in August and almost literally did not see them again for the next four months, until the conquest of a state championship ended in victory or defeat. And now it all seemed worthless.

His ear had been throbbing for about two months, and it was just one of several ailments that had come up during the course of the season. He was glassy-eyed and barely able to say a word, his thoughts still fixed on what had happened on the field, on what had gone wrong and whether it was somehow his fault.

235

Sharon handed him the medication for his ear. She hugged him briefly, her eyes closing tight. He didn't respond and she quickly withdrew, for she knew that he was lost to her, in his own world of shame and defeat. He hated to lose, absolutely hated it, and of all the losses, this may well have been the most devastating one.

She quietly left the field house and sat outside for a few minutes in the parking lot in her car. Her face peered out from the driver's window in the darkness and she too looked tired and exhausted, as if she had been out there with him on the field in those waning, helpless moments after the final pass from Winchell had fallen so pathetically incomplete and the ten thousand strong on the Permian side had collapsed into a shocked hush.

A wealth of feelings bubbled up inside her. She knew firsthand how high the stakes were in Odessa, how "goin' to State" was not something merely desired but demanded. It made her husband's job exciting and wonderful and it gave her some glamour as well.

If you took a poll, few people in town could tell you who the mayor was, or the police chief, or the city manager. Hardly anybody could tell you the name of a city councilman, or a county commissioner, or the head of the public works department, or the planning department, or the fire department. Those were jobs nobody cared about in Odessa unless a house burned down or a sewer line backed up. But just about everybody could tell you who the coach of Permian High School was, and that rubbed off on her.

Her daughter Nicole had often joked with her, "If Daddy dies, you would be nothing." But during the past three years, sitting in the stands week after week had become a nightmare for her as she listened to the fans tear apart her husband and the teenagers who played for him with unrelenting venom, not caring one whit that she, the wife of the coach, was sitting within easy earshot. Sometimes she couldn't stand it and had to move to one of the portals to get away from it all.

"I don't think they realize these are sixteen, seventeen, eigh-teen-year-old kids," she once said. "I don't think they realize these are coaches. They are men, they are not gods. They don't realize it's a game and they look at them like they're profes-sional football players. They are kids, high school kids, the sons of somebody, and they expect them to be perfect."

Yes, they did, and they had too much invested in it emotion-ally to ever change. Permian football had become too much a part of the town and too much a part of their own lives, as intrinsic and sacred a value as religion, as politics, as making money, as raising children. That was the nature of sports in a town like this. Football stood at the very core of what the town was about, not on the outskirts, not on the periphery. It had nothing to do with entertainment and everything to do with how people felt about themselves.

"They don't have any idea about the coaches and the time they put in and the dedication," she said. "They don't have any idea, and they don't care. They don't have any idea of what the families give up."

She remembered the cruelty of the 1986 season, her hus-band's first, when Odessa was going through the worst eco-nomic crisis in its history. Everywhere you looked someone was filing for bankruptcy, or throwing his belongings into a U-Haul to find another job up in the rustbelt or snowbelt or crimebelt from which he thought he had escaped. If there had ever been a time that the city needed a lift it was then, and Permian did not even make the playoffs for the first time in the entire de-cade. People had savagely ripped into Gaines then, as if the seven and two record the team compiled was the same as not winning a single game.

She remembered how, after that season, Nicole announced one day that she was too sick to go to school. Later that afternoon she bounded into the garage bubbly and obviously healthy. It then dawned on Sharon that there was nothing physically wrong with her daughter at all, that she simply did not want to go to school because of what other kids might say about her father. She had hated that year. She never wanted to relive it. And now it all seemed to be happening again.

With the 22–21 loss to Midland Lee there was a three-way tie for first place in the district with one game left. Since only two teams went to the playoffs, there was now the distinct possibility of Permian's not making it. The repercussions of that made her shudder. Her voice turned reedy and high-pitched as she imagined what might happen if Permian didn't make the playoffs. "If we don't, we may be saying goodbye to our sweet little ol' house," she said outside the field house, and the intent of her words was obvious: she was afraid that her husband was going to get fired, or simply be forced to leave because of the avalanche of criticism against him.

It wasn't an irrational thought, for there was no profession in the state of Texas with worse job security than that of high school football coach. Coaches were fired all the time for poor records. Sometimes it happened with the efficiency of a bloodless coup—one day the coach was there at the office decorated in the school colors and the next day he was gone, as if he had never existed. But sometimes he was paraded before school board meetings to be torn apart by the public in a scene like something out of the Salem witch trials, or had several thousands of dollars' worth of damage done to his car by rocks thrown by irate fans, or responded to a knock on the door to find someone with a shotgun who wasn't there to fire him but to complain about his son's lack of playing time.

When Gaines himself went home that Friday night at about two in the morning he found seven FOR SALE signs planted in his lawn. The next night, someone had also smashed a pumpkin into his car, causing a dent. It didn't bother him. He was the coach. He got paid for what he did and he was tough enough to take it. But he did get upset when he heard that several FOR SALE signs had also been punched into Chavez's lawn. Brian was just a player, a senior in high school, but that didn't seem to matter. "That's sick to me," said Gaines. "I just can't understand it."

The following Tuesday, as he drove downtown to the bus station to pick up some game films of the team's final opponent, the San Angelo Central Bobcats, he was still grappling with the loss. "It shakes your confidence, it shakes the heck out of it," he said. "It's been miserable, just miserable.

"I'm going to work as hard as I can and do the best job that I possibly can," he said. "If it doesn't work and I'm not needed, I'll move on. I have put everything I've got into it and if that's not enough, the good Lord can guide me in another direction." He was silent for a few seconds, and then he said something else about what it was like to have the job he had in a place like Odessa.

"You can't really describe how high you can be or how low you can be. I think that's a truism in coaching, but that's especially true here."

If he was looking for any reprieve from the fans in the succeeding days, he wasn't going to get it. A few, like Bobby Boyles, rose to his defense. Boyles was a die-hard booster, one of those who set his life each fall to the clock of the season. He and his wife sat there at the booster club meeting every Tuesday night and at the junior varsity game every Thursday night and at the varsity game every Friday night, wearing their black as proudly as a priest wears his collar. He needed Permian football as much as anyone, but he couldn't stand the attacks on Gaines. He was sitting at the Kettle restaurant over on Andrews when someone came round to the table the Monday after the game to ask him to sign a petition to get Gaines fired, and he bluntly told the person, "Go to hell."

"Lose two games by two points and they're ready to hang 'im," he said quietly at the booster club meeting that Tuesday night following the loss to the Rebels. "What it is, they're spoiled. They've won too damn many. They need about five years of losing and then they'd think Gary was great."

Boyles called Gaines at home to say he was still with him. "Gary," he told him, "They're ready to kill you, but I'm still your friend." But Boyles was clearly in the minority.

Phones rang off the hook. Ken Scates, who had religiously followed the team since its inception in 1959, couldn't remember a time when everyone had been so upset. Name the last time a Permian team had been favored by three touchdowns and had *lost!* You couldn't do it. It had never happened.

At the barbershop and on the practice field and in restaurants, fans and parents and even the boys who played for him had trouble looking Gaines in the face. He hadn't cheated anybody. He hadn't committed fraud. He hadn't physically harmed someone. But it seemed as if he had violated some sacred public trust.

"I got a different opinion of Coach Gaines," said Clint Duncan, the team's starting center. "I think he blew that game. I just can't look at him, because it still makes me mad. . . ."

How could he have called the plays he did? What had happened to him in the second half, going time and time again with those plodding, thudding sweeps? Didn't he remember the gorgeous bomb Winchell had thrown in the second quarter, so perfect it was like something in a dream, Hill's splitting three members of the Lee secondary like an ax to a log, and that ball lingering in those lights as twinkling and gorgeous as a shooting star? Hadn't he understood the power of that, the beauty?

The pressure had gotten to him, that's all Gaines's detractors could figure. The idea of beating Lee was too much for him, and that cocky son-of-a-bitch of a coach over there, Earl Miller, with that twang of his as thick as a T-bone, had done it to him again, sent him home like a scalded dog. Gaines had now not beaten Lee in any of his three seasons—three seasons! If there was anything more shameful to Permian fans, it was hard to know what it could possibly be.

In the minds of those against him, the Lee game only proved what they had suspected all along: under the heat of those Fri-

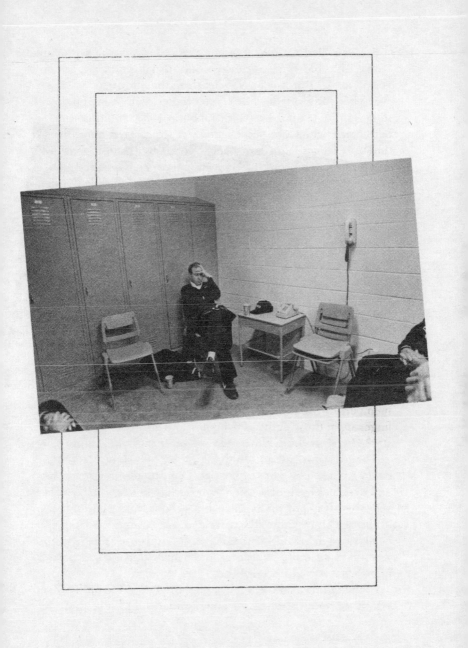

day night lights, lights that many a man had wilted under, Gaines had gone big-time belly up.

And there were many who thought it was time to do what had to be done, fire his butt and get someone else who could make these kids into winners, restore some discipline to this group that was too busy drinking their six-packs and getting horny on Ecstasy and listening to all that strange rap shit over their Walkmans to perform their job as football players for Permian High School. Where the hell had Mojo pride been in this game? Where had the fire in the belly been, the ability to suck it up and play four quarters, to do whatever it took to get the job done—all those things that had become part of the heritage of the town itself?

Following the circulation of the petition, a letter to the editor appeared in the *Odessa American* that said the following:

> *No matter how talented the team, Gary Gaines will never take a Mojo team to the state finals. What he said proves he is incompetent. Quote: "It doesn't matter if you win or lose if two good teams are playing." Never in the history of sports has anything been more ludicrously said. He talks like a coach, he acts like a coach, but he is not a football coach. Gaines could take the untied, undefeated 1972 Mojo state champions and play Lee's worst team, and Gaines would lose. You can bet on it. Around this area, there could have been several jackets with "state champions" on them. I feel so sorry for all the teams that could have had this. The downfall of mighty Mojo is going to be called Gary Gaines.*

There were many letters in the *Odessa American*, but none made a more personal attack than this one.

Gaines himself tried to shield his wife from seeing the letter because he knew that she would be hurt by it. They had been living this kind of life for seventeen years now, ever since Gaines had gotten his first coaching job in Fort Stockton, and over time Sharon had built up a certain immunity. The FOR SALE signs in the lawn didn't really bother her, since the same

241

thing had happened before in Monahans. On that occasion she had left a party over at the bank to get some ice when she drove by the house and saw them. She quickly pulled them up and threw them into the car, scratching it in the process. But that was the price she had to pay for not letting her children see them.

Her husband still knew that the hardest part of the criticism wasn't what it did to him but what it did to his family. "That's what I worry about," he said, "their ability to fight back at things they don't have any control over, hearing things you can't really refute, innuendos. I'm big enough to handle it. Certainly my hide's a little bit bigger than theirs is."

He hid the paper from her that night and put it in the trash, but when she got to her job as an elementary school teacher the next morning there were all these notes of condolences from other teachers as if someone had died. She read the letter and then called her husband. The second she heard his voice she started to sob. She knew the endless hours he put in, getting up at four-thirty every morning and often not getting home until midnight. She knew that he cared about the kids as much as any coach could within a system that demanded winning at virtually any cost. She knew the intolerable pressure he was under during the season. She called the publisher and canceled their subscription. The paper came for a few days after that, and her husband, aware of how upset she was, quietly read it on the porch instead of bringing it into the house.

Not every attack was so blatantly vitriolic as the letter, but around town came the suggestion that it was time to bring back the man whose initials had been A.G. when he had been here, short for Almost God.

His real name was John Wilkins, and he was a cold, aloof man with a pair of bottomless eyes that one coach up in the Panhandle said reminded him of Charles Manson's. Odessans had never paid too much attention to his eyes, or to the fact that many who played for him disliked him and felt little emotional warmth for him. They looked at his record, 148 games won

(55 of them by shutout), 16 lost, and two state championships over a thirteen-year period that had ended at the completion of the 1985 season, when he became athletic director for the county.

Wilkins, when he had been the coach at Permian, had had a very realistic view of his role. He knew that he wasn't close to the players, and he knew he sometimes rode them harder than he should. But he never believed the role of a coach was to build character or lasting relationships. The role of a coach was to win, because this was high school football and this was Odessa.

"You don't keep your job on how many good guys you turn out," said Wilkins. "In this state, in this community, the bottom line is how many games you win. All the other B.S. aside, a guy can't stay out there unless he's really successful."

His nickname hadn't always been A.G. When Permian failed to make the playoffs his second year in Odessa, there were many who thought he had had ample opportunity to prove himself and it was time to smoke *his* butt out of town. "It's tough, it's tough for your wife and children to sit up there and listen to some of the stuff they have to listen to," he said.

His pursuit to win a state championship became a ruthless obsession, say those who worked for him, for he knew that anything less would not be enough. It wasn't uncommon for players to see him throwing up before a game because not only did he want to win, he *had* to win.

"If you're gonna have a pleasant stay here, you need to win some ball games," said Wilkins. "You need to win. I don't think the school system would fire anybody. I don't think they'd have to. The situation would become intolerable for a man and his family."

When Wilkins was coach, fans had been afraid to speak during practice for fear he would shoot them down with those terrifying eyes and that lurched, stunted way he had of speaking, the words coming out in tiny sentences with long pauses in between, as if he was physically straining to stop the coils of his body from bursting open. Wilkins also got absolutely livid when something hadn't been done right, every now and then taking the little cards that had diagrams of plays on them and throwing them in the air in exasperation. Many of the boosters had felt intimidated by him. Many of the players had felt intimidated by him. After their careers were over they hated how he barely even said hello to them anymore, as if they no longer had value, as if all they had ever been were slabs of steak for the voracious beast of Permian football.

In temperament, Gaines was the complete opposite of his predecessor, for just as John Wilkins had been dubbed Darth Vader by some of those who worked for him, so Gaines was privately called Luke Skywalker. He did have many of the qualities of the *Star Wars* hero, a kind of wholesome purity that seemed too good to be true but was so natural as to make him appear almost delicate.

"No high is higher and no low is lower than what this game is, I'm tellin' you," Gaines said in the dressing room minutes after the game against the Rebels had ended. "A year's worth of work goin' down the tubes in a New York second."

A few minutes later Wilkins came in.

"Sorry, Coach," said Wilkins.

"Me too."

Gaines fell silent after that, looking boyish with his hand propped against the side of his neck and his black PERMIAN cap resting in his lap like a kitten.

Wilkins was quiet also. He stared at the floor and then pulled out his pocketknife and started whittling his nails.

II

"America can't even take care of America anymore," said Jerrod McDougal.

He had a shotgun lying across his lap and he was going hunting one fall afternoon with his dad and younger brother for white-tailed deer on a plot of land that seemed as vacant and exotic as a moon crater. They were near the town of Girvin, which had a population of fifty and a closed-up store with an outdoor concrete dance floor so smooth and sweet it seemed as if it only could have been built for ghosts.

"We bombed Japan in World War Two, and now they're kicking our ass," said Jerrod, riding atop a specially built bench on the back of a pickup that was a little like riding in a rickshaw. "Our smartest kids are average compared with Japan's smartest kids."

The pickup truck bounced along a dirt road, past jagged bits of rock that glinted like discarded razor blades, and strangling, spurting limbs of mesquite, and brittle branches with half-inch thorns like uncut fingernails, and draping braids of low-lying cactus. Jackrabbits weaved in and out.

"It was stupid not to let MacArthur finish off those rice eaters. Push 'em back."

In the front seat was Jerrod's father, Evert. On a wing and a prayer after quitting college he had scrounged up enough money to buy a dump truck in Crane. Starting with that one truck he had built himself a company that specialized in oil field construction—building roads and drill sites. In the good times the company had grossed $6 million a year, with yards in Crane and Odessa and Kermit. Evert had bought a house for his family over in University Gardens with ceilings as tall as in a cathedral and a pool out back and a beautifully appointed living room that had elegant figurines in the shape of elephants. But then the hard times of the bust had come and the gross of the business had been cut in half. He had closed one of the yards and was trying to get rid of that house with the ceilings as tall as a cathedral's if he could somehow find a buyer for it.

Jerrod's brother Jaxon was also in the front seat, with a shotgun hanging out the window. He was fourteen and he was still feeling the physical and psychological effects of a football injury two years earlier. It had come during kickoff practice in the seventh grade. A couple of kids had hit him high and a couple had hit him low. The right femur snapped. As a result of extensive surgery, his right leg had a steel plate in it with eight bolt holes. It had stopped growing. Because of that, his left leg needed surgery so that it would not become longer than the right one. He had been on crutches for about a year, and sometimes he cried because he wasn't able to play football. Given the chance, he would eagerly suit up again. Like thousands of other kids in Odessa, he wanted a piece of the dream.

"I don't know what America's thinking was," said Jerrod as the pickup edged its way to a little butte rising out of the stubble and the rock. "You go to war. We popped the atom bomb. That should have been it. No more discussion. We're on top and stayin' on top."

The wind was getting colder, but Jerrod seemed impervious to it. His jacket remained unzipped, and he stared off to a point that only he could see.

He thought about going to Australia.

"It's like the world's last frontier, like America was the last frontier," he said as the pickup got back out on the lonely highway and dissolved into the burnished hues of a red and purple sunset, past the buttes, past the endless fields of mesquite and thorns, past the ghostly dance floor of Girvin, on its way home.

Whenever Jerrod talked about the possibilities of life he dwelled not on what he saw, but on what he didn't. He couldn't help but feel how strange it was to be growing up in this country now, in this place that didn't seem like a land of opportunity at all but a land of failed dreams. How could he feel otherwise when he had seen what had happened to his father, how helpless his dad had been as all that work, all that sweat, all that go-for-it, take-a-chance fearlessness, had fallen victim to a crash in oil prices engineered by a bunch of people halfway across the earth? How could he feel otherwise when all he heard, all he read about, was how smart the Japanese were and how dumb Americans were? He could never do what his father had done, go out on his own after high school, start his own business, will himself into becoming an enormous success. It was like a fairy tale, something that just didn't happen anymore.

To think about it at all, about taking that terrifying plunge off the ramp of high school, scared him to death. But as long as he was in high school, doing what he was doing, he felt insulated. He felt safe.

Winchell described Jerrod as being "kind of emotional." Unlike most Odessans, he wasn't afraid to express his fears and vulnerabilities. But like many kids who lived here, anger raged within him, and he liked to cultivate an image of fearless toughness.

During lunch break from school he drove his jet black pickup, which looked liked something out of *Road Warrior* with its mile-high tires, at breakneck speeds through alleys and over curbs on the way to some fast-food Mexican place to wolf down food so quickly it was impossible to have tasted it. The sounds of Van Halen howled over the cassette player with the upbeat lilt of a dying wolf and his girlfriend of the moment sat next to him and giggled, "I love the way you drive."

He talked of how honored he was when the bat handed down by a group of senior players to the junior most likely to use it in a fight one night had been given to him. He talked of the time he and a kid from Andrews had gone at it over at B.S., a vacant spot over by the loop that kids used to hang out at to drink beer until the cops had finally busted it up. Someone had turned on one of those big flashlights and in the glare Jerrod could hear his friends yelling "Kick 'im! Kick 'im! Kick 'im! Kill 'im!" as he got it on with this fucker from Andrews who had pissed the shit out of him earlier that night. By the time Jerrod got off, the kid from Andrews was bleeding from his nose and lip and around the eye.

"We got two things in Odessa," Jerrod said once. "Oil and football. And oil's gone. But we still got football, so fuck the rest of you."

He went to school and he behaved well in class, because outside of his Saturday night fighting he was polite and quiet. But school posed virtually no challenges his senior year. He was taking mostly electives, and he breezed through them with ease. Then came the real work.

He got to football practice, where the demands and pressures were ceaseless the second he stepped on the field. Nothing he did went unnoticed. If he did something well, he received praise. If he did something wrong, it was pointed out in painstaking detail. And if it wasn't detected during practice, it was discovered afterward, when the coaches retired to their office to watch videos of the day's workout on the elaborate video machine that had been donated by the booster club.

Jerrod had done everything it took to become a starter for the Permian football team. He knew he had to because of the physical liability of being only five nine. He threw up regularly during the off-season workouts. He worked tirelessly in the weight room, his red cheeks bulging and his body vibrating. He religiously studied his blocking assignments for each game, because he was not about to make a careless mental error. He got up twice a week around six-forty-five to be at the early morning practice before school had even started. On Saturday mornings, he got up to listen to the five coaches tear the team apart during the critique of the game on film.

He routinely pushed himself beyond what he thought possible because he knew if he didn't, he wouldn't make it. In return there was a fantastic, visceral payoff—a single season of his life in which he became a prince, ogled at, treasured, bathed in the unimaginable glory of Friday night. It was he who described being a Permian football player as like being a gladiator, like walking into the Roman Colosseum with all those thousands in the stands yelling yay or nay, all wishing they could be you down there on that field.

All he thought about, all he dreamed about, was playing for Permian. Although he anguished over the future and worried about this country that seemed so impossibly hard to grow up in now, he tried to block it out of his mind. "If I had thought about it, I wouldn't have played very well," he said.

The house with the cathedral ceilings wasn't his home. The locker room was. "That is our place," he said. "There's days we come up here before the sun comes up and we don't come home until it comes down. It's ours, it's like our home. I've spent more time up there. . . . I've eaten more food up there than I have in my own dining room."

There were days when he didn't know if he could take it anymore, days during the off-season when it was time to do the dreaded mat exercises in the hot, sweaty weight room, those endless flips and somersaults at full speed. "I threw up whether I ate anything at lunch or not. There were days I didn't eat, it didn't do any good." But the image of Friday night always kept him going.

"I just think this is what I wanted to do, so let's go. Friday night, it's gonna be great, it's gonna be beautiful."

Beating the Rebels, said Jerrod McDougal, was the most important thing in his life. When Permian lost, it became the biggest disappointment in his life. "There was no doubt in my mind we were going to win that game," he said. "There was no doubt in anyone's mind in Odessa." He said he felt heartbroken, as if someone painfully close to him had died, and he said he had no idea what he would do if Permian didn't make the playoffs and the season suddenly ended in a few days. What would life without football be like? He knew he would be lost, just like his senior friends before him had been lost. He would feel as if it was no longer possible to keep balance anymore, as hopeless as if he was trying to ride a seesaw by himself. All during the season he had worried about it. "It's gonna suck," he said right before the Lee game, "but hopefully I can keep busy. The only way to make it decent is if we win State. For the seniors, it will be the fulfillment of a dream. But even then it won't lessen the pain." And now it had become an absolute mess.

His mother, Dale, felt the same way, for football had become as important to her as it had to her son. She went to every practice, and on Thursday nights she always invited a bunch of the players over for lasagna. She had sobbed after the loss to Lee just as hard as Jerrod had, for she feared the season's ending every bit as much as he did.

She blamed Coach Gaines for the pain she and her son were going through, and she simply couldn't face him anymore. "I told my husband, I'm sure he needs a friendly face right now. Unfortunately, I can't bring myself to do it," she said as she watched practice several days after the Lee game, her face filled with apprehension at the thought that the team might not make it to the playoffs.

"I'll be okay. I'll get over it," she said. "I thought he was a better coach than that and he got scared."

Like many others in town, she wasn't sure if Gaines had what it took to be head coach at a place like Permian, to withstand all the pressure, to win all the games that were requisite to survive. "It may have cost Jerrod what we consider a state championship team," she said in the soft afternoon light of the practice field, "but it may have cost Gary a career."

But there was a way for Gaines to salvage the season. There was a way to turn those who hated him into good, loyal believers again, to get all this incomprehensible pressure off him. He alone held the power to set his life, and thousands of others' lives, on the right track again.

It just depended on what his instincts told him as he lifted his wan, depleted face to the ceiling of a truck stop off the interstate past midnight and silently decided where he would rather place his fate: heads or tails.

CHAPTER 13

Heads or Tails

I

THE PERMIAN PANTHERS FINISHED THE REGULAR SEASON ON THE first Friday night of November by pummeling the San Angelo Bobcats. That same night, the Midland Lee Rebels finished the season by routing the Cooper Cougars, and the Midland High Bulldogs did likewise by beating the Abilene High Eagles. All three teams had identical five and one records in the district, and a numbing scenario was set up.

Since only two teams could go to the playoffs, the district's tiebreaker rule went into effect: a coin toss.

After all that work and all those endless hours, it seemed silly. But that's what the outcome of the season had finally been reduced to—three grown men still dressed in their coach's outfits driving in the middle of the night to a truck stop so they could stand together like embarrassed schoolboys and throw coins into the air to determine whether their seasons ended at that very moment or continued.

It was a simple process of odd man out. If there were two tails and a heads, the one who flipped heads did not make the playoffs. If there were two heads and a tails, the one who flipped tails did not make the playoffs. If they all flipped the same, they just did it again until someone lost.

It was hard for Gaines to find solace in any of this. But at the very least, the place wouldn't be a complete circus. By universal agreement among school officials, it had been decided not to disclose the location of the coin toss to the public. Doing so, they felt, would result in a crowd of several thousand waiting outside and a possible riot depending on who won the flip and who lost it.

"We are not releasing the place of the meeting," Midland school district athletic director Gil Bartosh had told the *Midland Reporter-Telegram* several days before the toss. "We are fearful that four or five thousand people might show up and we don't need a carnival atmosphere for this. After all, some people are going to be unhappy. There is no way around that."

As Gary Gaines drove along the dark ribbon of highway past Bobs Creek and Fools Creek after the San Angelo game, he knew he had no control over anything now. All he could do was pray that God felt mercy for all souls, even those who somehow found themselves needing it at the Convoy truck stop, where grim-faced men in white cowboy hats picked at plates of gargantuan steak fingers as if they were picking up rocks to see what might be buried beneath them.

To no one's surprise, Permian had just trounced the Bobcats 41–7. Winchell had thrown for 211 yards and two touchdowns, giving him a total of twenty for the season. Comer had rushed for 135 yards to up his total to 1,221 yards. If anything, the game simply proved how talented the team was. It gave Permian a regular season record of eight and two, and both losses had been by a single point each.

But it wasn't good enough without a trip to the playoffs and everybody knew it, most of all Gaines. This hadn't been one of those underachieving teams whose only hope was a fantastic combination of luck and miracle. This had been a can't-miss team, and if it didn't make the playoffs, it was scary to imagine the enmity that thousands in town would feel for him.

Unseen, on the edges of the undulating buttes, deer and wild turkeys stirred and every now and then the night burst alive with a shooting star that left a delicate and misty trail. It was a beautiful night and his car was just one of a steady stream of

vehicles belonging to Permian supporters making their way
back from San Angelo like worshipers returning from a pil-
grimage. They had prayed in San Angelo for a win. And now
they would go to their homes to pray that Gaines would have
the presence of mind to throw heads if it should be heads, or
tails if it should be tails.

He was in the front seat and next to him was Belew, nervously sucking one Marlboro Light after another as if they gave
him strength. They talked softly, their voices barely rising over
songs by Barbara Streisand and Neil Diamond.

> *Somehow*
> *Someday*
> *Some way.*
>
> *Time don't wait around forever*
> *We've got to do it right now*
> *Let's do it all together.*

A little later one of those songs from the sixties came on,
refreshingly tinny, made in a day when not all studio sound was
automatically reduced to perfect resonance.

> *Something tells me I'm into something good*

Was it an omen? Or was it pure silliness?

"It's a song of my era, Mike," said Gaines with a laugh, and
one could imagine him back in Crane looking pretty much the
same as he did now, with those liquid eyes and melt-any-heart
smile, captaining the football and basketball teams, throwing in
the half-court shot against Fort Stockton that forever made him
a legend, winning the Babe Ruth award for being best all-
around everything, distinguishing himself as one of those kids
you just knew would make their way in the world not because
they did anything with any particular flair but by the sheer will
of their own determination.

All week long Gaines had been nervous, almost snappish, but

now he was surprisingly relaxed, glad to be insulated from it all as the car spun its way toward the Midland loop.

A coin toss . . .

If there wasn't so much riding on it, if hundreds of people didn't already feel like running to the city council to get an emergency resolution passed legalizing lynching, it would have been laughable. But it wasn't.

Belew asked Gaines what kind of coin he was going to use, if he had some special one imbued with magical powers. He said he wasn't much of a gambler and talked about the time he had stopped in Vegas on the way back from a coaches' convention and couldn't bring himself to play blackjack.

"I was just an ol' country boy with my britches hangin' out," Gaines said to Belew with a little deprecating laugh. "I was kind of intimidated." Instead he had played the slots and also went to see the Siegfried and Roy magic act. He told Belew it was one of the most incredible spectacles he had ever seen, stumbling over his words as he described how some of the girls in the revue hadn't worn much in the way of lingerie.

He told the story the same ingenuous way he told the one about his trip out east when he was still at Monahans and had gone with another coach to look at artificial-surface tracks; they took a commuter plane from Philadelphia to Kennedy that was so tiny it looked for a moment as though the only way to get the other coach on board was to lasso him and throw him in the baggage compartment.

The car went past the twinkling lights of an oil rig lit up like a lonely Christmas tree, past the white clapboard houses of Garden City where the town sign heralded the seven and one record of the Garden City football team. The talk fell to snow skiing, to money, to what it had been like when they had gone to college, to anything but the coin toss.

They talked a little about the game, about who had played well and who hadn't. Belew related an anecdote about a player who had tried to quit the team earlier in the year and how his father had coaxed him back into playing by sharing a case of beer with him.

"I can't even begin to imagine that," said Gaines, who in his own life could only remember disappointing his father once, in seventh grade, when he had played a football game over in Kermit.

His father, who worked at a natural gas plant for Gulf as a shift supervisor, had not gone to the game that day. But he got back reports from friends saying that his son had broken free with the ball and then hesitated near the goal line, as if he was scared of getting hit. In the world of a small Texas town, where the four seasons of the year were football, basketball, track, and baseball, there was no greater condemnation. In stony silence later that evening, the elder Gaines sat down and ate his supper. Few words were exchanged, few words had to be exchanged, until he called his son into the backyard of their home.

He told Gary that if he couldn't be any tougher, he might as well not play. Suddenly he ordered his son into a stance and told him to fire off and start blocking. Over and over, Gary fired off into his father, who was much stronger than he was. Over and over. Then he tackled his father, and then his father tackled him. Over and over, with tears streaming down his face, scared that his father was going to hurt him, which he never would have, his mother listening to the painful commotion but not daring to interfere, because this clearly was a rite of passage between father and son.

Almost thirty years later, Gary Gaines recalled the backyard incident in his office one day with a sheepish half-smile on his face, describing the "bawlin' and a-squallin'" that had gone on as he tried, without success, to tackle his father. Looking back on it, it was the one memory of his youth he remembered above all others, although he wasn't even sure if his father had any recollection of it at all. But he did.

"I did it because I wanted the kid to be the best he could possibly be and I didn't want anyone to make the remark that he was shirking his responsibilities," he said. "If he didn't put out, he might as well not play."

If there had been a motto for Gary Gaines's life, that would have been it. It had always gotten him through, always enabled him to succeed, always given him a certain special edge.

Except now, as he left the serenity of the Concho Valley and headed for the Convoy.

Gaines pulled slowly into the driveway and seemed a bit taken aback. "Too many cars," he said. "I don't like this."

Two sheriff's cars from Midland were parked in front with their lights off, there just in case the location of the coin toss had leaked out and crowd control was needed. Gaines could stomach the police cars, but he wasn't necessarily prepared for the towering antenna rising up from the KMID-TV van.

The television station, recognizing the importance of the event for the community, had decided to broadcast it live even though it would not take place until after one in the morning. The last time it had broadcast a local event live at such an hour had been when a little girl named Jessica McClure was rescued from an abandoned well.

Inside the Convoy, cigarette smoke mingled with fumes of grease from the back-room grill to create a filmy substance that hung near the ceiling like a patch of stubborn fog. Gaines walked inside the restaurant and immediately went to the back, past the red and yellow leather stools that ran down along the white countertop like pieces in a checker game. He talked quietly with Wilkins, who was so miserably nervous he had become virtually mute, and Wilkins's wife, who wore a little pin that had a picture of their son Stan in his football jersey. At the other end of the room, Gaines's eternal nemesis, Earl Miller, and several assistant coaches from Midland Lee sat on chairs with the inscrutable look of Buddhas. They glanced up at their adversaries but didn't say anything.

Gaines was pale and sallow-looking. Away from the cocoon of the car with those velvety songs and that meandering chat-

ter, little beads of sweat began to form on his forehead. He fumbled with the handle of a pinball machine in the darkness of the game room, his liquid eyes as yearning and sincere as those of a puppy.

A little after one-fifteen the third coach to participate, Midland High's Doug McCutchen, arrived from Abilene. He was a roly-poly man, his stomach hanging amply over the bright purple shirt he wore.

The three coaches moved to the front of the restaurant and sat in little yellow chairs. The glare of the television lights immediately bore down on them, making the bags and circles around their eyes even more noticeable. Surrounding them in a hushed, solemn circle were reporters from television stations and radio stations and the two local papers. The men in the white cowboy hats looked up momentarily from their half-eaten steak fingers, trying to figure out what was going on in a place where excitement usually meant not getting charged for an extra cup of coffee, why all these hot lights were on at one in the morning when the world was supposed to be asleep unless you drove a truck for a living and why three grown men were now standing in the middle of the room solemnly listening to meticulous instructions on how to throw a coin and how it had to hit the dropped ceiling or it wouldn't be considered a valid throw. They stared back down again and returned to inspecting their food.

No one would have believed it anyway.

Miller was on the left. Gaines, feeling nothing but a numbness inside, was in the center. McCutchen, wearing a white cap that said BULLDOGS on it, was on the right. He had a look of sad bemusement on his face, as if to acknowledge that no job in the world was stranger than that of a high school football coach.

"Good evening, ladies and gentlemen," Big Two News sports anchor Skip Baldwin said in a hushed voice at 1:19 A.M. to begin the station's live coverage. "Welcome to an undisclosed location."

McCutchen held in his hand a 1922 silver dollar that he had

gotten from a friend. He claimed it had been successful in eleven straight prior coin tosses. Miller used a quarter that he had gotten from a player. He claimed that the player had told him, "Use this and we win." Gaines reached into the back pocket of his pants and fumbled for a 1969 nickel. He claimed nothing about it at all.

"Who's gonna caaalll it, caaaaallll it, Gareeee," barked Miller.

"One, two, three, go," said Gaines. They lifted their arms stiffly in the air with the same awkward motion of a bride reluctantly throwing her bouquet.

The coins flew to the ceiling, then ricocheted and spun around the room before landing on various parts of the red tile floor with tiny pings. Miller did a little skip to get out of the way of his quarter, which landed under a red leather booth against a wall.

Gaines's nickel took off from the ceiling at a forty-five-degree angle and ended up toward the back of the room under a camera tripod.

McCutchen's silver dollar landed smack in the middle of the room.

For several seconds there was silence as a dozen pairs of eyes frantically darted back and forth trying to pick up the outlines of the three metal objects.

"Heads," said Miller, pointing to McCutchen's coin.

Another voice said that Miller's own coin had turned up heads as well.

Now it was up to Gaines.

He went slowly to look for his nickel, as if he really wasn't sure that he wanted to see what it was. His hair was matted with sweat and he walked on the tips of his toes.

If the nickel came up tails, Permian was out of the playoffs, and the chorus of complaints and criticism against him would only intensify to the point that it might become unbearable for his family to remain in town. If it came up heads, it simply meant that the three men would have to line up in a row and make jackasses of themselves once again in front of the live television cameras.

Gaines bent down to find his nickel.

Perhaps for the first time in history, not the single clatter of a fork nor the clink of a coffee cup against a saucer nor the weary command of "Check please" to a bleary-eyed waitress could be heard inside the Convoy restaurant. Gaines finally saw it, wedged up against the tripod.

"Heads," he said in a loud voice.

It was a dead heat. They would have to do it again.

Skip Baldwin neatly summarized the action so far for viewers. "We got three . . ." But then he hesitated and didn't quite finish the sentence.

"Is that a heads on this one?" he said, gesturing toward the silver dollar in the middle belonging to McCutchen of Midland High.

"What is thaaat, tails? Thaaaat's tails, ain't it?" chimed in Miller, who looked ready to snap someone's neck.

McCutchen walked to the center of the room and slowly bent down to pick up his silver dollar. He looked at it momentarily, as if the deep sorrow of his gaze would somehow change what he saw. And out of his mouth came two words, spoken with the tone of a child sadly confessing to something that he had hoped and prayed would go unnoticed.

"That's tails," he whispered.

He was the odd man out.

"So it's Permian and Midland Lee in the playoffs," said Baldwin in a reverential whisper. "Midland High will not be going."

Gaines, still quiet and subdued, shook Miller's hand and then gave McCutchen a hug. He flashed a small smile and that was all.

"Congratulations," said McCutchen.

"Man, a cruel way to do it," replied Gaines.

For the next ten minutes he patiently answered questions from television, radio, and newspaper reporters, as if he had just become the second man in history to throw a perfect game in the World Series. He left the Convoy carefully and circumspectly, as if he was exiting a wake.

The second he got outside, he started scampering to the car

with the speed of a little boy going to open his birthday presents. He took off like a madman, doing eighty-five down Highway 80 without being aware of it, giggling and grinning, and had you been next to the car at that very moment you would have heard a grown man yell something that you didn't think grown men ever yelled, unless they had grown up in Crane:

"Hot diggety dog!"

At about two-twenty in the morning, the members of the Permian team arrived by bus from San Angelo at the field house. They had listened to the coin toss on the radio (KCRS had broadcast it live as well), so they already knew the outcome.

There were hugs and bear-sized claps on the backs of letter jackets that reverberated like yells in a tunnel. The season was still alive, the hope renewed of donning jackets with wonderful white patches saying STATE CHAMPIONS, jackets that would have everything on them except flashing markers.

Twenty minutes later, members of the Midland High team arrived home by bus from Abilene. They too knew the outcome of the coin toss before they arrived.

"I told you that we had no control over a coin flip," McCutchen said to his players. "I wish I could change the way things are, but I can't. It was out of our hands.

"I'm proud of each and every one of you," he said. As he tried to console them, there came a sound of high school football as familiar as the cheering, as familiar as the unabashed blare of the band, as familiar as the savage crash of pad against pad.

It was the sound of teenage boys weeping uncontrollably over a segment of their lives that they knew had just ended forever.

II

As all the commotion unfolded, Boobie Miles lay at home. He had officially quit the team earlier in the week, figuring it was better to undergo the knee surgery he needed at some point anyway and try to be ready to play in college rather than spend another hideous Friday night of his life languishing on the bench. When the doctor opened the knee up he discovered that Boobie had torn the anterior cruciate ligament. It seemed remarkable that he had been able to come back to play any games at all, since it was this ligament that prevented the lower leg from shifting forward and made it possible for a football player to plant his foot and cut.

Trapper thought it might take Boobie as long as two years to rehabilitate, and he still didn't know anyone who had ever come back 100 percent from it. The doctor had put in a replacement ligament, but it was hard to construct one that could handle the natural stress caused by the constant starting and stopping of running with the football. And the magic speed that had made Boobie so spectacular would be gone for sure.

By the time he got out of the hospital the town had come alive again, like the miraculous reblooming of a withered desert flower that all but a handful had given up for dead. There was no more talk of Gaines's getting fired, no more FOR SALE signs on his lawn, no more pumpkins smashed into his car, no more petitions passed around. The crowd that hung around the practice field was up and smiling again. People were making plans to go to Amarillo to face the Tascosa Rebels in the first round of the playoffs, and they knew in their hearts that by the middle of December they would be making plans to go to the great mecca to the east, Texas Stadium, to watch their boys in the state championship. Goin' to State was in the hearts and minds of everyone again, still at the center of the universe.

Except for Boobie. Football didn't entice or thrill him anymore. It just taunted him.

Football . . .

He couldn't stand the word now. Everything in his life reduced to a series of qualifying statements—could have done this, would have done that, might have been this, should have been that . . .

Are you gonna play college football?

It seemed as though everywhere he went there it came again, that awful question sounding like a nasty cackle as the wondrous universes of Nebraska and Oklahoma and Arkansas and Houston spun away from his touch. They were gone now, on to other specimens, and no amount of hoping and praying and wishing would ever get them back.

"Everywhere I went, everybody was askin' me, 'Are you gonna play college football?' Every time someone said *football,* I couldn't take it."

He came from a religious home and he believed in the lessons of the Lord. "Everything was goin' so good and he took it away from me just like that," said Boobie. There must have been a reason for it, an explanation.

But what was it? What on earth was it? And who was he anymore, besides a teenage kid who three months before had been beatified with a halo of invincibility and now was being laughed at and scorned because it was somehow his fault that his football skills were as fragile as the flesh of his knee?

"It's hard for me to feel sorry for someone who already shit in his bed," said Trapper, convinced that Boobie had been nothing but a quitter even before the surgery.

"The sad part is, there are thousands of Boobies all over this world," said Gaines. "A lot of them don't have a chance, welfare cases. He had several. He had a chance to fight back and he threw up his skirt."

On the practice field, a trio of men gathered one afternoon to joke about his plight. One of them suggested that maybe it was best for Boobie just to kill himself since he didn't have football anymore.

"No," one of them objected. "When a horse pulls up lame, you don't waste a bullet on him." There was unrestrained laughter and the three enjoyed the analogy of comparing Boobie to an animal. It was repeated.

"You don't waste a bullet on a horse."

Only Nate Hearne had a different perspective on it all. His

struggle to keep Boobie on the team when he had tried to walk out the door during halftime against the Rebels wasn't some act. He understood the psychological pain Boobie was going through, how unimaginably hard it was to sit there and watch someone else perform with brilliance a role that had once been his. He understood Boobie for what he was, a kid who had been through so much in his life that just to be standing in one piece was a terrific accomplishment. But he also understood the world of high school football: when Boobie got hurt, he became obsolete.

"He needed special, special, special attention, but he wasn't going to get it because he wasn't healthy," Hearne said. "He was expendable because we had a heck of a running back."

It was as simple as that.

When Boobie came home from the hospital, everyone was an enemy, an adversary, a contributor to the wreck of his senior year. Late that Saturday night, he and his uncle began to argue with one another in their home on the Southside of town. They traded words, their shouts echoing through the tiny rooms. There was a flurry of accusations, both of them lost in the misery of what wasn't and the painful reality of what was, Boobie feverish, despondent, with a puffed-up knee that no longer contained the God-given gift of speed as sweet as the wind, L.V. heartsick at how all that work, all those attempts to mold his nephew into the next winner of the Heisman, all those hours spent teaching him the spins and the jukes and the angles for the corner, had ended up like this.

At ten-thirty, Boobie announced that he was going over to his aunt's house. L.V. told him he was crazy to get up and go somewhere after major knee surgery.

"I'm through working with you," said L.V.

"I'm through with you," said Boobie.

"Then get your stuff out."

And Boobie did just that, because nothing meant anything to him anymore, not even his uncle.

L.V. waited for him to return. It had just been an argument

and surely he would come back once he calmed down, once he got hold of himself. But then hours went by and then a day, and then another one and then another one. And it became clear to L.V. that there wasn't much use waiting for the crooked front door to open on Boobie standing there with that infectious smile on his face begging for forgiveness.

He wasn't coming back.

L.V. felt pain. He felt anger. He felt rejection. But like everything else in his life, he ultimately accepted it as another disappointment that would somehow settle in, just like the wall in Crane that fenced him and the other blacks in like cattle, just like not being able to play high school football because he wasn't allowed to go to the white school, just like not being able to find a job. "I miss him, but as time goes on, I'll learn to live with it," he said. "It kind of wears away, but it's somethin' you think about all the time. Boobie was just like my own."

Boobie came by the house after about a week. L.V. was livid and told him he was never going to make it, but Boobie was in no mood to listen. He packed up the rest of his stuff and just left. When L.V. looked into his room, it was bare. Boobie had taken virtually everything with him, the poster of his idol Michael Jordan, the one of Lawrence Taylor that had been given to him by the coaches as an inducement to play defense, even the recruiting letters that had once glowed so powerfully.

But the dream still floated, still beckoned, as beautiful and elusive as the green light at the end of Gatsby's dock. "He's got the physical ability to play pro football," said L.V. one afternoon, lingering by the practice field even though Boobie wasn't there. "Everybody in the world knows that. But he's got to have the mental attitude. I hate to see it all go up in smoke. Three or four more years, I would have had 'im ready.

"It's a bad situation," he said, his voice as soft and sorrowful as an autumn leaf slip-sliding to the ground, "but I'll let it go."

264

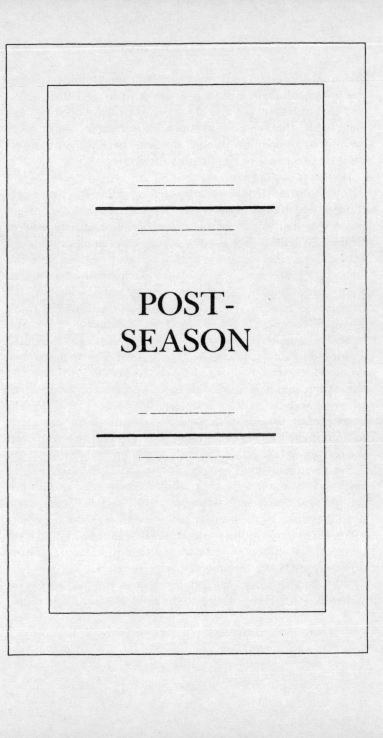

POST-
SEASON

CHAPTER 14

Friday Night Addiction

I

Permian beat Amarillo Tascosa in the first round of the playoffs with ease, 31–7. Then the team flew to El Paso by chartered jet to face the Andress Eagles. Everything seemed off that night. The temperature was freezing with a bitter wind and little flecks of snow, and the ten thousand or so fans in the stands of the gigantic Sun Bowl looked like little bits of paper swirling in a vacant street. Gaines, usually so silent and focused on the strategy of the game, prowled the sidelines with fury. He had gotten his reprieve and made it to the playoffs, but there was no room now for mistakes or sloppiness.

"That's horse crap and you know it! . . . Crap! Absolutely horsecrap! Can't make a foot because you can't block anyone, Mannix! . . . Quit tacklin' like a girl, Ivory! . . . Hustle off the field! Get your heads out of your ass!"

His anger extended to the locker room at halftime, when the score was only 21–7 in Permian's favor. He yelled at Winchell for throwing two interceptions. He yelled at Steve Womack and Billy Steen for not being able to tackle anyone. Then he started screaming at the top of his lungs and it didn't seem like some calculated tantrum.

"We're not gonna win a state championship playin' like that! We are not going to win a state championship playin' that way!"

Permian was easily victorious with a 41–13 score, but if the

267

outburst was designed to steer the players toward greater discipline, it didn't work. Back in Odessa, the players celebrated with a party at one of their houses (since they had traveled by chartered jet, they got home way before their parents, most of whom made the 286-mile trip by car), and there were reports of one player wandering around dead drunk in the middle of the field house parking lot at three in the morning.

The following Wednesday, with school out for the Thanksgiving break, the players found a mysterious note in their lockers when they came in for morning practice to prepare for the third-round playoff game against the Irving Nimitz Vikings.

AN OPEN LETTER TO THE 1988
PERMIAN PANTHER
FOOTBALL TEAM

Gentlemen:

It has become quite evident in the last few weeks that the 1988 edition of the Permian Panthers is blessed with a great deal of physical talent. Impressive performances have indicated this and many of your opponents will testify to your physical prowess. But we fear that your continued success is in much jeopardy.

What we make reference to is the obvious lack of moral integrity and discipline among several members of your group. It has become painfully evident that the winning of a State Championship is not a high priority of every member of this team. The primary goal of many of you appears to be seeing how intoxicated you can become, while others of you try to see how many rules you can flaunt and get by with. The tradition of MOJO was built over a period of several years. Each succeeding team has contributed to this tradition. All of them have not contributed, for example, the 1986 team, but the vast majority of the teams have contributed in many different ways.

At this point in time all the 1988 team is doing is feeding off of what was done in previous times. As a team you have not made a single contribution to the tradition. In fact at the present rate of decline this Saturday will probably be the end of your season and then you will join the 1986 team in history. That place is marked by a large sign with one word on it

!!!!!!!LOSER!!!!!!!!

> *Senior class, the choice is yours. No one can play the games for you.*
> *You must make a commitment to winning the remaining games or be*
> *prepared to have the stigma of being called a loser attached to your*
> *team for the rest of history.*

The letter was unsigned, but most of the players suspected it
had been written by one of the coaches.

"I know those cocksuckers wrote it," said Jerrod McDougal,
the key tip-off being the use of a four-syllable word. "*Intoxi-
cants*, that's a coaches' word."

He didn't find the letter amusing at all. Here it was, the day
before Thanksgiving, and there they were on a field that had
turned from lush green to stunted yellow, practicing, just as
they had done the day before, and the day before that, going
over the Nimitz defenses, 80 Loose C-5, 80 Solid C-5 Invert
Weak, 68 Storm C-3 Man, and the Nimitz offenses, Right Pro
Strong, Right Squirm, Right Tite F Bump to Unbalanced, until they were blue in the face, just as they had done for every
other opponent, like they were robots or something, or me-
chanical arms on an assembly line. They had started practice in
the middle of August, those wretched two-a-days when every
muscle ached and it wasn't unusual to lose five or six or seven
pounds from one practice to the next, and they were about to
play their thirteenth game of the season. It was impossible not
to feel mentally and physically exhausted. But more than that,
they were also scared to death.

"We've dedicated our lives to it. And they've already fucked
it up once," said Jerrod, the memory of the loss to the Rebels as
searing as it had ever been. And now he had to contend with
an unsigned typed letter in his locker as untraceable as a ran-
som note accusing him of being a loser in capital letters if the
team didn't win the state championship.

Several days later, starting linebackers Ivory Christian and
Chad Payne found jerseys with the numbers of Irving Nimitz's
starting running backs on them. Nimitz's backfield was the fin-

est in the state. There were notes attached to the uniforms; the one to Payne said, "I'm gonna wear your ass out!"

The one to Christian, who because of his religious beliefs and his preaching hated profanity, said: "You ain't shit and I'm gonna drive your dick in the dirt. MOJO my ass and you ain't shit." The source of these notes wasn't discovered either.

On Saturday, about an hour before game time, Coach Belew met, as usual, with the defensive ends. He went over basic strategy, how to read the keys for the six sweep and the ten tackle trap and the waggle at eight, what to do depending on how Nimitz lined up on offense.

"Okay, twenty-nine cover five versus one back or no back, we're just stayin' straight twenty-nine unless you get a swap call, okay, right? Get a swap call and then you play a foot technique. Other than that cover five means nothing to you, it means nothing, cover five means nothing unless your linebacker gives you a swap call and then of course that means you're in a foot technique on the tackle or if you have a tight end you're in a seven technique, okay, that's all that means. Bump to eight flip, like always, check loose to B over, okay, not strong set, okay?"

There were no questions. Everyone understood perfectly because it was something everyone had practiced and studied religiously. Belew then continued in a slightly different vein.

"Hell, guys, there's only sixteen teams [left] and hell, there's only gonna be eight teams remaining after tonight. You guys are in the elite few in the state of Texas. Hell, I'm proud of you, real proud of you.

"Hell, play balls out, it's a great chance to show your stuff, okay. If we beat these guys and we play great defense, hell, everybody's gonna know it, right? All the eyes are on us. All the eyes are going to be focused on you, all the sportswriters, all the TV, all the fans, everybody, there ain't nobody else playin'. Okay? So you got a chance to really stand out, okay?

"One thing about it, I've been associated with state championship teams. In eighty-four we won a state championship and in eighty-five we played for it. God dang, guys, there's nothin' else like it. There's nothin' else like it and I still hear from those guys. One of them called me last night just to wish me good luck. . . . It's still a real special feeling and those guys are twenty-one, twenty-two years old, twenty-three, they're grown men now. It's still real important to 'em and it still means a lot.

"I know it's been a long season, hittin' and runnin' and gassers and all that stuff, I know it's not any fun. Hell, it never has been and it never will be any fun but it's the reward that you get for payin' the price, payin' your dues, okay? That's why you do it and that's why we want you to do it and that's why we ask you to do it.

"And there's nothin' else like it. There's no other feeling like it that you can feel from being on a championship team and playin' with a group of guys like you've played with. It's somethin' you always have. Later on in life they can take your money away from you, they can take your house, they can take your car, they can't take this kind of stuff away from you, somethin' that you'll always have and you'll always be proud of.

"Let's play hard today and let's knock the hell out of 'em. Rodrick, okay, let's light 'im up. Let's see how good he really is, okay, let's put some helmets on 'im."

Rodrick Walker came into the game the state's leading rusher in Class AAAAA with 2,048 yards and 196 points. Coach after coach paid him the highest possible praise: they pulled out every possible time-worn cliché to describe him. He was unstoppable. He was as good a runner as they had ever gone against. He was poised to assume his place in the state record books with the stud duck list of other great schoolboy runners—Billy Sims, Eric Dickerson, Earl Campbell, Kenneth Hall.

After the team meetings, the atmosphere in the Permian locker room seemed more grim and determined than it ever had been. The players finished dressing with the methodical pride of a bride preparing for her wedding, every piece of equipment adjusted and pulled until it was perfect, and as they slowly paced back and forth on the black carpet they glanced at the new spate of quotations that had been tacked to the bulletin board. From Sam Huff:

People pay money to see great hits.

From Howie Long:

They call me Caveman because of the way I attack people. I like to think of myself as being relentless.

And from *Chariots of Fire*:

Let each of you discover where your chance for greatness lies. Seize that chance and let no power on earth deter you.

In the trainer's room, Alan Stewart, the Odessa police chief, was on the phone making sure there was a police escort for the buses. Two police cars showed up and the buses made their way to the stadium in a swirling wind that sent little veins of dust down the empty road like slithering snakes.

About fifteen hundred fans from Nimitz were already there, some of them having made the 330-mile trip in chartered Greyhound buses that were shoe-polished on the side with the words WE LUV YOU BLUE. When the first group of Nimitz players took the field for the pre-game warm-up, the blue-clad, bell-ringing, flag-waving supporters rose to their feet.

"*GO VIKES GO! GO VIKES GO! GO VIKES GO!*"

On the field, Walker ran side by side with his teammate in the backfield and best friend, Byron Miles. They ran in such beautiful sync that they looked for a moment like Siamese twins, and they had the cocky jaunt that all athletes have when they want to draw attention to themselves quietly, the stride smooth and effortless.

The enormous phalanx of the Permian band, led by the majorettes in their black velvet costumes, unfolded like the Russian army in a Victory Day parade in Moscow. Not a single person was out of step. Not a single costume looked droopy or saggy. The band made its traditional circle around the stadium, not even remotely rattled by the tireless efforts of the Nimitz fans to drown it out with their continued rosaries.

"GO VIKES GO! GO VIKES GO! GO VIKES GO!"

Minutes before the kickoff, Gaines called the team around him in the stadium dressing room. For the first time all season, he had the players exactly where he wanted them. The letter, whoever had written it, had achieved its intended effect. They were angry, enraged, humiliated. You could feel it. Losers?

They would show the world who was a loser.

"They're out there hollerin' for Mojo," said Gaines of the Nimitz fans. "We're gonna give a little dose of Mojo. You got it?!"

"Yes sir."

"Mojo's gonna be the eleven on the field wearing black jersies, you understand that?"

"Yes sir!"

"I hope all of you have prepared yourself to call on somethin' extra, call on somethin' extra from within you that's gonna allow you to play even better than you've ever played in your life, a supreme, fanatical, wild-eyed effort that it's gonna take to win this football game! Emotion! Enthusiasm! Intensity for four quarters! Four quarters! Can you go four quarters?!"

"Yes sir!"

He bent down in the middle of the circle and led the team in prayer, as he did before every game.

"Dear God, we're thankful for this day, we're thankful for this opportunity you've given us to display the talent that you've blessed us with. Heavenly Father, we thank you for these men and these black jerseys, thank you for the ability that you've given 'em and the character that you've given 'em. We ask your blessings on each one of them this afternoon. Help them, dear God, to play to the very best of their ability. Help them to play with some quality that they've never played with before, give them that something extra that they've never had to call up before."

On the first play from scrimmage the great Rodrick Walker took the ball on a pitch. He moved to the right side, looking for the tiny sliver of space he needed to break upfield with his 4.4 speed, just as he had done against Trimble Tech and Arlington and L. D. Bell and Haltom. But he wasn't prepared for the mass of black shirts coming at him in a crazy blur, like hungry rats jumping over each other's backs to get to a speck of food. He tried to dodge, to somehow get out of the way, at least make it to the sideline and regroup a bit, but who the hell were these people? What possessed them? Defensive tackle Billy Steen clawed into him first and Payne came from the outside line-backer position and dove into him at full speed. On Payne's back, dying for a little piece of the meat as well, was Ivory Christian. And right behind Ivory were other tacklers equally desperate to dismember Rodrick Walker.

Jerrod McDougal was right. It was like imperial Rome, like the Christians and the lions, violent, visceral, exciting, crazy. And Walker was about to become a sacrifice with twelve thousand fans screaming at the top of their lungs to finish him off, their thumbs raised so high to the sky they could almost touch it.

Walker was crushed, a pile of black shirts burying him so you couldn't even see him anymore. The roar of the crowd grew louder and louder. A helmet hit him where he cradled the ball. It popped into the air like a lazily floating balloon. It was caught by defensive back Stan Wilkins for the fumble recovery.

Two plays later Comer took off for a forty-nine-yard touch-down run. With twenty-two seconds gone, the game was over.

The vaunted Walker managed a total of one yard on seven carries in the first half as Permian went into the locker room

with a 27–0 lead against a team that had come into the game ranked sixth in the state. The final score was 48–7. Walker ended up with seventy-one yards on fifteen carries. Comer had 221 yards on twenty-six carries and four touchdowns.

The Nimitz fans, shamed but loyal to the bitter end, started chanting *"WE LOVE YOU! WE LOVE YOU!"* to their ever-noble heroes. On the other side the Permian players marched about giving each other high-fives, eager to take advantage of the fact that they still owned the town for another Saturday night as if they were legally licensed desperadoes, and some of them seemed doubly inspired by the letter they had found in their lockers, as well as by the discovery of a new, far more elegant word for the more traditional *shit-faced*.

"Shit no," said Don Billingsley when asked if he was going to cut down on the post-party celebrations that night. "I'm gonna party, see how intoxicated I can get and how many rules I can flaunt. That's my motto."

After the game ended, the trophy commemorating the win was held aloft, a golden football mounted on a pedestal. Permian had so many of these by now that there was no longer room for them in the school trophy case, and some of them sat atop the refrigerator in the coaches' office as ignominiously as empty pop bottles. But there was still something magical about getting one, and dozens of hands reached out to touch it, to feel its smooth, gleaming surface and draw sustenance from it, to keep the wonderful moment going forever, to join the illustrious pantheon of those who had actually made it, who had gone to State. It was during times like this that they suddenly became resurrected again: Bizzell, Shipman, Mann, Hassell, Dale, Hix, Williams . . .

Their pictures appeared on the Wall of Fame as in a shrine to eternal youth, men who no matter how old they were, no matter what they had done or hadn't done, whether they had become lawyers or car thieves, whether they were happily married or had the beaten, sucked-in look of divorce, whether they were successful or were still groping to rekindle that indescribable moment when everything was all right and the entire world flickered beneath them with outstretched arms and every man looked jealous and every woman looked like a lover, whether they missed the game beyond their wildest dreams or had come to hate it beyond their wildest dreams, would always, always, be thought of in cleats and pads and a helmet with a *P* on the side that burned as brightly as the sun.

II

He remembered the turning point, as everyone who had ever been there always did.

"Here's the pass."

On the video Jerry Hix faked to the fullback, dropped back, and hit the tight end for a touchdown.

"At that point right there, I knew we had 'em."

The play had taken place eight years before, five days before Christmas.

The breathless voices of the announcers came on over the video. He sat on the couch and listened in silence.

All season long we've talked about Jerry Hix to an extent making this Panther team go. . . .

"Sitting there and watching this, still, it gives me a feeling. . . . Feel kind of odd all over, like you're down on the field sweating."

And Hix scores! From a yard and a half out.

On the screen he dove into the end zone for the touchdown, impossibly small to be playing football, five eight and 135 pounds. And yet not only was he playing football, he was excelling at it. He was the embodiment of the myth that had made

Permian so enormously popular—small, overachieving, white, fearless. Two teammates helped pull him up to his feet like a beaten-up rag doll. On the screen he got up slowly and there was the slight shaking of a fist.

"I guess I'm reliving."

He reached to the coffee table to check his stats. He remembered halftime when Coach Kennedy came in and kicked a trash can across the room with the team down 19–7.

He knew the plays before they appeared on the screen.

"We got here and ran thirty trap up the middle. . . . then we throw the little dunk pass. . . . Try a reverse right here. . . . Two-thirty-six pass. . . . I hit the flanker on this one. . . . I think we ran twenty-nine here, sent the back in motion."

He watched the team score to take the lead.

He watched the defense hold, only to fumble on the very next play.

"This is a play I hate, I felt like crap when I went to the sidelines. That killed me, I thought I saw the hole inside and it closed up. I went to the sideline and took off my helmet and was damn near in tears."

On the screen, the team scored late in the fourth quarter to ice the game for good.

Everyone knew Permian had done it, achieved one of the great upsets in the modern history of Texas schoolboy sports. They had won the state championship.

"I'd give anything to go back out there."

It was wrong to think that life had been unkind to him. It was just different now from how it had been then. He had a nice house he had gotten on a mortgage repo for $48,000. He had a lovely wife and a lovely baby girl and two adorable stepdaughters. He had run the forty in 4.7 and he was All-State, but because of his size he knew there wasn't a college in the world that had use for him as a football player. He had gone to the junior college in town, Odessa College, but then left after a year to work full-time at Odessa Builder Supply. He rose to shop foreman and then had quit the previous summer to start his own company, Brazos Door & Hardware. But something was missing, and he wasn't ashamed to admit that the only way to remember what it was like was to pull out that worn video every month or so. It was a way of getting back there, just as his parents still kept his room filled with memorabilia—a picture of the championship team, a statue of a black panther that he had carefully put back together after it had been broken, a framed article and picture given to him by the booster club, a collage made for him by his Pepette.

"We were hoarse from screaming and yelling. We didn't want to leave the field."

When he finally did, he remembered dozens of kids calling to him for his chin strap or his mouthpiece or his arm pad or his earpiece, all these kids begging for a piece of Jerry Hix, begging for a piece of the quarterback of the state champions of Texas. It wasn't a matter of feeling like Roger Staubach, or Terry Bradshaw, or a quarterback who had just won the Super Bowl. It was a matter of their not knowing what Jerry Hix felt at that incredible moment, unless they too had gone to State and won it.

"I miss it. Like I say, if I could, I'd go back and relive that moment. Nothing can compare. I miss it. I guess that's why I have season tickets and go to the games. I don't want to be apart from it."

At the public pep rally out at the stadium the Thursday before the quarterfinal showdown against the Arlington Lamar Vikings, Hix stood on the glittering field. About five thousand people were there, and when he came to the microphone to give a short speech they rose and honored him with a standing ovation, because they would be thankful to him forever.

"There were a lot of people who didn't think we had much of a chance to win District, let alone a state championship," Hix told all those loyalists in the stands. "But we believed in ourselves and each other. We believed in our hearts."

There were several more introductions of former players that night and there were dozens more who would have gotten the same adulation, the same standing ovations for deeds done five or ten or fifteen years ago, still remembered by everyone as if they hadn't changed a single bit.

They were players like Joe Bob Bizzell, the Golden Boy of golden boys, the one against whom all others were measured. Said one former classmate of him with dreamy reverence as he remembered Joe Bob's place and time in high school in the early seventies, "You couldn't touch 'im." He had been All-State three years, making it as a sophomore, as a junior, and then both ways at receiver and defensive back as a senior. No one else at Permian had ever done that and no one had an instinct for the ball like Joe Bob Bizzell, something that rose beyond a rare gift, a natural talent, and had become a very part of him. "Before they even snapped the ball, I knew what play they were going to run," he said. "It was weird, but that's how it was done."

He wasn't big, five seven and 132 pounds, but he had become the Paul Bunyan of Odessa, no story about him too tall, no feat too outlandish. On the edge of the practice field, boosters gently argued with one another over how many people he had knocked out on a single play. One booster pegged it at one. Another said two. Another said three. They smiled as they re-called the glory of Joe Bob Bizzell, and it was impossible not to think of the little picture of him on the Wall of Fame in which he was adorable-looking, his easygoing smile seeming to imply that he knew exactly where his life was headed.

Despite his size, he had been too good a prospect to pass up. He got heavily recruited and ended up going to the University of Texas in 1973 when the legendary Darrell Royal was still the coach. Toward the end of his senior year at Permian he had had an accident in the school parking lot when he drove his motorcycle while drunk and skidded. He lost a lot of blood and skin on the left side of his face and the left shoulder and left knee and Darrell Royal called him up, of course, to see if he could still play and when he said he could, everything was okay again.

He had played for Texas as a freshman on a team that went to the Cotton Bowl and had on it two future big-time pros, Doug English and Raymond Clayborn. In a Thanksgiving day rout of Texas A & M, he intercepted two passes that helped set up scores. In a 19–3 Cotton Bowl loss to Nebraska, he started at safety and was in on nine tackles and intercepted a pass. Darrell Royal bragged about him on national television, and Joe Bob Bizzell seemed to have it made until the following fall, when Raymond Clayborn, who was faster and bigger than Joe Bob Bizzell was or ever would be, became the starting safety. Shortly afterward, campus police stopped Joe Bob in his car and found a marijuana pipe. Darrell Royal responded by kicking him off the team two days before the season opener against Boston College. Raymond Clayborn returned a touchdown ninety-five yards for a score in that game, indicating that when it came to football, Darrell Royal had shrewdly gauged the expendability of Joe Bob Bizzell.

He had come back to the team in 1975 and returned a kickoff fifty yards in the Bluebonnet Bowl against Colorado. But it was too late by then for Joe Bob ever to get on the right track again. He was arrested by campus police for public intoxication and expelled from school for a year in 1976. When he tried to come back to play football in 1977, the coach then, Fred Akers, told Bizzell he didn't want him back. He thought about transferring to North Texas State, or to Hawaii, but it got complicated and hopeless.

"My life's never been the same since," said Joe Bob Bizzell one afternoon day fourteen years later of that moment when Darrell Royal had told him he was through and cut off his lifeline because of a marijuana pipe. "It ruined my career. I thought I was going to play football. I was good at football. It just changed my life."

His face bore little resemblance to the one on the Wall of

Fame, with little webbed feet around a pair of eyes that looked like brittle coals. He had a drooping, saggy mustache and black hair that fell below the neck. He looked weary and exhausted and he gave off a deep laugh every now and then that came out of nowhere. He was home watching his kids and a "Ghostbusters" cartoon wafted over the television.

Hold your fire, Peter. I think he wants to talk.

He worked as a production operator, which was a fancy name for a pumper, for Amoco over in the North Cowden field west of town. The work was hot and dry and as monotonous as the maddening, slowpoke motion of the pumpjacks themselves. He checked them to make sure they worked correctly. Although his name was a household word among Permian fans, he didn't have season tickets anymore. Although he had been on a state championship team, he never saw any of his old teammates, nor did he ever hear from them. Although just about everyone in town knew his name, he almost never went out because it was hard to find a babysitter, which was all right because he loved his wife and three boys. But there was also a limited amount he could do with them.

The Texas Longhorns had washed their hands of him and let him go after they found someone who played safety better than he ever could, but he still carried the legacy of the Longhorns with him.

He felt it during the mornings when he couldn't bend over to tie his shoes. He felt it when it became painfully difficult to throw a ball. He felt it when he had to stop playing flag football because his body couldn't take it.

Bizzell traced the problem to his freshman year at Texas. He had been playing on the freshman team and was hit head-on in a game against Baylor. He couldn't walk for three days because of pain in his back. And then he was called up to the varsity. He showed up in street clothes, and Bizzell said it was made clear to him that if he didn't make good on this opportunity, he could go back down to the freshman team and rot there for the rest of his life. He said he was fitted in a corset and played in it all year on the presumption it was a sprain. But he said a doctor had looked at his back recently and told him he needed fusion surgery if he wanted it to get better.

"I've learned to live with it, I know that," said Joe Bob Bizzell. "My wife don't like that, but shit, I'm not gonna get cut on." In the meantime, he had finally come to grips with what had happened in his life and what hadn't. But it had taken a painfully long time, and it wasn't until the year before that he had finally explained it all to his wife after she repeatedly asked him what was wrong, what was eating away at him.

He had cried when Darrell Royal told him he was kicking him off the team. Football was his identity, his life, the one and only thing people knew him for. "That's all I knew how to do was football," said Joe Bob Bizzell, the Golden Boy of golden boys. "It had been my life."

He felt he had been used as an example, and it was hard for him to see the evils of having a marijuana pipe when you could purchase them all over Austin. There had been other players on the team who smoked dope and did drugs. But there were those who got away with it because of who they were, and those who did not.

Had he been given the chance, he believed that he could have had a career like the one he had had at Permian. After that he believed he would have had a shot at the pros. He even tried to walk on with the Cowboys in 1978, but they told him he was too slow and didn't bother to give him a tryout.

"I wish I could have had an opportunity to play pro. Not a ten or thirteen-year-old career, but maybe one or two years . . . and maybe get a different job."

At Permian it had been victory after victory. It was one exciting week after another, and the world seemed only to consist of cheers and praise and glory and rules that had no meaning. He made twenty-odd interceptions his sophomore year and in one game alone against Abilene Cooper took down five. It was hard sometimes not to wish those days were back because there seemed something so old-fashioned, so wholesome, so simple and unfettered about them. It had all fallen apart after that, and though he wished it had turned out differently, he wasn't so much embittered by it as hurt.

"I'd do it all over again," he said. He looked up with those sad eyes and then came the deep laugh out of nowhere that didn't sound like a laugh at all, rising over the scratchy rattle of "Ghostbusters" on the television screen.

Daniel Justis would have been another to receive a standing ovation at the pep rally that night. He was All-State and had also gone to State. But Justis hated the game of football and wanted his son to do the same and had programmed him to think that anyone who played it was a fool.

"I'm gonna have a negative influence on him," said Justis. "If he wants to play, I'm going to steer him into every other sport. I don't think he has to play football to get an education. He doesn't have to play football to be somebody or not. Maybe in my mind, I didn't think I was anybody unless I played football."

He was the first to admit that football had helped him become a dentist. It was also a nice drawing card for his practice since just about everyone knew he had been the star running back on a Permian team that went to the finals in 1970. It was hard to forget, with the messages on the sign of Temple Baptist that said GIVE ARLINGTON "JUSTIS," NOT MERCY or the banner headline in Pearl Harbor black that said JUSTIS FOR PERMIAN, 22–19." But he still hated the game.

As he told it, it may have been because of the arthritis in both hips or the one arm that was shorter than the other or the constant pain in his legs. It may have been because of the two separated shoulders. It may have been because he "threw up and shit all over the place" before games with the realization that "you're going out on the field and getting the shit knocked out

283

of you." It may have been because of the coach in ninth grade who thought he was faking a broken arm and wouldn't let him leave the practice field until the fluid built up.

But it also may have been, as his wife Janet suggested, that despite how much he hated it, or tried to hate it, he couldn't get it out of his blood, and he missed the adulation and attention, missed the woman in Dallas who had commissioned a black panther statue for him, missed the Pearl Harbor–black headlines, missed the church-sign slogans.

"You live in a fairy tale for that one year of your life," said his wife. "You're worshiped, and that year is over and you're like anyone else.

"We all feel that our husbands have been unhappier with everything after they got out of it. You see your name up in lights and people follow you and they put your name in the newspaper and then all of a sudden the season is over. . . ."

It was a phenomenon that Trapper had seen dozens of times before, a kid so caught up in it all that there was no room for anything else, another kid for whom nothing in life would ever be so glorious, so fulfilling as playing high school football. Trapper didn't see the game as being a savior for these kids. He saw it as "the kiss of death."

"These kids think they're invincible. They put that *P* on their helmet and that black and white, they think nobody can kick their ass. It doesn't matter what state you're from, how many players you got on your team.

"They're popular. They're in very hot demand, like a hot rock group. No matter what they do, it's a hit. Everything they do is right. And they just can't find that again. What other job can they find that has that glamour?

"What's the substitute? Find the substitute for it. The only consequence of it is a mentally crippling disease for the rest of your life."

Trapper knew the amount of sacrifice that kids went through to be Permian football players, how they were willing to play, with the blessing of their parents, with broken feet and broken ankles and broken wrists.

"How much better would it be if they concentrated that into school?" he asked. "How much better would it be if they concentrated it into a job?"

A graduate of the University of Iowa, he had been a student trainer there on a wrestling team that won the national championship. Iowa was a wrestling-mad school, but the intensity was nowhere near what it was in Odessa over football, the relationship nowhere near as intertwined.

Trapper loved Friday nights as much as anyone, he got caught up in the game as much as anyone. But he always had another season to look forward to if this one didn't happen to work out.

He knew these kids had no soft cushion. The second the season was over they became vague, fuzzy shapes, as indistinguishable as the thick clouds that skimmed across the sky into the horizon. They might come back to the locker room after a big game. Their favorite coach would give them a big, sincere hello and then quickly drift off because of more pressing needs, and they would paw around the edges of the joyous pandemonium and it would become clear that it wasn't theirs anymore—it belonged to others who had exactly the same swagger of invincibility that once upon a time had been their exclusive right.

Trapper knew he would get paid for what he did no matter what happened during the course of a season. If this particular one ended Saturday in the quarterfinals of the Class AAAAA Texas playoffs against the Lamar Vikings, there might be some hurt, some disappointment at what could have happened, because this team clearly had the talent to go to State. But before long the delicious anticipation of another season would come again. A new set of kids, a new set of faces, a new set of hopes, a new set of heroes would be paraded atop the shoulders of the town as gloriously as the Greeks honored their gods.

"That's my salvation," he said. "What's their salvation?"

But he also knew it was too powerful, too intoxicating to ever get away from, for those who played and also for those who sat in the stands cheering week after week, month after month, year after year.

"It's the Friday night addiction," said Trapper.

III

"This needle gonna hurt?" asked Ivory Christian as he lay on a table in the trainer's room. "I hate needles."

"I know," said team doctor Weldon Butler.

"Don't look," said Trapper.

"It will give you some strength the second half," said Butler.

"I hate needles, Doc," Ivory said again, his voice quavering, scared.

"I know, I do, too."

"I'm afraid of needles."

"Don't jump, Ivory. Make a fist and hold it."

He had come off the field at halftime against the Lamar Vikings exhausted and complained to Butler that he didn't know if he was going to make it. He was quickly ushered into the trainer's room next to the dressing room and the door was closed.

Ivory, dressed in his uniform and smelling of sour sweat, groaned as the needle attached to the IV bag slipped into his vein. One of his feet hanging over the edge of the table began to shake, and it was clear he was terrified. The IV bag contained a solution of lactose; such a procedure was a common method of replenishing depleted body fluids. It also had the psychological effect of making Ivory think that some magical, power-packed supply of energy was coursing through his veins, a miracle potion to get him through the second half of a game in which a loss would mean the end of the season.

"Don't move," Butler said again. "You'll play the best second half you've played all year."

"I hate it," said Ivory.

"How long is the halftime?" asked Butler.

"Twenty minutes," said Trapper.

"Long enough to get one in there," said Butler.

"I hate needles, man," Ivory said again. "They scare me."

But it didn't matter. The Lamar Vikings hadn't wilted at all under the hot sun of Odessa. The Permian lead at halftime was only 7–0, and the team could not afford to have an exhausted Ivory Christian at middle linebacker. If an IV solution normally used in hospitals and at the scene of accidents was now being used during the halftime of a high school football game to ease complaints of exhaustion, so be it.

Only a month earlier, the atmosphere surrounding Ivory had been so different. Sitting on the bench in the middle of the last regular season game against San Angelo, he had said he could care less if he played anymore. During halftime, one of the coaches had criticized him for failing to play the trap correctly with the score 28–0 in Permian's favor, and he was seething over it. He was tired of studying the play sheets that filled a thick notebook, tired of being picked at and probed and poked for every detail. He was also upset when a fellow teammate at linebacker, David Fierro, suddenly got benched after starting all year.

"I do not like the Permian football program," he had said. "I don't want to play six more games. I'm ready to go home.

"They think you're a super athlete just because you're black," he blurted out angrily. "They expect me to make the tackle. . . ." When asked if he wanted the team to win the coin toss or not, he said nothing.

Later in the week, anger had given way to the familiar feelings of ambivalence. The playoffs were coming up, and he knew from the year before how exciting that could be. But there was also a part of him that truly wished the season was over. He questioned his own commitment to the game, wondering if he hit as hard as he had in the past.

"If someone held me, or cheap-shotted me, or called me something, I went off on 'em. No mercy. No prisoners. That's how I got my reputation as a brute." But he wasn't sure if the same instinct was still there.

"Mojo used to be serious to me, before I got up here," said Ivory. "It's just another football team to me now. It's got a winning tradition. It's got good players. But I got other things to do besides football and getting people psyched up. . . ."

His interest in preaching seemed as strong as ever; it was the only area, as he saw it, that he could freely express himself. Just as there was a part of Ivory that didn't think he hit people hard enough on the football field, there was a part of Ivory that felt he hadn't dedicated enough of himself to the church. He said he looked forward to the moment football ended and he could spend all his free time "working with Jesus, working with Christ." He dreamed of someday becoming the pastor of the largest Baptist church in California, with a congregation of a thousand and a four-hundred-strong choir behind him. He dreamed of how he would get a bachelor's degree in communications or business management and then a doctorate in theology. He dreamed of the day people would respectfully address him as "Dr. Christian."

And then, with a phone call from a college football recruiter, all those dreams began to fade away.

Around the time the playoffs started, Texas Christian University, a Southwest Conference school, spoke to Ivory. A recruiter told him they were interested and that a good showing in the playoffs might cement a scholarship, and it was hard to think about anything else after that.

Once the team got caught up in the playoffs, Ivory never preached again. His aspirations in life also changed. He saw a new light now, a new path, and it didn't come to him in some fantastic, surreal dream, as the call to preach had.

He wanted to be a major-college football player. The thought of playing for another six weeks in the playoffs no longer filled him with questions. Like everyone else, he wanted the season to go on forever. In the past he had had the reputation of being recalcitrant, stubborn, a player who marched to his own beat and always seemed to fight off the brainwashing aspects of the Mojo mystique.

But it was hard to see any evidence of that behind the closed door of the trainer's room, silent except for the dripping of a spilled cup of Coke into a drain like the sound of rain falling against a windowpane in the dark of the night, where a student trainer stood above him squeezing on the IV bag to send that clear fluid through Ivory's veins as fast as it could possibly go.

He played a wonderful second half against the Lamar Vikings. The heat, which had turned him laggard in the first half, no longer seemed to affect him. Lamar scored a touchdown early in the third quarter to tie the game 7–7, but Winchell threw a twenty-eight-yard touchdown pass to Hill to once again take the lead. The crowd of fourteen thousand five hundred, sensing the kill, rose to its feet on almost every play, the cries of *"Mojo! Mojo! Mojo!"* louder than they ever had been, almost scary.

J. J. Joe, the highly touted Viking quarterback with an arm that was even better than his name, became rattled by the deafening, frenzied sounds enveloping the stadium. And Ivory was everywhere, lunging to make an arm tackle, speeding past blockers to break up a pass and push the receiver to the ground as if he were a little kid. He was truly inspired, and so was the rest of the team.

Permian beat the Lamar Vikings 21–7, and with the win the team was on its way to the final four, the semifinals of the Texas high school playoffs, a breath away from the promised land that some of the players had dreamed about since they were old enough to walk. What Belew had talked about the week before, how there was nothing else like winning a state championship, wasn't something abstract now, but something they could feel. After all that work they were so close, so magically close.

But an enormous obstacle lay in the way. Their opponent the coming Saturday was a school from Dallas that had the most talent of any team in the state of Texas, perhaps the most talent of any team in the country.

The Carter Cowboys had the best high school linebacker in the country and maybe the best defensive back, along with ten other players who were sure to be recruited by major colleges. They valued football every bit as much as Permian did, perhaps even more if that was possible, and they had become imbued with a power every bit as special as the Mojo mystique. Most teams felt intimidated playing Permian because of all the tradition and its history of winning. But this team was different, very different. The Carter Cowboys were scared of no one, absolutely no one, and just as the Permian players walked around with a shield of invincibility, so did they, a shield ten times stronger. "We don't care about Mojo. They can have their Mojo," said Derric Evans, the All-American defensive back. "We've got mo' of everything else."

They were fast and strong and they talked with relish of knocking opposing players to the ground and making them bleed. They had been undefeated during the course of the season, and their performance on the field was truly remarkable.

The only thing more remarkable was their performance off it.

CHAPTER 15

The Algebraic Equation

I

IF YOU WERE A FOOTBALL PLAYER AT DAVID W. CARTER HIGH School in Dallas, you didn't have much to worry about, and since Gary Edwards was a football player, he didn't have much to worry about. He and his teammates were the Princes of the City, only they were high school kids instead of New York City narcotics detectives, their domain not the drug-infested streets of Manhattan and Brooklyn and the Bronx but a nondescript building on the southern fringe of Dallas that was nestled in the midst of a pleasant residential neighborhood with street names like Algebra Drive and Indian Ridge Trail. But they had the swagger, the feelings of immunity and invincibility, the giddy laughter that came from riding on clouds and knowing that no one could ever touch them, ever get to them no matter what they did.

"It was paradise," said Gary Edwards of the life he and some of the other Carter Cowboys led at school. "You walk around, you break all the rules. The teachers and administrators, they see you, they just don't say anything to you. It was just like we owned it. Everybody looked up to us, it was just a great life."

If Gary Edwards and his friends felt like missing class and going to the lunchroom, they went to the lunchroom. If they were bored and felt like leaving class early before the bell, they just got up and walked out before the bell. If they felt like walking around the halls without the required hall pass, they walked around the halls without the required pass. If they felt like leaving school, even though it was a closed campus, to go out for lunch or go home, they left school.

A few teachers did try to stop them and put some reins on their behavior. One even wrote Gary Edwards up once and sent him to the principal's office with a referral, but it had no impact and Gary marched right back into class as if nothing had happened.

He was no fool about any of this. He knew he didn't get treated this way because he had any special intellect, because he was a merit scholar, because he had the chance of an academic scholarship to Stanford or Rice, because he was poet or a painter or a musician. His endowments were of a purely physical order—a 4.4 speed in the forty, a skillful ability to play both defensive back and running back, a reputation for hard, tireless work on the field. It was football that gave Gary Edwards a halo and made his whole life there like a ride in the backseat of a limo, and he wasn't about to pass on it.

In the classroom, the road for Gary Edwards and his friends also seemed paved with gold, their life as free, as effortlessly easy as the Bobby McFerrin tune that had become the rage during the school year—"Don't Worry, Be Happy."

There was a controversial policy in Texas called the no-pass, no-play rule. If a student didn't have a passing grade of 70 or better in each class at the end of each six-week grading period during the semester, he was not allowed to participate in any extracurricular activity for the next six weeks. The rule, which had been signed into law in 1984, was designed primarily to force football players to have some accountability in the classroom as well as the athletic field and rekindle the notion that the purpose of going to high school was to learn something besides the intricacies of defending against the option offense. Football coaches hated the rule. They thought it was unfair and would ruin their programs. But they accepted it because they had no choice, and it took its toll. Smack in the middle of the season, star linebackers and star quarterbacks were suddenly lost to the team because of a grade below 70 in algebra or English or biology.

But Gary Edwards and some of his friends on the Carter Cowboys didn't seem likely to have that problem. Gary had found that out during test day in one course. The class started out routinely enough. The teacher passed the tests around the room, and Gary of course got one just like everyone else. But then he got something else that no one else got: the answer sheet.

The teacher realized the situation might be confusing for Gary, since exams usually came only with the questions. So he took him out into the hallway just to make sure Gary recognized what it was that had been thrown on his desk. At first Gary thought it was a setup, but the instructor assured him that it wasn't, just a little extra teaching aid. Gary went back into class, and as it turned out he really didn't need the answer sheet anyway, looking at it once or twice.

That had been the only time Gary got an answer sheet during the football season, but there were several other occasions on which he went to a classroom to take a test, only to have the teacher tell him that there was no reason for him to do so. This happened three times in two different courses during senior year. "They just really excluded me from it," was the way he described it. "I wouldn't ask any questions about it." It would have been wrong to say that Gary Edwards abused the rules, because by his own account and those of others there were no rules for football players. It would have been wrong to say that the players' behavior posed a constant challenge to authorities, because by their account authorities made no effort to stop them and in many cases protected them.

Gary Edwards certainly wasn't the only one who had benefited by being a Carter Cowboy. His best friend, Derric Evans, was an even better football player than Gary was. He was six three and weighed 190 pounds and had once been clocked in the forty in 4.37 seconds, an astounding time for someone of his size. He was also something of an assassin on the football field, one of those players who loved to hit a quarterback on a full-speed blitz and then tower over him as the quarterback lay crumpled on the ground and tried to figure out who he was and where he was. One college scouting service rated him the second best defensive back prospect in the country, and after the season was over Evans became one of three defensive backs named to the *Parade* All-American team. It was because of attributes such as these that over a hundred schools wrote to Derric telling him that they would be privileged to have him on their college campuses the next year.

If the rules didn't apply to Gary Edwards, they certainly didn't apply to Derric Evans. Derric wasn't a violent kid in school, but he wasn't above sassing off in class, or getting others into trouble because of his verbal antics. Some teachers thought he was a troublemaker, but among his fellow students he was a hero, the kind of kid that everyone wanted to be, and when the school year was over he was named Most Popular.

As it was for Gary Edwards, the notion of rules, of restraint, seemed ridiculous to Derric. One time during the year Gary and Derric and a third football player left school, not to go to lunch, not to go home, but to have sex with a sophomore girl. So honored was she by the presence of these three stud football players, according to Derric and Gary, that she insisted on Polaroid pictures being taken to commemorate the occasion. Later she passed them around school to prove that she had done it, she had made it with three of the baddest Carter Cowboys on the very same glorious afternoon. Gary and Derric never saw the pictures, but they knew they were out there. When asked about the incident they said it had happened, both of them giving embarrassed smiles as if they had been caught with their hands in the cookie jar.

Derric also didn't have much to worry about at Carter High School. There was homework, but whether or not he did any seemed to be up to him and not the teacher. Given the option, Derric thought his life would be better by not doing it. "I never did homework," said Derric. "The kids in the classroom, they knew it. Each day a teacher would assign a certain student to go around and pick up the homework and they'd go right around me and keep on going. They knew I wasn't going to have mine."

Since he didn't do any homework, there was no reason for him to bring books home from school. On a few occasions he did reluctantly carry them home, not to study but to appease his mother when she asked him how come he never had any work to do.

He too received an answer sheet for certain tests, and he knew in general that the taking of exams was irrelevant, because the teacher was going to give whatever grade he or she deemed appropriate regardless of his performance.

"Sometimes we wouldn't even take our exams, we'd just get a grade," said Derric. "We could take 'em but it didn't matter how we did on 'em because they were going to give us whatever they wanted to." Four or five times during his senior year he didn't take the exam but just sat back and waited for the honor grade. "I was getting nineties, eighties, whatever, they just give me a grade," he said.

Under conditions such as these, Derric Evans, just like Gary Edwards, loved David W. Carter High School. "I loved goin' to school because I didn't have to do nothin'. I just went," said Derric.

Sometimes the Carter Cowboys' football coach, Freddie James, lectured his talented subjects on the evils of what would happen if they acted too wild and showed no respect for rules and order. They listened, but they didn't pay much attention because they knew that after the season there would be a bevy of college recruiters begging for them as desperately as a baby begs for his mother's milk—regardless of their performance in or out of the classroom.

And if answer sheets and waivers from homework weren't enough to pass, they also had something else to fall back on—the unusual grading policy that had been especially approved for Carter by the Dallas Independent School District.

Carter had always been a troubled school, with test and performance scores that fitted the profile of an inner-city minority school. It was 96 percent black, but it wasn't in the inner city, and most of its students did not come from deprived backgrounds but from middle-class ones. They drove nice cars and they dressed in beautiful clothes, and as Gary Edwards put it, the school had a reputation of being the "fashion show" of the Dallas school district.

The solution to the problem of poor performance scores had been a new system of grading that would encourage students to stay in school as well as improve their self-esteem. Beyond these important, admirable goals, it also had a more immediate purpose: it would undoubtedly reduce the school's notoriously high failure rate, which had become an embarrassment to the school and to the school board. Under the plan, equal weight was given to class participation (which to some teachers meant simply showing up, because how on earth were you supposed to quantify participation?), homework, weekly tests, and a final exam at the end of every six-week period. A student could flunk every weekly test as well as the final exam and still pass a course for that period.

In lofty bureaucratic doublespeak the policy was called the School Improvement Plan. But to many educators, a more honest title would have been the School Futility Plan, a concession to the notion that simply showing up for class was all students had to do to pass a course at Carter High School. Others suggested that the true purpose of the Carter plan was to make sure that none of its football players fell victim to the no-pass, no-play rule, particularly this season, when the team was obviously loaded with the talent to go all the way. After all, if a student could flunk every exam he took and still pass, how hard could it be?

But then something unexpected came along, an unforeseen roadblock. It started as a small dispute, something that could be quietly taken care of in-house. But it spilled out into the open, setting off a series of events that even by the hyperbolic standards of Texas became quite incredible.

By the time it was over, the name of Gary Edwards, a seventeen-year-old with a face that still looked boyish, would become a household word in the state of Texas. The name David W. Carter High School would become a household word also. The newly appointed Dallas superintendent of schools, representing an outraged black constituency, would become hopelessly mired in it. So would superintendents from surrounding school districts, representing outraged white constituencies. So would the state's highest education official, trying to uphold the integrity of the no-pass, no-play rule. So would Dallas school board members. So would state legislators. So would legions of lawyers. So would just about every person in the state of Texas, where attitudes on the subject became quickly defined on the basis of whether you were black or white.

Suits would be filed over it. Hearings would be held over it. Depositions would be taken over it. Emergency injunctions would be sought over it. Black versus white. City versus suburban. Local control versus state control. The right of blacks to determine the best educational course for their children without whites telling them what to do. All these issues spilled out into the open as a result of something that seemed shockingly inconsequential: Gary Edwards's grade in algebra II.

Had Gary not been a high school football player, it wouldn't have a made a whit of difference. No one would have cared, except for him and his parents and the teacher who had taught him.

But he *was* a high school football player. And it therefore made all the difference in the world.

II

There was one teacher at Carter who didn't pay homage to the Carter Cowboys.

His name was Will Bates and he looked like his name, rotund, sallow-looking, with the exact mannerisms that one might expect from a man who had dedicated his life to the teaching of math and industrial arts. He seemed intent on not turning his classroom into a mill where everyone passed regardless of how much or how little they knew. He had a notoriously high failure rate, which of course made him the anathema of Carter High School.

Will Bates was Gary Edwards's teacher in algebra II, which seemed amazing given the fact that Edwards was a Carter Cowboy and Bates was a hard-nosed grader who made no bones about flunking kids.

Bates tried to follow the school policy guidelines for grades in daily participation and homework. But that proved tricky in Gary Edwards's case when he missed class one day so he could watch game film in the coaches' office. Should he receive a zero for class participation that day? Or should the grade for class participation be waived because the absence was a valid one?

Edwards clearly struggled in algebra II. He got a 40 on the first weekly test, and then a 60, and then another 60, and then a 35.

A crisis was developing, not because Gary Edwards was having desperate trouble in algebra II, not because he might need a tutor or remedial help, not because the enormous rigors of football were interfering with his ability to do schoolwork and maybe he should think about quitting football. The concern was much more basic than that. At the rate he was going, he would no longer be eligible for football once he received his grade for the six-week period. He wasn't making a 70.

With little more than a week left in the six-week grading period, school principal C. C. Russeau transferred Gary Edwards out of the course to one with another teacher. And he reported Bates, who had a doctorate and thirty-five years' teaching experience, to the school administration for not being in compliance with the so-called School Improvement Plan. Because of the lateness of the transfer, and because he was behind, Gary Edwards didn't receive any grades for homework or participation with his new teacher. This was also against the School Improvement Plan, but no one seemed to mind. He scored an 80 on the six-week exam, and with the transfer grades that he received from Bates he managed to pass algebra II for the six weeks with a 72. It wasn't the lowest grade he received for the six-week period. That came in Spanish, where he had scraped by with a 70. It also wasn't the highest. That came in football (the actual name of the course), where he got a 100.

In the meantime, the Carter Cowboys kept on winning. They finished the regular season with a record of eight wins and a tie and number-six ranking in the state. As they headed into the playoffs, many considered them a serious contender to win it all. Until the anonymous phone call.

Take a look at Gary Edwards's grade in algebra II, state investigators were told over the phone. See how it was calculated. Try to figure out how he came out with a 72 when the only way he could have gotten it was by the people over at Carter inventing a new math in which precious points were plucked out of the air for football players needing a 70 to stay eligible. Get the teacher who had passed him, an algebra teacher no less, to do the computations again. Find out that Gary Edwards hadn't passed algebra at all but flunked it. Conclude from that that Gary Edwards had actually been ineligible for the past three weeks, which meant, under the rules, that Carter would have to forfeit all three games played during that period. Now do new computations. Take Carter's district record of four wins and a tie and change it to two wins and three losses, a record that would no longer be good enough to make the playoffs.

Agatha Christie couldn't have erected a more chilling, more perfect plot. It was one thing for Gary Edwards to be ineligible. It was another for him to be discovered to be ineligible at a time when he would take the whole Carter team down with him.

The anonymous caller turned out to be exactly right. When the grade was recalculated, it came out to 68.75.

Marvin Edwards, the newly installed superintendent of the Dallas schools who had come from Topeka, Kansas, arrived at a simple conclusion based on the obvious proof in front of him. Gary Edwards was ineligible to play, Carter had to forfeit the three games in which he had played, and Carter was out of the playoffs. It seemed straightforward enough, but Marvin Edwards apparently forgot one thing: he wasn't in Kansas anymore.

Supporters of the Carter Cowboys were livid at his decision. Several angry meetings were held that night, and people arranged for some of the city's most powerful black lawyers to represent them and immediately begin preparations to file suit to prevent the Carter Cowboys' ouster from the playoffs. They got on the phone to school board members, and Marvin Edwards himself (no relation to Gary) came to one of the meetings and saw just how upset people were.

As long as Gary Edwards had a failing grade in algebra II, there actually wasn't much that could be done. But Russeau, the Carter principal, then came forward with a solution of his own to the problem.

He changed Gary Edwards's grade.

Peering into Bates's grade book, a document that was later brandished about in the courtroom as if it were a murder weapon, he saw the notation "NC" for one of the daily homework grades. To Bates, that "no credit" was the equivalent of a zero, because Gary never had made up the homework by the time he was transferred out of the class. Russeau decided it should have been a 50. It was a fortuitous number, because it meant that Edwards's grade in algebra, as changed by Russeau, was now 70.4.

Gary had now passed algebra II by four-tenths of a point and the Carter Cowboys were back in the playoffs, if the superintendent of schools could somehow be convinced that Gary Edwards had in fact not failed algebra II.

A day later, after seeing grade reports provided by Russeau, Marvin Edwards reversed himself. Gary Edwards had passed algebra and Carter was back in the playoffs for the opening-round game that night against Plano East.

In later weeks, as the controversy raged, Marvin Edwards defended his decision by saying that it had nothing to do with football. At issue, he said, was local control and the right of a school system to determine in good faith the grade of a student without interference from anyone else. But many felt that Edwards had been unprepared for the outrage that greeted his initial decision to keep the Carter Cowboys out of the playoffs. The motivation for him to change his mind, they felt, was a desire to appease a constituency whipped into a frenzy over high school football. The issue wasn't local control. The issue was a state championship, which hadn't been won by a Dallas school in thirty-eight years.

"The superintendent was pushing it because he was going to get lynched if he didn't push it," said assistant state attorney general Kevin T. O'Hanlon, one of more than a dozen lawyers who eventually became caught in the quagmire. "The Dallas Independent School District hadn't had a state champion in I don't know how long."

Edwards's reversal set off great celebrations of joy as black students from Carter held hands and danced at an impromptu pep rally. It also set off protests of fury as about five hundred students from South Grand Prairie, the school that initially was supposed to go to the playoffs in Carter's place, staged a walkout and had to be urged to go back to class.

Back in the playoffs, the Carter Cowboys beat Plano East 21–7 with two touchdowns in the fourth quarter. Gary Edwards scored the go-ahead touchdown, intercepted a pass to squelch a Plano East comeback, and then scored again.

The following week, the Texas Education Agency ruled that Carter should remain in the playoffs. The same day, the school board of Plano, a predominantly white suburb outside Dallas, announced that it was filing suit to seek an injunction preventing Carter from continuing in the playoffs the next night. That Friday, the scheduled day of the playoff game, Texas education commissioner William Kirby, the state's highest education official, became the latest in a long list of people trying to figure out Gary Edwards's grade in algebra II, and also figure out what on earth was going on in the state of Texas.

III

Peering out into the crowd in the hearing room, one contingent of which was black and from the city of Dallas and another contingent of which was white and from the suburbs, Commissioner Kirby couldn't help but wonder if the priorities of the public had gone slightly mad.

American education was faltering and Texas was no shining exception. The state ranked thirty-fifth in the nation in expenditures per pupil for public education. Its average SAT scores ranked forty-sixth in the nation. Earlier in the year, a landmark $11 billion lawsuit that would determine how local school districts were funded by the state had played to an empty courtroom. Here, with the issue of whether the Carter Cowboys would stay in the playoffs or be replaced by the Plano East Panthers, the place was packed and frothing.

"The secretary of education spoke here in Austin on Monday and decried the academic achievement of American children when compared with other industrialized countries. We ranked thirteenth out of thirteen in science," Kirby noted before beginning the hearing. "Yes, football and extracurricular activities are important, but shouldn't we also concern ourselves with science, and math, and reading, and writing? Tonight I'm told there may be forty thousand people in the Cotton Bowl watching a [high school] football playoff. Today this room has many interested and concerned individuals. The papers have been filled with stories of the controversy. All of these are appropriate and all of these should have been done.

"But I urge you all and all of the people of Texas and America, don't leave the weightier matters undone. Put some of your time and effort and attention and energy on improving academics and on emphasizing academics."

After saying that, Kirby then plunged into the morass. It seemed a trivial thing for the state's highest education official to spend time doing, but Kirby felt compelled to uphold the integrity of the no-pass, no-play rule. If a principal could come in and simply change a grade from fail to pass without any compelling reason, then what was the purpose of the rule and how could it possibly achieve the intended purpose of shifting the focus of Texas high schools away from the gridiron to the classroom?

Kirby patiently listened to the testimony and ruled that Gary Edwards had flunked algebra II and was ineligible to participate in football under the rule of no-pass, no-play. An hour later, the University Interscholastic League, which sanctioned high school sports in the state, kicked Carter out of the playoffs and replaced it with Plano East. Supporters of Plano East cheered and said that justice had been done.

But lawyers for Carter and the Dallas school district weren't about to quit. With the kind of frantic behavior that is usually associated with trying to stay the execution of a death row inmate, they rushed to the Travis County Courthouse in Austin and asked district court judge Paul Davis to grant a temporary restraining order delaying the playoff game until the court had had an opportunity to consider all the issues in the case. Among their legal arguments, the lawyers said that depriving the Carter Cowboys from competing in the playoffs would cause irreparable harm.

With ninety minutes left before the game, Davis granted the order.

The Carter Cowboys had been saved from the electric chair. They were back in the playoffs. The game was rescheduled to Saturday, and Carter won 28–0. A week later, Carter easily won its third playoff game against Lufkin, 31–7. Gary Edwards scored a touchdown and intercepted a pass.

The following week, a hearing began in Judge Davis's courtroom to consider once again Carter's right to play football. Carter supporters had raised $17,000 to help pay legal fees, and the number of lawyers representing Carter and the Dallas school district in the case, eight, was more than the number of lawyers who had represented the school district in various stages of a federal desegregation suit filed against it. There were some other unusual developments as well.

Will Bates, who a month before had been an unheard-of math teacher, was suspended from his job with pay, reportedly because of concerns over his safety if he continued to teach at Carter. Gary Edwards, a high school senior, suddenly found himself as hounded by the media as Ollie North.

"I didn't have any privacy," he later said. "I would walk into my classes and there they were, right there in my classroom. I was walkin' down the hall, there they were. I would go to football practice, there they were at my locker. I'm standin' there naked and there they are trying to nail me. I go out to practice, they want to ask questions, this and that.

"Then I go home and the phone's ringing and they want to talk to my mother, my father, and me and drive by. Sometimes, I just snuck out the back door and went to my grandmother's or somethin'."

By the time the Carter Cowboys were scheduled to face the Marshall Mavericks in the quarterfinals, the hearing hadn't ended. Carter went ahead and played Marshall, who was undefeated and ranked tenth in the country. Blessed with a certain magic at this point, the Cowboys won on a touchdown pass in the final three seconds, 22–18.

That put them into the semifinals against the magic of Mojo.

As the contest approached, it didn't seem as if Permian and Carter were playing a football game at all, but were representing two vast constituencies desperately intent on bludgeoning each other, one exclusively black, the other exclusively white.

To whites across the state of Texas, Dallas Carter was a no-good bunch of cheaters who didn't deserve the honor of playing for a state championship. What else could you expect from a bunch of niggers whose idea of passing a course was showing up for class? To blacks, Dallas Carter was being persecuted by whites who did not want to witness a black school with black players and black fans go to State and win it. What else could you expect from a bunch of racist rednecks who couldn't stand the fact that the best damn team in the state of Texas didn't have a white starter on it?

In any playoff contest there were always several issues that had to be negotiated before the game. They were normally taken care of over the phone, but that proved impossible in this case. Instead, Permian and Carter agreed to a sit-down the Sunday before the game at the Midland airport.

Four members representing Carter flew into town, where five members representing Permian were waiting to meet them. With the suspicion of warring Mafia families, they exchanged bloodless greetings. Then they moved to the back room of the coffee shop where they could have some privacy and try to re-solve the various issues associated with playing high school foot-ball in this particular instance—money, where the fans should sit to minimize possible outbreaks of violence, how many offi-cials should be black and how many white.

They first tried to settle the thorny question of where to hold the game. One possible option was for each side to agree on a neutral site. Another was for each side to pick a mutually agree-able "home site" and then flip a coin for it.

Carter initially picked Texas Stadium as its home site. "What would it take you to come to Texas Stadium?" asked Carter coach Freddie James.

"Sixteen," replied Wilkins, the athletic director for the county. He wanted $16,000 up front to defray transportation costs, which included a chartered jet for the team and hotel expenses the night before the game as well as the costs of travel for the band and Pepettes.

Permian in turn picked Ratliff Stadium as its home site. The Carter contingent said it would only consider playing there if the Permian band, Pepettes, and student section were moved from their normal location on the visitor's side to the home side. It said the move was necessary because of a concern that noise from the Permian band would distract the Carter coaches when they tried to talk to their players. But a few minutes later they indicated it wasn't noise from the band they were worried about at all, but the ramifications of putting white supporters of Permian next to black supporters of Carter.

Permian principal Jerald McClary said police were always on duty at the stadium to handle any crowd control problems. Bringing in the police, the Carter contingent responded, would only make the situation worse.

"We've got an all-black community," said Loie Harris, a representative from the Dallas school district athletic director's office negotiating for Carter. "You send police over there and it says—"

"You don't want police over there or what?" snapped Wilkins, his lower jaw throbbing up and down, those bottomless eyes shooting off darts.

"We have a lot of problems we don't want to get into this table," she reiterated. "It's just different. We have a different community than you-all have."

Wilkins then asked Carter how many tickets they wanted set aside if the game was held in Odessa.

Russeau, the Carter principal, sat up in his chair and abruptly gave the answer.

"Two thousand student, six thousand adult," he said.

Wilkins considered the request ridiculous. There was no way that many people from Dallas would come to a football game 350 miles away in Odessa, and he did not want to tie up such a large number of tickets. The only people who traveled such long distances to games in massive numbers were Permian fans.

"There's no way you'll sell six thousand," he told Russeau in a tone that was terse and scoffing.

Russeau shifted in his chair and became slightly indignant. "You don't understand the gravity of what's been going on in this community and we do," he said.

"It isn't just the Carter community, it's the whole black community," added Harris.

"The issue's not football anyway," said Russeau.

"It's the attack on the black community all over Dallas," said Harris. "The football game is just a catalyst."

The negotiations became more and more tense, and the Carter contingent changed its mind. Forget the thought of ever playing in Texas Stadium in the white suburb of Irving. Think now about playing in the Cotton Bowl, deep in the heart of Dallas. That was Carter's new choice for a home site if it came down to a coin toss.

The Permian side was momentarily stunned. Even Wilkins became speechless, and his face smoldered to a deep red.

The Cotton Bowl.

Of all the places Permian wanted to play the Carter Cowboys, the Cotton Bowl was the last. Its location, a little east of downtown Dallas, made it a magnet for the city's black community. The place would be crawling with them.

"If it's the Cotton Bowl, they'll have the whole black community," said Permian assistant Hollingshead in a private meeting out of earshot of the Carter contingent.

The two sides finally agreed to play the game at a neutral site in Austin at Memorial Stadium of the University of Texas. In the meantime, both coaches agreed that a crew from San Antonio would officiate the game, with the stipulation that at least two of the officials be black.

When Harris, jotting down conditions of the game that would have to be written into the contract, heard that, she blanched a bit. God forbid there was any hint, on paper at least, that race had been a factor in the negotiations.

"Let's not say *black*," said Harris. "Let's say *mixed ethnic crew*."

Finally, the only thing left to decide was the color of the teams' uniforms. The Carter Cowboys had their sacred red. The Permian Panthers had their sacred black. But someone had to wear an away uniform, and in this case, Permian didn't mind at all giving up black. It wasn't a problem.

They would just wear white instead.

IV

If a curious spectator had walked into courtroom 509 in the Travis County Courthouse in Austin the next day without knowing a single detail of the case, it would not have mattered. One look at the charged, tense atmosphere would have made the facts abundantly clear.

Obviously, the man on the stand with the soft voice and gray hair had gone berserk. He had undoubtedly shot someone in a psychotic rage, maybe a child, maybe a cop, maybe more than one person. That would explain the jammed courtroom and why it was almost impossible to find a seat. That would explain the presence of half a dozen lawyers inside the room solemnly passing documents back and forth to one another, which they culled from the filled cartons surrounding them. That would explain the way he was being grilled on the stand, ominously reminded by the angry lawyer in front of him that he was under oath, that what he was saying today was different from what he had said previously.

His denial of his heinous crime would explain the presence of television and newspaper reporters from Dallas and Austin and the Associated Press furiously scribbling down his every word. He was apparently a teacher, so he must have killed someone in his classroom. That would explain why Dallas school superintendent Edwards was there in the front row grimly listening to every word with obvious discomfort. That would explain why Texas commissioner of education Kirby was there. That would explain why Dallas school board member Yvonne Ewell was there. That would explain why parents of some of the victims were there, having gotten up in the wee hours of the morning to make the two-hundred-mile drive from Dallas to Austin.

Clearly, the man on the stand had done something so awful, so abhorrent, that it must be a death penalty case. But if the curious spectator stayed around long enough, it would have become evident that the crime of the man on the witness stand had nothing to do with murder. It had nothing to do with rape or robbery or assault or even a parking ticket.

It had to do with a grade in algebra II.

And the curious spectator would have found that the man on the stand wasn't a murderer, or a child molester, or even a parking violation scoff-law who had taken a power saw to a boot.

He was Will Bates the math teacher, and his crime had been giving a flunking grade to a Carter Cowboy football player who had a 49 average on his tests, had missed at least one class to watch football films, and hadn't tried to do all his homework.

The hearing reached absurd, numbing proportions as lawyers tried to ascertain Edwards's algebra grade in a court of law. Yvonne Ewell sat and tried to calculate the grade as she listened to hour after hour of testimony from Bates and Russeau and others. But Ewell gave up. There were just too many numbers—daily grades, weekly grades, grades for participation, grades for homework, grades for tests—all part of the bewildering Carter grading system under the School Improvement Plan. The transfer from one teacher to another didn't help either. Nor did the account of the meeting between Bates and Carter Cowboys defensive coordinator Arvis Vonner in which they sat down and figured out all the grades that Gary could possibly merit under the School Improvement Plan, as if the grade was little more than a tool of barter.

It was too numbing to try to figure out the grade; too exhausting. What did become clear was that, given the Carter grading plan, it was possible to give Gary Edwards just about any grade. He could have passed. He could have flunked. Just about the only question that wasn't asked during the hearing was whether Gary had actually learned any algebra or not. To Yvonne Ewell that was a salient issue, but no one seemed the slightest bit interested in it.

"This case has taught me two things," said Judge Davis in rendering his decision. "First, that grading is not an exact science. Second, this case has demonstrated amply the absurdity of setting grades by public hearing."

But Davis ruled that Carter had acted responsibly in determining Edwards's grade and that education commissioner Kirby had no standing to determine that Edwards was ineligible. Kirby's purview, said Davis, should be educational policy, not the setting of individual grades.

"The commissioner should have been looking at: did the school act responsibly? He ought not to be in the business of establishing an individual grade in an individual six weeks because he will be overwhelmed by students who don't like the grade they got."

Carter, Judge Davis ruled, would stay in the playoffs. The game against Permian would go on as scheduled.

There were tears and hugs by Carter supporters at the decision, and in the aftermath, many who supported Carter and the Dallas school district couldn't help but believe that the whole issue had been racially motivated.

"I think the issue of race is paramount in it," said Ewell. "If we had a white superintendent, the commissioner never would have done such a thing. I think race was an essential component in the whole procedure."

But Kirby said his involvement in the case had nothing to do with race, or wanting to get Carter or the Dallas school district. Instead he described Russeau's changing of Edwards's grade as a "blatant" example of grade-fixing to make sure that a football team would be eligible for the playoffs. And he said he entered the case not because he was interested in determining the grade of an individual student, but because Russeau and Carter had made a travesty of the no-pass, no-play rule.

It was hogwash, he said, that this case had anything to do with preserving local control of school districts. It had to do with one thing and one thing only: keeping the Carter Cowboys in the hunt for the state championship.

"We have a song down here that says Bob Wills is still the king," Kirby said. "Well, this decision today says football is still the king, at least in the [Dallas Independent School District]."

Even Ewell, who did see the court decision as an important victory for local control of schools, couldn't help but feel overwhelmed by it all.

Had it involved anything else—the educational rights of a student who was a writer, or a poet, or a merit scholar—Ewell acknowledged that "it would never have gone to court. It would not have gone to court. It would not have been up for debate. We got our goals skewed. That's why I think schools are in a dilemma all over the United States.

"I just hope we can carry that enthusiasm to the more substantive issues, particularly those schools which serve children of color," she said. "I'm afraid that when it's over, it will be over and it will be back to business as usual, and that would be a tragedy."

Out of the whole saga, there was one substantive change that was made rather quickly.

Will Bates was drummed out of Carter and reassigned to teach industrial arts in a middle school. He was given an unsatisfactory evaluation rating, placed on probation for a year, and had his salary frozen. And, of course, he was forbidden to teach math to prevent further threats to the sanctity of football.

Fervent supporters of the Cowboys, realizing, perhaps, the unseemliness of going to court and shelling out thousands of dollars on legal fees over high school football, said the victory before Judge Davis could serve as a great civics lesson for black kids that democracy does work.

But the victory in court, instead of inspiring faith in the system, seemed to inspire the exact opposite. It seemed to fuel the belief of certain Carter Cowboys to a greater degree than ever that whatever they did, there would always be someone to rally around them and protect them, to provide them with a safety net that would avert the consequences of any act. If anything, some of the Carter Cowboys felt more than ever that there was something sacred about them, something invincible.

With the court proceedings out of the way, with Gary Edwards's passing grade in algebra sealed in cement by a state district court judge, the Carter Cowboys were on their way to

311

State with messianic fervor, ordained and blessed not only inside the school, as they always had been, but now by the entire black community of Dallas.

Three hundred and fifty miles to the west, there was no need to find a catalyst for the zeal that could be created by a winning high school football team. Such zeal was firmly in place, just as it had been for the past sixty years.

"Between the referees' whistles, I guarantee you, we'll get after their ass," Gaines told his players several days before the two kingdoms would face each other for the right to go to State. "If you're not up to it, we'll find a place for you somewhere else."

No one came forward.

CHAPTER 16

Field of Dreams

I

As a child Mike Winchell had dreamed of it, right down to the shoelaces that he wore. And now he was here in that mystical place, the huge oval of Memorial Stadium at the University of Texas, with those smooth flanks of concrete curving to the sky.

During their road trips across Texas together, his brother Joe Bill had always made a point of showing Mike the great football baronies of Texas—Texas A & M, the University of Texas, Baylor. "Hey, if you work hard, you can go here," Joe Bill told him. Of all those trips, and all those schools, it was the University of Texas that had made the greatest impression. He wore shoelaces with little orange Longhorns on them. He fought for its honor when other kids dared to sully it.

Joe Bill had first taken him to Memorial Stadium in 1981. They had gone there other times since then, and Joe Bill remembered the time Mike got to try on the helmet of one of the Longhorn players. When Mike was a junior at Permian, his brother took him to meet David McWilliams, the Texas head coach, and an assistant later took Mike into the field house and showed him the weight room.

"That's all he wanted to do," said Joe Bill, "was go to Texas."

And now he was in that field house again, not as some gawking, starry-eyed kid, but as a football player, preparing for the semifinal game against the Carter Cowboys.

Since the beginning of December, college recruiters had been coming to Permian to see who might be worth running after. They were interested in Ivory Christian, and they were particularly interested in two other black players who were only juniors, Hill and Comer, because it was never too early to start laying the foundations. When Gaines spoke to them, he also tried to steer them in Winchell's direction.

There was no doubt that Winchell had exceeded all expectations. As a senior he had come into his own. After fourteen games, he had completed 97 of 203 passes for 1,881 yards, twenty-four touchdowns, and only five interceptions. And there were moments when he had thrown the ball so exquisitely, with such a soft, intangible touch, that it was hard to believe he couldn't make a contribution somewhere.

Beyond the statistics, Gaines also thought they would never find a player who was more dedicated or disciplined. He was a one-in-a-thousand kid who would work tirelessly on the football field and then go back to the dorm to work tirelessly on his homework, a kid who actually believed that the purpose of an athletic scholarship was not only to play football but also to get an education.

But football games were not won with noble role models and the cotton candy that college presidents liked to spin out for the media. They were won with kids who had rockets for arms and hydraulic pistons for legs and biceps and triceps and quadriceps that could carry refrigerators home from Sears and cross-eyed looks suggesting that to maim someone was sublime. Mike Winchell wasn't at all what the college recruiters were looking for, and the fears that had always haunted him were probably right: he wasn't fast enough, or tall enough. He didn't possess a good enough arm, and no amount of work was going to make up for that.

"I gave everybody his name," said Gaines in his office one day, obviously discouraged. "Nobody has stepped forward and said they're real interested."

But Mike was in the place of his childhood dreams, and he

314

was at a time in his life when dreams still did come true, when David whipped Goliath, when unexpected pleasures fell from the clouds, when surprises rained down daily, when every feeling seemed like the most important on earth. He was still in high school.

And who knew what might happen if he had a great game, riddled the nation's finest high school defense, threw his passes true and straight and on a bead, made the right audibles at the line of scrimmage, didn't wince once under the blitz that had knocked many a quarterback into terrified submission?

Maybe the college recruiters in attendance, maybe even one from the University of Texas, would take their eyes off the Carter Cowboys and say silently to themselves that there was something about this Winchell kid, something indescribable, something that was worth taking a shot on. . . .

The morning of the game, the weather in Austin was cold and rainy. As the starting time drew nearer and nearer, as he walked along the field where the Longhorns played and now he would play, his head became filled by a nagging feeling that he couldn't get rid of, couldn't let go of. He grew silent, as he always did on game day, and the familiar strains of agony began to show, the face so tight, the eyes filled not with the glitter of the challenge but the pressure of it, and he imagined a likely scenario for what would happen:

It was too wet. He would never be able to throw the ball, never be able to get a grip on it. It wouldn't be a field of dreams at all, but one of nightmares.

II

The locker room, laid out the night before by the student trainers and managers, was stunning.

Each of the uniforms hung from the fourth mesh hole at the top of the locker. Each was turned the same way, with the names of the players across the back in black letters, just like in

college, just like in the pros, but better, those uniforms symbolizing something richer, something deeper, because if they lost
they would never wear them again.

*Winchell, Christian, Chavez, Billingsley, McDougal, Payne, Sweatt,
Dean, Wilkins, Brown, Johnson . . .*

There was a stool in front of each of the lockers. The shoes
were propped up against one of the rungs like Cinderella's slip-
pers. The pants and socks had been placed on top of the stool,
each laid out the exact same way. On top of the pants and socks
was the helmet, each turned the same way.

Jerrod McDougal picked up his helmet and gently thumbed
it. It wasn't a corny gesture, but a gesture of awareness.

"Damn," he said in a whisper. "It's here.

"Win this one and we're there, where we want to be."

Everything followed in the same sequence, as it always did, the
ritual sounds of getting dressed that now seemed so automatic,
so reflexive. The quick, bloodless tears of tape on the trainer's
table. The rustling sound of pants being pulled to the waist like
the fitting of a wedding dress. The clapping sound of shoulder
pads transforming a scrawny kid into a larger-than-life football
player. The scratchy sounds of the psych-up music from the
Walkmans, Bon Jovi for the whites and Public Enemy for the
blacks. The fixed, familiar looks of the players, Winchell furtive
and nervous; Billingsley tapping his legs up and down, those
beautiful eyes alive and electric and darting; McDougal biting
down on his lip, wanting to get it on so badly, bring those Carter
Cowboy motherfuckers on; Christian trying to remain calm as
his stomach boiled and churned, seething like a cauldron;
Chavez stony and silently receding into his special, momentary
world of violence.

Outside on the soggy, spongy field, the Carter Cowboys con-
ducted their pre-game warm-ups. They wore bright red uniforms that were the color of blood, and it was obvious just by
the physical look of them that Permian hadn't faced a team like

this all year. Their best defensive player, linebacker Jessie Armstead, six two and 205 pounds, would be named national high
school player of the year by *SuperPrep* magazine after the season and would sign a football scholarship with the University
of Miami. Six other players on the defense would sign scholarships, with Oklahoma State, Tennessee, Houston, Baylor, and
two with North Texas State. On the offense, the Carter line
averaged six one and 243 pounds, and two players would sign
scholarships, with SMU and Houston.

With Boobie lost to the team, Permian, if it was blessed,
might have one player sign a scholarship with a Division I
school. Maybe Winchell. Maybe Ivory Christian. Or it might not
have any at all.

As the Carter Cowboys went through their warm-ups, the
Pepettes arrived. They had traveled to Austin in a caravan of
buses along with the band. A patrol car had followed them the
entire 340-mile trip after the school received a series of phone
calls threatening to sabotage the buses.

The Pepettes arrived in their short skirts and letter jackets,
their hair, usually so buoyant, falling in damp strings because
of the rain. About five thousand Permian fans were already in
the stands even though the game was an hour off, and at the
sight of the Pepettes they started yelling their familiar chant.

"MO-JO! MO-JO! MO-JO! MO-JO!"

The Carter team, for no apparent reason, edged over to the
Permian sideline en masse. They started making low, guttural
sounds that sounded like dogs barking or the arfing of seals,
then started clapping in unison. Several of them wore dark
green visors over their helmets, a new equipment feature that
served no obvious purpose other than to make football players
look more menacing and killerlike than they already did. They
started chanting something, and it was hard to make out what
they were saying. Some said it was "Oreo! Oreo!" directed at a
Permian teacher who was black. Then they started chanting
something else, something that sounded like "Fuck O! Fuck
O!"—perhaps a version of "Fuck Mojo! Fuck Mojo!" The Pep-

ettes looked intimidated, scared, as the Carter Cowboys moved closer and closer in their bloodred uniforms, the claps getting louder and louder, the chant rhythmic and taunting. When some of the Carter players were asked what they were saying, they just smirked contemptuously through their green death masks and walked away.

The Permian band came in and began to make its traditional march around the stadium. It played "Grandioso," with those stirring, rising notes. It moved to the very edge of the Permian side, as if it was a demilitarized zone, and then stopped and came back the other way. The band always went all the way around the stadium—that was a Permian trademark—but a decision had been made not to go over to the Carter side, presumably because of fears of trouble.

The Carter band came in led by a drum major, the music sweet and jazzy. The Carter crowd, far smaller than the Permian crowd even though they had a much shorter distance to travel, broke into exuberant cries.

"CAR-TER! CAR-TER! CAR-TER! CAR-TER!"

The Carter band moved into the stands and members of the crowd started swaying dreamily back and forth as if they were dancing.

The stadium filled up with more fans. Some came in through portal 17, right smack in the middle. Occasionally they went in the wrong direction, but they were quickly able to right themselves. In the waning minutes before game time there was a small stream of black passing white to get to the Carter side, and white passing black to get to the Permian side.

The coaches gave their pre-game speeches in the locker room.

From Gaines with Winchell, methodically going over the checks and the three-play packages. From Mayes with the linebackers, filling up an entire blackboard with defenses and read responsibilities that looked like an equation for nuclear fusion. From Belew with the running backs and the defensive ends.

From Currie with the linemen. From Hollingshead with the receivers and defensive backs.

"We're one game away from playing a state football championship game. We deserve it, because we've worked our ass off in off-season, worked hard in August, had two-a-days, came up to practice in the morning. You got to have it in your heart that you want it worse than Carter does. It is a team sport, football is a team sport, the team that wants it the worst is gonna win this football game."

There was no other moment like it, and anyone who had ever played high school football could still recall it with perfect clarity, that emotional peak, that time in life when all energy was concentrated on a single point and everything was crystal clear. Whatever happened afterward, whatever success, or failure, or happiness, or horror, it could not be forgotten.

Just before the team had left to fly to Austin, a final message of inspiration had been placed on the bulletin board of the field house. It came from Don Meredith, who had been an All-American quarterback at Southern Methodist University and an All-Pro quarterback with the Dallas Cowboys. But the game he felt proudest of took place when he had played quarterback for the Mount Vernon Purple and White Tigers in the homecoming game against Sulphur Spring.

> *I knew at that moment I'd given everything I had to give, total commitment. Not holding back anything. Like being truly clean and truly free as far as maximum effort. It's an emotional feeling, an emotional high that is basically unparalleled.*

There wasn't a player in that locker room who didn't innately understand exactly what Don Meredith was talking about. They had felt that feeling before, and they knew in their hearts they would feel it today in the gray drizzle of Memorial Stadium. As they huddled around Gaines, there wasn't one who didn't think that Permian, somehow, some way, would win.

That was their great cutting edge. That's what made them

different. And they would not give it up, not against the Carter Cowboys with their 4.4 flyboys and their All-American hotshots and the wild-eyed fervor of their fans fueled by all those Kafkaesque court battles to stay in the playoffs, not against anyone.

"There's four teams left in the state of Texas, and the Permian Panthers are one of those four," Gaines softly told his players moments before it was time to take to the field. They huddled around him on one knee, their faces so earnest, so filled with nervousness and hope, and they truly did seem like a family, the bunch of brothers that Gaines had talked about so long ago before the Odessa High game. It seemed corny then, the kind of sentiment coaches always tried to invoke. But it didn't now. They were together, white and black and Hispanic, rich and poor, and they would stay that way for as long as they were a team, as long as they had another game to play.

"We got to go out with the attitude that we are not going to get beat," said Gaines. "We are not going to accept anything less than a win. That's the attitude that we have to have. They've played some good football teams but I don't think they've played anybody capable of getting after 'em for forty-eight minutes like we're capable of getting after em."

Everything was in place for that to happen. Nothing was absent, not even the painful retching of Ivory Christian.

His heaves echoed in the locker room as if he was choking, the sounds more horrible and violent than usual, but by now they had become reassuring, an encouraging vital sign.

It meant that he, like everyone else, had come too far and been through too much not to win it all, not to go to State.

III

"Fuck you . . . motherfucker . . . bitch . . ."

The words came out of Derric Evans in a frothing torrent, anything he could think of, it didn't really matter what it was, just as long as he whispered something every time he fell over

Mike Winchell, just as long as it was foul and filthy, just as long
as he let Winchell know that every time he took the snap from
center there would be Derric Evans again, the All-American
High School Hit Man, ready to hold him up again and whisper
sweet nothings into his ear. It was all part of the rite, all part of
the image, all part of the Intimidation Trip.

"Pussy . . . bitch . . ."

It defined the savage spirit of the game.

The Carter defense was every bit as good as the college scouts
said it would be. Slivers of space closed instantaneously. Comer
was buried under by five, six, seven Carter Cowboys as he tried
to cut up to the outside. Billingsley, despite a noble effort,
looked like a Lilliputian trying to block defensive ends and linebackers who were seven inches taller and forty pounds heavier.
They were too big, too quick, too fast as he dove in front of
them, flinging his body in a vain effort to stop them. Sometimes
he got a piece of them, but most of the time they just side-
stepped him like toreadors or pushed him away as though he
was a bothersome younger cousin.

Winchell was having tremendous difficulty throwing the ball,
and it was hard to know why—the rain, or the nervousness of
playing in Memorial Stadium, or his own silent prophecy of
failure. The ball skittered off his hand, underthrown, over-
thrown, nowhere near its intended target.

For the first time all season, Permian was having trouble moving the ball at all, punting on three of its first four possessions.
But so was Carter.

Compared to Carter, the Permian defense had no individual
talent at all except for Ivory Christian at middle linebacker and
Hill at safety. But that didn't matter. Like an exquisite machine,
the defense fell for nothing, not the play fakes, not the flea
flicker, not the three receiver-side formations or any of the
other seventy-odd formations that Carter had run during the
course of the season. The Permian players had been trained
and molded to perfection, every ounce of skill extracted and
made into something, and it showed stunningly.

321

It was going to be a football game after all, a mean, relentless, thudding fight in the gray and the rain.

With about three minutes left in the second quarter and the game scoreless, Permian faced a second and thirteen from the Carter 31. Comer got the ball on a pitch and moved around the right side. McDougal hung up the defensive end with a good block. Billingsley, using his entire body, momentarily wrapped up Derric Evans. Comer had daylight to the outside with Hill and Winchell running interference ahead of him. Hill got a piece of one defensive back. Winchell dove into another one and wiped him out. Comer was off now, the legs pumping, in full stride, furious, strong.

A Carter player came from behind and lunged, grabbing hold of his jersey. Comer refused to go down, dragging the player along for several yards to the 15. The grip finally came loose, the player slipping to the ground as if he was sinking into a swamp, and Comer broke off into the end zone.

The extra point was no good, but that was all right, because each of the Permian fans who had driven on icy, dangerous roads to come to Austin knew at that very moment that the only thing in the world better than the vaunted Carter Cowboy defense was the magic of Mojo. The Carter side fell silent, pulling out umbrellas to ward off the miserable rain that now started falling again. The only sounds came from the band, not spirited or militaristic, but an almost mournful wail.

The Cowboys came right back, moving fifty-eight yards in a minute to tie the score, the touchdown coming on a seventeen-yard pass from quarterback Robert Hall to flanker Marcus Grant.

The Cowboys' extra point was good, giving them a 7–6 lead, and the Carter side reverberated with newly discovered enthusiasm:

"MO-JO! YOU GOT TO GO! MO-JO! YOU GOT TO GO! MO-JO! YOU GOT TO GO!"

Permian got the ball back at its own 20. Aided by a twenty-five-yard scramble on third down by Winchell and an interference penalty against Carter, it moved down to the Carter 14 with four seconds left before the half.

Alan Wyles, a talented kicker who absolutely hated to kick, came in to try a thirty-one-yard field goal. The kick reflected his angst. It fluttered painfully, like something in slow motion, taking forever to reach the crossbar. Finally, the referees gave the signal. It was wide to the left.

Permian was down by a point with two periods left to play.

McDougal walked through the locker room at halftime with an almost frantic look on his face.

"This is it!" he yelled, angry, his eyes ablaze, filled with a mixture of venom and fear. "You want your last game to be here? These punks are just askin' to be rocked! Let's rock 'em and go home! What else do you have to do over Christmas holidays?"

"Play football," several players answered back.

The defense had performed wonderfully, holding Carter to 14 yards on the ground and 117 passing. On offense, Comer had already gained 109 yards. But Winchell was only 2 of 16 passing for 42 yards and 1 interception. He was losing the struggle to the old, familiar demons.

Right before the second half began, Gaines gathered the players around him once again, his voice rising as he spoke.

"We gotta hammer 'em. We gotta keep hammerin' at 'em. Our conditioning's gotta pay off for us. Our discipline's gotta pay off for us. Our mental toughness has to pay off for us.

"Keep diggin'! Keep scratchin'! Keep clawin'! Give a fanatical effort this second half! That's what it's gonna take! A fanatical effort! Better than you've ever given in your entire life! You all understand?"

"Yes sir."

Comer fumbled to begin the second half. The Cowboys took over at the Permian 49 but couldn't move the ball and had to punt.

The kick was blocked by Steve Womack.

Permian had a first down at the Carter 17.

"MO-JO! MO-JO! MO-JO! MO-JO!"

The cries from the soaked-to-the bone fans carried to the heavens.

But the Permian drive sputtered and it was time for Wyles to agonize his way through another field goal, this one from the 30 instead of the 31.

The kick fluttered painfully, just like the last one. It took forever to reach the crossbar, just like the last one. But it was good.

Permian had regained the lead, 9–7.

The defense played with even more fire, swarming, running for their lives. A reverse snuffed out perfectly by Ivory Christian for no gain. Billy Steen, who bore no resemblance whatever to a football player but had become one through sheer will, fighting off an offensive lineman four inches taller and fifty pounds heavier to sack the quarterback. Felipe Davila looping around a lineman thirty-five pounds heavier than he was to force the quarterback into an off-target throw. Chad Payne diving to trip up a running back and stop a draw play from going all the way. The Carter offense was fidgety, nervous, rattled. But so was the Permian offense.

Billingsley on a pitch and immediately smothered by the two All-Americans, Armstead and Evans, for a loss of two. Comer on a pitch, smothered by defensive end Joseph Tips. Evans sacking Winchell and lying on top of him after the play so he could whisper into his ear, let him know that he was a pussy, a motherfucker, a sissy bitch. Hill open for the first down over the middle but the ball floppy and fluttering and out of his reach.

The third quarter ended with Permian still ahead by two points.

Carter's Hall dropped back to pass with a first and ten at the Permian 48. The rain was falling in sheets, and there were puddles all over the field. He threw deep and the ball sliced through Marcus Grant's fingers and fell to the turf, but Grant deftly cradled the ball in as if he had caught it. Television replays unquestionably showed that the ball had been dropped. But the official in charge of making the call ruled it a completed pass. It gave Carter a twenty-five-yard gain and a first down at the Permian 27. Permian supporters, accurately noting that the official had never been in position to see the play in the first place, later grumbled that he made it the way he did because he was black and favored Carter. Whatever happened, the Cowboys had just gotten a wonderful gift.

The beat of drums started up from the Carter side. With a second and ten, Hall dropped back to pass. He made a spin move to escape outside linebacker Greg Sweatt on a blitz and then threw a little dump-off pass to fullback David Jones. He got the block he needed and ran untouched down the left sideline for a touchdown. He knelt down to pray afterward in the end zone before several delirious teammates went to pull him up. The extra point was good.

Carter led 14–9 with eleven minutes left.

Permian got the ball, stalled, and punted. Carter got the ball, stalled, and punted. Permian got the ball, stalled, and punted. Carter got the ball, stalled, and punted. Permian got the ball at its own 48-yard line.

There was a minute and fifteen seconds left.

It had stopped raining and the field glistened under the flood of the lights, looking like an empty skating pond. For a moment everything seemed stopped in time. There was a strange sense of detachment in the air, as if no one was there at all, just these two teams having it out with such relentless bitterness, and the rain and the cold temperatures made everything seem fuzzy and out of place. There was no glory here, no pomp, just the raw-boned sound of bodies crashing into bodies.

The Permian fans were on their feet, yelling with an urgent poignancy. The season was slipping away, the fabled cry of "State in eighty-eight!" that had been etched on the backs of cars and scribbled in yearbooks a minute away from becoming a failed dream. The rain-soaked hair of the cheerleaders looked lifeless. The band, sitting in an upper corner of the stadium to escape the rain, played its familiar marches, but the music seemed muffled and miles away. And yet there was still the chant.

"MO-JO! MO-JO! MO-JO! MO-JO!"

Fingers were crossed. Eyes were raised to the dull gray sky. In the cavernous stadium, the cheers seemed distant, tinny. But still there was hope, because there had to be.

That was the very point of it all.

Dale McDougal couldn't bear the thought of it ending.

Soaked through, wearing a black jacket with a pin that had a photograph of Jerrod on it in his uniform, she had been on her feet most of the game, cheering, yelling. Mojo magic. Mojo pride. Mojo tradition. It could not fail her now. She couldn't imagine what she would do if the season was over now. She had built a life around it, a whole routine—the lasagna dinners, the booster club meetings, the practices in the dappled afternoon light with that sweet breeze blowing across, and of course, those wonderful games, so glorious, so exciting, the power of a million stars shining down on Odessa on a Friday night. She knew it had to end sometime, but she wasn't ready yet, not in this final minute, not for her, not for her son, not for her town.

"This is the last minute of your life," said offensive lineman Ronnie Bevers in the huddle. McDougal talked about how hard they had worked. Winchell said little. He refused to look at the clock. He just knew the seconds were ticking away and to look at it would only make the tension worse. Normally the Permian team held hands in the huddle, but Winchell resisted. "Don't touch me," he snapped nervously, because he didn't want to get his own hands any more wet than they already were.

The first play, a sideline pass to Hill, went for four yards. It was the first pass Winchell had completed the second half, and it eased the pressure a little. The next play, a pitch to Comer, went for seven yards and a first down to the Carter 41.

They were in a rhythm now. They could move the ball. They could sense a change in the momentum. It was about to happen like something out of a storybook, like something out of a Greek myth.

Shawn Crow stood in the rain, wishing he could be out there.

The year before all these same people dressed in black in the stands had been focused on him, his play in the quarterfinals of the playoffs against Arlington so magical it drew sobs of joy. No one had ever seen anything like it and he would always be remembered because of it, have a tiny place in their hearts and a picture up on the Wall of Fame. But with the herniated disc he had subsequently suffered, he still wasn't in college yet, and it wasn't just the herniated disc that football had given him, but the broken leg, the broken arm, the smashed-up thumb.

He wasn't sure he had wanted to come to Austin to watch Permian play. It wasn't his season anymore, it was someone else's, but he decided to go to the game at the last second. He cheered as hard as anyone and now, in the final minute, he thought about the Arlington game, how Permian had come back from 28–7 to win it when everyone thought the game was over, how he and several others had drawn from deep inside themselves a strength and endurance they never knew they had. And as he watched, he would have given anything to return to that high school field again, to take that ball and lower his helmet and show the remarkable balance that had once made him so invincible.

The front four of Carter was exhausted and barely charging. Winchell took a quick drop back and hit Hill on the sideline. Hill eluded defensive back Gary Edwards and went out of bounds after a nine-yard gain. Permian had a second and one at the Carter 32 with fifty-six seconds left.

Gene Ater had been yelling so hard he had already driven away a couple of fans sitting in front of him.

He was a state district judge when he wasn't rooting for

327

Permian, and it was he who started every booster club meeting with the hoglike call of *"Mojo!"* that came out of him like a great spiritual release from all the problems of the world.

He had come to Odessa from Dallas twenty-seven years before, so he had been in the town long enough to know exactly what it was like, tight-clenched, blue-collar, conservative. He didn't expect any miracles as a result, but even so, it was hard sometimes not to get discouraged. When the bond issue to renovate the dilapidated civic center failed not once but twice he could not help but wonder if there could ever be any real progress in a place like that.

But Ater, like thousands of others, found something to fall hopelessly in love with in Odessa, something to keep him going. Maybe it was his playing days as a 135-pound linebacker and guard at Pecos that did it, or maybe it was just a tendency to cling to what was there, but Judge Ater loved these boys playing for Permian as if they were his own children. He knew about their backgrounds. He knew about their grades. He beamed when he saw them and he cherished the fantastic myth of them, how they never gave up, how size meant nothing to them, how beautifully they played together. Wearing a black sweater, a PERMIAN BOOSTER CLUB jacket, and a MOJO cap, he hadn't given up in the final minute. He had seen these boys do it before and he knew they could do it now. He tried to ignore the cheers across the way from the Carter fans, cheers that sounded to him "like a bunch of African natives," and instead yelled as loud as he possibly could.

"Let's go, Mojo! . . . Get your blocks, let's go!"

Winchell threw incomplete on the second down, the ball slipping off his hands and landing out of bounds. Permian had a third and one at the Carter 32.

Ken Scates huddled by the radio at his home in Odessa, trying to keep calm.

He actually had two radios going, one in the bedroom and one in the den so he could walk around and settle himself down and not give his heart any more trouble than it already had. In thirty years, he had never missed one of Permian's sixty-nine playoff games. But his ride had fallen through that morning and by the time he tried to find another one, everyone had already gone. He was heartbroken over it, but he rooted for the team as if he was there.

He had moved to West Texas in 1949 from California when the Snyder boom was on and had settled two years later in Odessa. He had hated it when he first got here. He thought it was at the very end of nowhere, filled with honkytonks and little better than the cesspool of Snyder. But it grew on him. There was something about it that touched him, or as his wife Mary put it, "They say when you get the sand in your craw, you never want to leave." No, it wasn't very pretty. Yes, it was still pretty much at the end of nowhere, but it had the things he wanted in a hometown—it was simple, friendly, God-fearing, patriotic.

He had built his own oil field service company. It did wonderfully during the boom, but then he got trapped in the bust. The bank had called in a note he held, and it had been one horrible, humiliating headache after another. He had already developed an ulcer, and then he needed heart bypass surgery. He came to realize that any business in the oil patch was an enormous gamble, even when prices were sky high, and he really wasn't much of a gambler. He didn't have the stomach for the constant ups and downs that never let a man truly know where he stood.

But through it all, he had always had something to fall back on, ever since 1959 when he had gone to that first practice. "I get out to the football field, everything wipes clear in my mind," he said. He kept all the booster club programs and the newspaper clippings from Dallas. He was a familiar sight on the ·practice field, sometimes standing by himself, watching in si-

lence as the boys silently shadow-danced across the field, and
sometimes in little groups with men as devoted as he was, where
the reminiscences came out sweetly and proudly. "You know,
there's not a lot to do in West Texas," he said. "I've made more
friends and acquaintances through football than anything."

Despite his best attempts to remain calm, he was still as jittery
as he could be in the final minute. Over the radio, with the
pauses and the strains of the crowd noise, it was hard to tell
exactly what was happening. It wasn't like being there. Yet he
knew the Carter Cowboys were about to join the list of those
who should have beaten Permian, but like every other team,
would succumb to the magic he and ten thousand others had
created.

Comer dove forward for four yards and a first and ten at the
Carter 28-yard line. Winchell backpedaled on the next play.
He had good protection and saw Chavez break free down the
middle of the field from his tight end position. There was no
one within three yards of him. Winchell threw the ball with
more authority than he had all day. Chavez ran to grab it. It
was a perfect call, and up in the press box Belew thought they
had a sure six points. And then he saw a hand shoot up out of
nowhere. It belonged to Jessie Armstead, and it showed why he
was the best high school football player in the country. Covering the field with his fantastic quickness, he swatted the ball
down. A run by Comer went nowhere. Permian had a third and
eight at the Carter 26 with thirty seconds left.

Boobie Miles could feel himself getting nervous.

Living with friends, he hadn't seen L.V. in a month, and he
had also lost all contact with the football team. He was still going to school, but he had missed over a week of classes because
of the knee surgery. With the close scrutiny that football players' grades received because of the no-pass, no-play rule, he
had always passed his courses. Now that he wasn't playing any-

more, he found himself flunking three classes at the end of the second six-week grading period. When the coaches saw his name on the failure report, they quietly snickered.

Boobie himself tried to take it all in stride. Sitting in the empty bleachers of the gym one day watching basketball practice, he said he enjoyed his newfound life—going home early in the afternoon, "chillin' out" with his girlfriend, not worrying anymore about his knee.

But when asked if he regretted his decision to quit, he became morose and silent, the glassy-eyed look on his face the same as it had been in Lubbock when he sat on the bench with a knee that had just been torn to shreds, the same as it had been during that Friday night against the Rebels when everything in the world stirred so brightly without him.

"I don't think people sympathized with him," said Callie Tave, the college counselor for the senior class at Permian. "I don't think they understood what he was experiencing. This was going to be *his* year. He was really going to be the star, and it just devastated him. I regretted so much what happened to him. I was hoping for nothing but good for him."

But her soft voice was in the minority. Many fans still remembered that image of Boobie in the Lee game, but they didn't see an eighteen-year-old kid doubled over in pain on that bench. They saw someone who was selfish, who openly moped during the game and didn't show the slightest concern for his fellow players. Among the team members he was almost never mentioned anymore, as if all record of him had been expunged; there was no trace of who he was, and what he had done unless you had witnessed it.

He had no link to Permian football anymore, but he felt the familiar anxiousness during that final minute. He still wanted his teammates to score and win the game. And there was a part of him that could never leave the field, no matter where he was. He could feel the vestiges of the invincible fire, the urge to be out there on the field to take on Jessie Armstead and Derric Evans and let them know there was one player in the state of Texas who could match them size for size, strength for strength, who wasn't scared of them at all.

"I wish I was out there with 'em," he thought to himself.

But too much had happened for Boobie to be anyplace other than where he was, listening to the final minute on a car radio 340 miles away back in Odessa, cut off from L.V., cut off from a season that instead of bringing him the cheers of thousands, had only brought him silence.

Hill took the hand-off from Winchell on an apparent reverse, then stopped and looked to the far sideline to throw. No one was open, so he took off, and made it all the way to the ten before getting pushed out of bounds. Permian had a first down at the Carter ten with twenty-two seconds left.

Sharon Gaines paced up and down on the sidelines.

All football seasons were hard and took their toll on her. It had been a condition of life ever since she had married Gary Gaines. But it was difficult to remember any season more emotionally wearing than this one. The letter to the editor crucifying her husband had hurt her terribly. Then came another letter, this one to school officials from an irate fan who ripped into her for standing up too much during games and blocking his view. She knew she stood up a lot during games, but it wasn't through selfishness. She just felt the tension and the pressure every bit as much as her husband did—she had been through the nightmare of the 1986 season when the team didn't make the playoffs—and she felt humiliated having to defend herself over something like this. "I don't think people realize how much that team is a part of my life," she said. But she also knew that most people could have cared less anyway, even if they did know. They weren't interested in her feelings, or her husband's. They were interested in winning.

She looked at the clock and watched the seconds disappear.

She watched Hill move downfield and her heart leapt, so close were they, just ten yards away!

And then the Permian crowd turned sour and she knew something horrible had happened.

Center Clint Duncan was called for holding. Jessie Armstead had been flying by him on the play, and desperate to do something to stop him, Duncan had tackled him. Permian had a third and seventeen at the Carter 35. They ran another trick play with Hill throwing to Winchell for an eleven-yard gain. It gave Permian a fourth and six at the Carter 24 with ten seconds left. Carter called time-out.

Ronnie Bevers knelt to the ground to pray. Winchell was still afraid to look at the clock. Duncan, dwelling on the holding penalty despite efforts to block it out of his mind, said nothing. Winchell called the play that had been sent in from the sidelines, sixty-one pass. During their six-year careers they had practiced and run it a thousand times. The players were aware of nothing, the frantic yells of the crowd, the clock, the dwindling light, the gray sadness of it all. They were only aware that this was where they either went to State, or turned into has-beens as quickly as the golden coach turned into a pumpkin. Right before coming to the line of scrimmage, McDougal turned to Bevers and said simply, "This is it."

Winchell, lining up over the center, saw Hill double-covered and knew he would not be able to get the ball to him. He would have to look instead for flanker Robert Brown over the middle. Duncan hiked the ball and went into his pass block stance. He didn't look up, because the sound of the crowd would tell him whether the pass was complete or not. Brown turned toward Winchell, a signal that he was open.

Winchell threw the ball.

Duncan waited and listened.

And he was exactly right, the sound of the crowd did tell him who had won and who had lost, a sudden, joyful eruption that came from one of the sides like a blast of bullets to hail a surrender. As Clint Duncan later related it, he could also tell from something else.

"I saw a bunch of cocky niggers jumping up and down."

Dale McDougal ran to find her son. They both started sobbing and walked off the field clutching each other. Near the door of the field house a Carter fan started gleefully chanting.

"NO MO' MOJO, MOJO NO MO! NO MO' MOJO, MOJO NO MO! NO MO' MOJO, MOJO NO MO!"

The taunts felt like daggers, and several players went toward the fan to lash back. But they were herded back and entered the field house in silence, where the bright lights and shiny equipment made the interior seem like a hospital. Television and newspaper reporters from Dallas and Midland and Odessa milled about, ready to interview them.

In the place of his dreams, Mike Winchell had just had the worst performance of his Permian career, four for twenty-four passing for fifty-seven yards and one interception. Reporters came up to him and he answered their questions dutifully, quick to heap blame on himself and acknowledge that he couldn't put a tight spiral on the ball because it kept slipping off his hands in the rain. He showed little outward emotion, but according to his brother, who later spoke with him, he was distraught over what had happened, for there was no place he wanted to reach the heights in as much as this one. But there wasn't anything he could do now, except look back. It was over.

"You make some bonds for life," he told a television interviewer of his career as a high school football player. "The real sad thing is, we'll probably go our own separate ways."

Chavez, weary and tired, sat in the locker room in silence. He was upset and melancholy, but life, instead of ending at this moment, was just beginning for him. McDougal and Billingsley were in tears, and Ivory had a strange smile on his face, not because he was glad it was over, but because it was hard to imagine that after all the personal agony and angst it actually *was* over.

For the last time, Gaines gathered the players into a circle. All around him, bent on one knee, there were teenage boys in tears, their great, compelling belief in themselves punctured.

"I'm very proud of you as a person, I'm proud of you as a team," said Gaines, his soft voice barely rising over the sobs. "To be one of the final four teams left in the state of Texas playing football at this December date is quite an accomplishment. We fell one game short of where we wanted to be, to be playin' for it all, and it hurts, it hurts all of us." Then he led the team in prayer.

"Heavenly Father, we pray that you be proud of the effort we've given, that you be proud of the way we played. Father, it hurts so much because we did so many things good and came up short. We pray that you would help each one of us to overcome this setback, that you lessen the hurt, that you give all of us strength and comfort that only you can give us. We thank you for these young men that it's been our pleasure to coach. We pray that you be with these seniors and go with them. Thank you for the leadership that they have displayed, the leadership that they have given this team. We love each and every one of them, dear God."

Later that night, when the team returned to Odessa, emotions were more in control. There were no more tears, just dejected silence, except from Jerrod McDougal. He lingered by his locker and started to sob again. "That's why it hurts so much, to lose to someone you know hasn't worked as hard as you," he said as he closed his eyes and tried to fight back the tears.

He thought back to the time he had been a sophomore and had walked into the locker room for the first time, how nervous he was, how excited he was, how much time he thought he had until he became a senior and had a chance to drink in the glory. And then, just like that it seemed, it was over, the time moving

335

so fast it was hard to hold on to it. "These sophomores think it's a long road," he said as the tears trickled down his face, "but it ain't." And suddenly he wasn't a high school football player at all, but a high school kid with absolutely no idea of what he was going to do with his life.

The locker room was empty and polished, the black carpet free of the tape and the tobacco spit and the shoes and the shoulder pads. During the season, there had been a ceaseless cacophony in that room of songs and stories and pleas for fifty cents to buy a soda. There had been laughter and occasional fights. There had been the wonderful gyrations of Boobie, in better times, when he would imitate a striptease dancer. There had been the killer's grin of Billingsley and the little-boy grin of Winchell and and the stoicism of Ivory Christian and the admiring laughter for Chavez when he got up during the captains' speeches and swore profusely. There had been the serious faces staring intently at Gaines as he tried to inspire them with herculean stories of Civil War heroes and Olympic swimmers. There had been Belew telling them that everything could be taken away from you in life, your house, your car, everything except a state championship. There had been the solemnity of the pre-game ritual, when all the players lay on the floor as if they were soldiers in the hull of a ship. And there had been the effusion of the post-game ritual, screams and cat-calls followed by eager plans for the glorious remainder of Friday night. Now there wasn't a sound, and the carefully cleaned room looked as if it had never been inhabited.

Jerrod clearly didn't want to go. He stood in front of his locker, fumbling with the lock. But he had no choice. He put on his coat and walked into the soggy cold. After he left, only a few of the coaches remained. They ruminated a little over the game and how close they had come. But already their focus was somewhere else.

On the far wall of their office was a depth chart. It had the names of each of the players on little magnets that could be constantly juggled, from first string to second string, from tackle to guard, from fullback to tailback, from offense to defense, or removed altogether.

They went to work immediately, because there was no time for sentiment, no reason to postpone it.

Boobie's name had been taken off long ago. But now the others joined him as well. WINCHELL . . . MCDOUGAL . . . BILLINGSLEY . . . CHAVEZ . . . CHRISTIAN. . . . They and all the other seniors were placed in a neat little pile at the bottom, and suddenly there was no sign of them at all on the board, just black, empty spaces that would soon be filled by other magnets at quarterback and tailback and middle linebacker and all the other positions. The season had ended, but another one had begun.

People everywhere, young and old, were already dreaming of heroes.

Epilogue

The Carter Cowboys won the state championship a week after defeating Permian in the semifinals.

As expected, a dozen players on the team, including Derric Evans and Gary Edwards, were heavily courted by college recruiters. If life at Carter High School was like an endless amusement ride because of their stature as football stars, getting recruited was like taking a roller coaster to the moon.

"I was promised money, credit cards, apartments, come home on weekends when I wanted to," said Derric, one of the finest high school defensive backs in the country. "Everybody was promisin' something. It was just who was promisin' the most."

Over a hundred schools had beckoned to Derric, and when it came time for him to decide which ones to visit personally, some coaches tried to lure him to their campuses by asking what type of woman he wanted when he got there. "The coaches would tell us, they would ask us, what color do you want, black, white, Mexican," said Derric.

He decided to visit four schools, the University of Tennessee, Michigan State, Baylor, and Arkansas. For the Tennessee visit he was picked up at his home in a limousine and sat in the backseat talking to his girlfriend over the phone as he was taken to the airport. "I was back there all by myself, looking at the TV, talkin' on the telephone," said Derric. "It was like I was on top of the world."

At Michigan State, he and some other recruits were taken by their player hosts to a strip joint. Once there, hey paid for Derric to have the educational experience of a so-called couch ride, where he went into a back room and sat on a couch while one of the women at the club stood over him and made various enticements.

At Baylor, he went to a party where a woman he had never met before came up to him and said, "I know who you are. You're Derric Evans." She seemed eager to sleep with him, which struck him as slightly unusual because she was white, but he eagerly accepted since it seemed part of the package.

At all three of these schools, he said he was taken to one of the local stores to pick out tennis shoes or sweaters or jersies or running suits, not only for him, but for his mother, his girlfriend, whomever he wanted. He finally settled on Tennessee, a fairly easy choice because, he said, coaches there offered the best deal by promising him an off-campus apartment and telling him he would never have to worry about money.

Gary Edwards, fully recovered from the controversy over his algebra grade, made trips to Nebraska, Tulsa, Arkansas, and Houston.

The promises of what he would reap were not as bold as they were to Derric because he was not the physical specimen that Derric was, but there were obvious hints—an assistant coach at Nebraska telling Gary to look at what this player and that one had, a player at Tulsa openly discussing what the coaches could do for you if you were good enough. Gary himself saw players at some of the schools driving Cadillacs and BMWs, and he was savvy enough to know that these cars did not come from a college player's salary, which presumably was nothing.

Gary accepted a scholarship from Houston. The whole recruiting experience had been something he could never have possibly imagined. The phone had rung constantly with recruiters, all begging for a piece of him. "I don't know anyone who would have the same hat size after that," said his father.

But it didn't stop there. Because Derric and Gary had been on a state championship team, the first from Dallas in thirty-eight years and also one that had become a gigantic cause célèbre in the black community, their star status only intensified.

Kids asked them for autographs. When they went out to eat in the neighborhood, restaurant managers ripped up the check. Once when they were pulled over for speeding, the Dallas policeman who stopped them recognized them. After giving them a lecture about not letting the state championship go to their heads, he sent them on their way. At school, as usual, they came and went as they pleased. Neither of them drank. Neither of them took drugs. Instead they lived on a better high, the high of invincibility at the age of eighteen.

"We was on top of the world," said Derric. "We had [all these] recruiters and a state championship and we thought there ain't nothing can happen to us."

They committed their first armed robbery together on May 18, 1989.

The idea came from another Carter Cowboy, who had already committed several armed robberies of his own and bragged in the school lunchroom about how easy it was. Gary and Derric did not wear masks and their getaway car was Derric's mother's white BMW. They got around a hundred bucks apiece and it took them several weeks to spend the money because they were both from comfortable, middle-class homes and did not want for anything.

They did a total of seven armed robberies in the space of a month until they were arrested by police. Their motive, as far as anyone could tell, was that they had done it sheerly for kicks; something to do before it was time to play big-time college football. Nor did they give any thought to the consequences.

"Me and Gary, we were sittin' in the police car and we weren't even worried," said Derric. "We thought we're gonna go to jail for a little while and our mothers would come bail us out and we'd go back home and it would be over with."

Besides Derric and Gary, three other members of the Carter Cowboy state championship team were charged with armed robberies. These five, and ten other black teenagers, committed a total of twenty-one robberies in a loosely organized ring.

Just like the grade controversy, public opinion over the case broke almost strictly along racial lines. Whites, finding the robberies perfect justification for their original feelings that the Carter Cowboys had cheated their way into the playoffs, had no sympathy for the defendants at all. They were thugs and criminals who deserved to be put away. Blacks, hurt and humiliated at what had happened, prayed that some mercy would be shown for these kids who had made a colossal, inexplicable mistake.

Walking into the courtroom for his sentencing on September 22, 1989, Derric Evans thought the very worst he would get was ten years, and he still had hope for probation. Gary Edwards, convinced that he would get probation, had already made plans to watch a friend play high school football that night.

"I believe much of the media attention on these trials is because some of you were on a state championship football team, and a few of you have scholarships and great potential," began state district judge Joe Kendall.

"I can think of, but will not name, off the top of my head three former Dallas Cowboys and one former Miami Dolphin who have two striking things in common. They all four have Super Bowl rings and they all four have been to the penitentiary.

"Although it sometimes may not seem so, the criminal justice system really doesn't care who you are. The typical American male lives vicariously on Sunday afternoons in the fall and winter through the lives of football heroes. However, when it comes to violating the law, at the courthouse it simply doesn't matter that you can run the football."

Derric Evans was sentenced to twenty years in prison.

Gary Edwards was sentenced to sixteen years.

The three other defendants who had been members of the 1988 Carter Cowboy state championship team received sentences of thirteen years, fourteen years, and twenty-five years.

Marshall Gandy, the prosecutor on the case, was generally reluctant to blame outside factors for any crime. No single, pat explanation could explain what caused these kids, the children of good, hardworking parents from middle class homes, to go out and rob fast-food places and video stores just for fun. But he didn't believe Derric Evans and Gary Edwards exhibited typical patterns of criminal behavior, and he wondered what favor had been done these kids by placing them on a golden pedestal. He found it remarkable that Derric Evans had signed his letter of intent to Tennessee in a hot tub with a passel of gold chains around his neck. The only aspect more remarkable was the presence of Dallas television and newspaper reporters to cover the signing because of Derric's stature as a high school football star.

"You look at how we treat them in high school, and how we treat them in college, and everyone asks why they act like children," said Gandy.

"How would you expect them to act any other way?"

Brian Chavez applied to Harvard after the season ended.

He ranked at the top of his class and had scored a 700 on the math portion of the SAT. He also hoped that his football career at Permian would enhance his chances of admission. The coaching staff at Permian did not contact the Harvard football program on his behalf. When asked by a Harvard coach to supply a game film of Brian, Gaines sent film of the first game of the season. It certainly wasn't Brian's best game of the season; he hadn't even played in it because he was injured.

The problem was discovered when a Harvard coach called Brian's father and said he was having trouble figuring out what number Brian wore.

Gaines said he sent the wrong film by accident. His father accepted that but was still upset. "How could you make a mistake with something as important as that?" Tony Chavez asked, and he worried that his son's chances for admission to Harvard would be diminished.

Brian himself was deeply hurt, considering the sacrifices that he had made to play for Permian, like the time in the playoffs junior year when he had played an entire game with a broken ankle. He had injured it the previous week, but it was purposely never x-rayed because the discovery that it was broken would have kept him from playing. To get through the game, the ankle was tightly taped, an air cast was put around it, and he said he was given painkillers right before the game and also during halftime. About a week later, a doctor who examined Brian told him the ankle had in fact been broken.

On April 14, 1989, he was admitted to Harvard.

Brian went out for the freshman football team in September, but quit after one day after coming to the conclusion that the program was on a par with the junior high one in Odessa. He also found it hard to adjust to the idea of playing games in front of a handful of people when he had played in front of twenty-five thousand at Texas Stadium.

Permian still exerted a hold on his life. During the annual football banquet to commemorate the 1988 season, a video of highlights of the season had been shown. A song by Billy Joel called "This Is the Time" was used for part of the soundtrack. When one of Brian's roommates at Harvard played it one day, chills shot down Brian's spine and he could almost feel tears welling in his eyes. It all came roaring back, the wins and losses, the glories and pains shared with his teammates.

When he went out for the team at Harvard, it no longer felt right. It wasn't the purpose of his being there, and for the first time in his life he was in an environment where football had no special cachet. When he was at Permian, Winchell and Ivory Christian and he had once received a standing ovation at an elementary school assembly, with all those gaping nine- and ten-year-olds wanting so desperately to be just like them some-day. But when he stepped out onto the playing fields of Harvard in the fall of 1989, he knew such moments were over. He felt no magic or history in those fields, just an awareness that there were more important goals that he wanted to accomplish. He didn't rule out playing as a sophomore, but not when a new phase of his life was starting.

"I was only out there because it's football, Brian Chavez is out there because he's a football player."

Jerrod McDougal tried to adjust to a life that no longer in-cluded Permian football.

"A lot of people tell me to let it go, to let it go," said Jerrod.

"You just can't let somethin' like that go. It's like you're married for thirty years and all of a sudden you get a divorce. You don't just stop lovin' somethin'. You just don't give the better part of your life away and just stop thinkin' about it. You just don't do it.

"I'm only eighteen. I spent six years working for it, and all the time before thinkin' about it. When I got to the eighth grade, I found out I wasn't going to be able to play college ball. Shit, high school ball was the best thing for me. And now it's history.

"I've got no idea what I want to do. I've got no idea what school I'm going to go to. If I had a choice. I don't have a choice. My SAT won't be worth a shit. And no football school wants me. I'm just average, really. I won't be valedictorian like Brian. The thing was, grades weren't that hard for me to make. I wish now I had tried harder in my studies."

Jerrod toyed with the idea of going to Australia, but elected to stay in Odessa and in the fall of 1989 was working for his father's company. During the football season he went to the game against crosstown rival Odessa High.

"I want to play football bad," he said on his way to the game, still driving his praying mantis of a pickup and wearing his letter jacket. "There isn't a day I don't think about it. There isn't an hour."

The stadium was filled to capacity, with over twenty thousand fans shaking the beautiful night. "Man, it gives me the chills," said Jerrod as Permian quickly scored to take a 7–0 lead. But as he continued to watch all the sights, the images, he grew quieter and quieter.

"What hurts so bad about it, I was a part of it for a while. The thing is, it always goes on, it will never stop," Jerrod said. "Permian will have good teams when you and I are dead and gone."

A month later he stood on the sidelines as Permian played the Rebels in Midland, and he sardonically referred to himself and the other former teammates who showed up as part of the "has-been club." This game too had a capacity crowd. Tears came to his eyes when the Permian band played the old psych-up song, "Hawaii 5–0." Late in the fourth quarter, with Permian desperately trying to hold on to a 17–13 lead and beat Midland Lee for the first time in four years, he cheered crazily. When Permian staved the Rebels off on the last play of the game at the five-yard line, pandemonium broke out.

The Lee players were in tears, doubled over in agony. The Permian players were in tears, standing with their helmets held high. And in the middle of it all was Jerrod. The moment the game ended he ran out onto the field and draped his arms around a player. He hugged him as hard as he could, and his eyes closed tight.

For the briefest of moments, he was back where he wanted to be.

Don Billingsley split up from his father shortly after the season ended. Their living together had always been a rough road, and without the common bond of football it seemed harder than ever for them to stay together.

After graduation he returned to Blanchard, Oklahoma, to live with his mother and stepfather. As had been his habit through much of high school in Odessa, he continued to drink heavily. He went through a bottle of whiskey every other day. But one night, after he came home so drunk he did not know where he had been, he decided to quit.

"I started gettin' afraid that I was gonna die," said Don. "I was just tired of drinkin' and druggin' and women. I just needed somethin' else." He turned to religion. He was saved and then baptized in July 1989.

Don believed he had been on the verge of becoming an alcoholic. The past three years he had spent in Odessa were wild ones, and he thought it would have been almost impossible to quit drinking there because of the peer pressure and the need to maintain his reputation as the ultimate party animal. A further impetus for his reformation came when a former Permian player he had known killed himself.

He received no scholarship offers and decided to walk on at East Central University in Ada, Oklahoma. The program there didn't compare to Permian's. The weight room was the size of a shower stall. The games attracted three hundred fans instead of the thousands that he was used to. "In high school football there's a bond," he said. "Here, it's just someone you see every day. In the field house it was like a family, more family than I had in three years."

Don sometimes wondered what his life would have been like if he had stayed put in Oklahoma instead of moving to Odessa for the sole purpose of playing football for Permian. He had been a starter on the Blanchard team as a freshman. By the time he was a senior he would have been the big star, and that might have put him in a better position to get an athletic scholarship.

But Don would not have traded his Permian experience for anything. Like many players, he talked about it as if it had been a fantastic dream. He missed all of it, the locker room, the games, the girls who adored him and followed him through the school corridors. And he also talked about how hard it was to go back to the locker room after it was over and realize that you weren't a part of it anymore. Like Jerrod McDougal, he couldn't help but feel like a has-been.

Don made the team at East Central. But in the middle of the 1989 season he had arthroscopic surgery on his knee. Ever since he had injured it while playing for Permian his senior year, it hadn't been the same.

Mike Winchell, despite setting career records at Permian for most yards passing, most passes attempted, most passes completed, and most touchdown passes, was not offered a single scholarship.

"It's just so frustrating to me that I can't get anything going. It just bothers me," said Gaines. But he also wondered if the perspective placed on football in Odessa sometimes created a false reality.

"We have a unique situation here because football is so im-

347

portant," said Gaines. "I guess there's such a thing as just being a good high school football player. And I guess being a high school football player doesn't mean you're going to be a good collegiate player."

When a recruiter from Yale called to see if Permian might have any potential candidates, Gaines eagerly gave him Winchell's name. He seemed to possess the football skill, and he had the grades, with a class rank in the top tenth. But his board scores, although significantly above the Permian average, were 1000. He filled out some forms and did some reading on Yale to find out where it was and what it was like.

When one of the coaches called, Mike answered the phone with a mouthful of doughnut, and he became painfully self-conscious of his West Texas twang. He was convinced the coach thought he was the dumbest hick ever to walk the earth. But, the accent of the coach sounded foreign to Mike as well.

He heard nothing back from Yale, and it was all for the best anyway. "I'd never been around nothin' like that," he said. "It would be too much culture shock. My mind would go berserk and I wouldn't be able to study. I wouldn't fit in there, that's what it was."

Mike's brother, Joe Bill, did what he could. He called the University of Texas coach, David McWilliams, almost a dozen times, but was always told he was in a meeting and couldn't come to the phone. He called the University of Nevada–Las Vegas, but after a flurry of correspondence no one there was very interested either.

"I knew I wasn't a hot commodity," said Mike, "but I thought there'd be a little interest." And he felt that most recruiters viewed him as the typical Permian player—disciplined, well trained in the technique of the game, with all talent already drawn from him.

During the summer, while hammering in nails to build a fence, he thought about himself and his life. He realized that he agonized over everything all the time, and he admitted that part of the problem in the Carter game had been his own lack of belief in his abilities. He knew the reason why he was like this, that it was the price he had paid for carefully watching out for himself ever since he had been a little boy. "I've never taken a chance in life," he said. "I need to run in front of traffic buck-naked and get arrested."

He went to Baylor and joined the team as a walk-on. He practiced but did not make the traveling squad. There were no miracles at Baylor, just the same haunting inconsistency, which Mike summed up with his own characteristic assessment.

"One day I throw the ball like Roger Staubach, one day like Roger Rabbit."

Ivory Christian was offered a football scholarship by Texas Christian University in February.

He was the only player on the Permian team recruited by a Division I school. He expected to be red-shirted and not play his freshman year, but because of injuries he saw a great deal of time at middle linebacker for the Horned Frogs. He made nearly a dozen tackles against Southwest Conference rival Texas A & M, and then started against both Southern Mississippi and Southern Methodist. With several games still left in the 1989 season, he was happy with his performance and playing time. But he found it did not match the feeling of playing for Permian. Although he had vacillated between loving Permian football and despising it, he found himself missing it more than he had ever imagined he would, and he said that playing against the Midland Lee Rebels had been more exciting than playing against Texas A & M.

He was treated well at TCU and lived in a nice dorm along with other athletes and had a nice room. Because of TCU, he had become the first person in his family to go to college. But it was hard not to feel unsettled. When he looked around the campus the only blacks he saw were athletes, and sports seemed to be their only reason for being at the school. And sometimes, it often felt as if he wasn't playing football so much as working at it, getting up every day at six to make study hall, then going to practices and meetings from two in the afternoon to six-thirty in the evening.

But Ivory now knew exactly what he wanted to do. He no longer preached. He no longer had the aspiration of becoming the pastor of the biggest Baptist church in California, or getting a doctorate in theology, or being addressed as "Dr. Christian." He had also dropped the ambition of majoring in business administration—it seemed like too much work considering the demands made on him in football. He had decided instead to major in criminal justice so he could become a policeman if he couldn't realize his newfound dream of playing pro football. Although he was a superb athlete, the odds of that happening seemed remote because of his relatively small size. At five eleven, he would have to be nothing short of remarkable. But that was his new aspiration.

At Permian, he had felt a strong sense of comradeship with those he played with. He missed the magic of those Friday nights. The wearing of the black and white, as he looked back on it, had meant something special. At TCU the feelings were different. "Out here," he said of the life of a major college football player, "it's who can stand out and can make it to the pros."

Boobie Miles moved back home with his uncle a few days before Christmas in 1988.

Although the big-time schools had stopped calling, several junior colleges in Texas were interested, and L.V. thought maybe that was better anyway for his nephew. "Boobie ain't no book genius, and the transition [to a four-year institution] might be more than he could handle."

Far from becoming soured on football because of what the two of them had been through, L.V. was as positive as ever. "I told him what we're gonna do now, we're going to start working towards the Heisman." Boobie received a scholarship offer from Ranger Junior College in Ranger, Texas, and accepted it. He too tried to be as positive as possible.

"I think it kind of teaches me a lesson," he said of the injury that had ruined his senior year. "I had fame and glory and all that and the Lord took it away. I kind of had the big head, and he took it away from me."

But it was still impossible sometimes not to wonder what would have happened if he hadn't gotten hurt. "We could have gone to State. I could have had a better scholarship. But right now, I'm happy with what I've got. I've got a scholarship I didn't think I was gonna get. If I do good, I could go somewhere in a year."

Most of the Permian coaching staff gave Boobie little chance of playing effectively again. They figured he would get to Ranger and quit in a couple of weeks when he wasn't coddled.

After graduating from Permian, he went to Ranger and became the only freshman starter in the backfield.

On a clear November day in 1989, the Ranger Junior College Rangers took on the Navarro Junior College Bulldogs before a homecoming crowd of five hundred. The fans sat on a pair of rickety bleachers. In the press box the announcer, standing up with a microphone in his hand, gave the players funny nicknames and made up fake scores from the Mexican Hockey League. A sharp wind came in, past the yellowed grass of the field, past a little metal fence, past the barracks-style buildings that comprised the tiny campus.

Boobie wore number 3 and looked gorgeous and powerful. But he was buried mercilessly by the Bulldogs, the number-one-rated junior college team in the country. He juked and spun and did all the things that L.V. had taught him, but without much success.

"Com'on!" yelled a teammate from the sideline. "Lower your shoulder and run over his ass! Stop jukin!'"

L.V. watched silently from the bleachers. He had gotten off the late shift at the Exxon station where he was working and had made the two-hundred-mile trip to Ranger from Odessa with some friends. "Couple of years of this, he'll be ready," said L.V. as he watched Boobie get battered by the Navarro defense on the way to a 31–0 loss.

Navarro was a strong team, but Boobie clearly wasn't the same runner he had once been. He was as fearless as ever, but his knee was still weak and swelled up easily with fluid. Because of the protective braces that he wore on both knees to prevent further injury, he no longer had the breakaway speed that the big-time college recruiters had once upon a time found so enticing.

A person like me can't be stopped. If I put it in my mind, they can't stop me . . . ain't gonna stop me.

See if I can get a first down. Keep pumping my legs up, spin out of it, go for a touchdown, go as far as I can.

Those words were just a memory now.

"I've never seen that burst of speed," said the head coach of Ranger, Joe Crousen. "I don't know how many times he got caught from behind.

"It's hard when you have greatness and it's taken from you and you just can't get it back in your hands."

Boobie seemed frustrated and discouraged after the Navarro game. But L.V., as always, was there to console him and give him support and keep the dream alive. He told him that his offensive line had been just about hopeless and there wasn't much a running back could do if the people in front of him didn't know how to block.

They stood together, talking softly, sometimes not talking at all, but drawing strength from one another in the absence of anyone else. In the fading afternoon light of Ranger, Texas, with that bitter wind blowing across the field, flanked by the malarial yellow of the dormitory where Boobie lived, they looked quite beautiful.

The city of Odessa moved forward with some signs of economic relief. The price of oil itself hovered around $20 a barrel for much of 1989, an improvement of roughly $5 a barrel over 1988, and there were even predictions that a worldwide shortage might push the price of oil even higher. People in Odessa had been burned so many times by predictions that they tended not to pay much attention to them, but there was a belief that at least things could not get worse.

Whatever happened, it seemed clear that the fate of Odessa lay in the hands of others. Like the automobile industry, and the steel industry, and the semiconductor industry, the domestic oil industry had become a follower on the world market. The decline in U.S. oil production in 1989, 6.8 percent, was the largest drop ever in any single year. Imports rose to 46 percent, their highest level in twelve years, and OPEC's noose around the West Texas oil patch was as tight as it had ever been.

Outside of the economic news, there wasn't much change in other areas. A new quality-of-life study came out in the fall of 1989, and as usual, Odessa distinguished itself. The revised volume of the *Places Rated Almanac* rated Odessa the second worst place to live in the country out of the 333 that were studied. Odessa, according to the almanac, had the worst health care in the country and ranked in the bottom twenty-five in the categories of transportation, jobs, and recreation. Some folks were upset with the ranking, but after a few outbursts life went on as normal, and people latched on to the same things they always had.

The speeches were the same, and so were the looks on the faces. It could have been Brian Chavez, or Jerrod McDougal, or Mike Winchell, or Ivory Christian, or Boobie Miles. But it was December of 1989 now instead of December of 1988 and the names were Arvey Villa and Kevin Mannix and Chris Comer and Stony Case and Johnny Celey and Jeff Garrett. Otherwise, everything seemed untouched, a cycle destined to repeat itself forever, an interchangeable set of boys all captive to the same dream. *Goin' to State.*

About an hour before game time, Mike Belew met with the defensive ends.

"They say they're gonna shut us out and say they're gonna beat us like Yates did and all that. That's hard for me to live with, men. That hurts my pride a little bit. It hurts for myself. It hurts me for you guys, and for everybody from West Texas, everybody from Odessa. They slandered us in the paper, and now, by God, we're gonna take care of business out there on the field, okay? We're gonna make it all even on the football field today.

"This is something that you dream about and I'm sure you're just like every other little boy that grew up in Odessa, you thought about playin' for Permian. Golly, men, here you are in the big 'un, in the big house, it's gonna be on TV, you got all the elements.

"Let's get after these guys, okay? Let's get after 'em. Let's win it for ourselves. Let's win it for our school, win it for our parents. Let's win it for West Texas."

Minutes before game time, Gaines called the team to gather around him.

"Everybody in this room has paid a dear, dear price to be where you are," he told them. "That ought to make your effort that much more intense, that much more fanatical, because of all the hard work and sacrifice that's gone into gettin' you here. It ought to make you play that much harder.

"You represent a lot of people. We're gonna represent 'em well, and we're gonna win this sucker."

They huddled in that long tunnel of Texas Stadium amid cries of "Let's go, baby, let's go!" They broke through the banner made by the cheerleaders that took up almost half the end zone. They heard the cries of *"Mojo!"* and the enormous swell of the band. They played with a flawlessness and sense of purpose that had been building inside them all their lives. After it was over tears flowed freely down their faces, and also down the faces of the grown men and women who depended on them year after year after year.

It was hard to fathom the shock of what Odessa had gone through during the eighties, from a world where everything seemed possible to one in which it was hard to hold on to anything with certainty. So much had happened. So much had changed. But one anchor was still there, as strong and solid as ever. It didn't really matter who was playing, or who was coaching. It would always go on, just as Jerrod McDougal had realized, because it was a way of life.

The Permian Panthers ended the decade exactly the same way they had begun it.

Two days before Christmas, they became the state football champions of Texas.

Afterword

TEN YEARS HAVE PASSED since the publication of *Friday Night Lights*, and still its words continue to influence and reverberate. Barely a week goes by without my getting a call or comment about it. Over the past decade I have heard strange and remarkable stories of the book's impact—a man who left his job in Brooklyn so he could become a football coach in Texas, a songwriter who wrote a ballad inspired by the book, teenagers forsaking Florida to make spring break pilgrimages to Odessa. When readers tell me they have been touched by this book in a way that no other has ever touched them, their words leave me humbled.

How did it all happen? Why did it all happen? In light of the controversy that erupted in Odessa after the book was published and the accusations of betrayal that still ring in certain corners today, are there any regrets about what I wrote?

I have had ten years to think about it all, ten years to examine what it was that catapulted this book into the reading consciousness of so many, ten years to examine the harsh judgments made of me as well as my own decisions about the words I chose and the words I did not, ten years too to think about this team that I grew to know so intimately during a remarkable year of my life. I adored the players on the Permian Panthers, whose lives I followed during the 1988 season. It is a feeling that still stays with me. Memories crease through me at unexpected times—the awesome silence in the locker room with those eyes locked tight, the gleaming shape of a playoff trophy held high as another rung on the ladder of goin' to state is climbed, the thrust of a fist into a wall in the helplessness of defeat, the silence of the plains suddenly broken by adoring screams.

I still think of how it all began, in the rocket ship of Ratliff Stadium, on a sweet and still night, when those teenage boys crashed through the handheld banner that had been made for them by the cheerleaders and a sea of fans drenched in black came to their feet. I still think of how it all ended, in spitting rain and misery, when the hand of Jesse Armstead came out of nowhere to swat down a pass that should have been the winning touchdown for Permian against Dallas Carter, the same Jesse Armstead who is now an All-Pro linebacker for the New York Giants.

In particular, I think of the six players who so graciously allowed me to intrude on their worlds. Our lives have all spread in different directions. But I still keep up with several of them on a regular basis, and both directly and indirectly, I am familiar with the roads their lives have taken.

Brian Chavez returned to the football field at Harvard for his undergraduate house tackle football team. He graduated Cum Laude in 1993, and I was honored to be at his graduation. He successfully navigated a monumental transition from Odessa to Cambridge (it is hard to imagine any two places in the world at more opposites), and it was a special delight to watch Brian receive his diploma under the proud gaze of his family. Brian looked at the east coast with a combination of curiosity and anthropological interest, as if he were studying a different species, and he concluded that it was no place for a human being to actually live. At the personal invitation of the dean, Brian went to law school at Texas Tech University on a full scholarship. He started the Mexican-American Law Student Association there and graduated in 1996. Afterward he returned to Odessa to his family's law practice. He opened a satellite office in El Paso and has aspirations of becoming a federal judge. Although he seems eternally wed to the haunted plains of West Texas, he is also thankful he spent time beyond its borders.

"It was hard as shit for me to adjust and hard for me to deal with, but Harvard changed my life. It showed me that there's more out there than West Texas."

Jerrod McDougal went to Odessa College in the spring and fall of 1990. He did not play football because Odessa College does not field a team, and he was not invited back to school after the fall semester. "I didn't have any enthusiasm for it at all," he said at the time. Jerrod also went to Midland College, as well as several community colleges, but he has never received a degree.

He went to work full time for his father's oil field construction company in Crane at the beginning of 1991. In 1999 he moved to Bandera, near San Antonio, to work for Roger Stevens, a contracting company acquired by his father. He has had his personal traumas over the years, including a serious car accident that shattered his ankle. But he has still maintained his West Texas spirit of passion and emotion.

At one point he tried to erase his memories of playing football for Permian because he felt emotionally stunted by it. But he realized it was impossible. "It will never be lifted off of me," he said, and if it was football that consumed him at Permian, it was also football that kept him in school. "Otherwise I would've been down on dynamite crews blowin' shit up, because that's what I liked," he said. Sometimes Jerrod thinks about the 1988 season with the wincing anger of not winning a state championship. But mostly he thinks of the private beauty of what he and his teammates shared and will always share.

"I got a group of brothers, a set of friends that you could never ask for and get. There's nothing I wouldn't do for any of 'em and there's nothing they wouldn't do for me."

Don Billingsley, the Permian player targeted by the coaches and teammates as most likely for an early grave, proved that the worst predictor of future behavior is behavior in high school.

Don stopped playing football in the fall of 1989 after arthroscopic surgery to his knee. Instead of falling prey once again to alcohol and drugs, he began to actively study for the first time in his life. "It feels good to be learnin' somethin'," he said at the time. Don also went through a religious reawakening during that period of his life, and he has kept the keenness of his faith ever since.

Don remained at East Central University, graduating with a bachelor's degree in public relations in 1993. He then received his master's in human resources counseling from the university in 1995 and did counseling work in Oklahoma City and Norman. In April of 1999 he married Melanie Fannin and moved to join her in Dallas. Melanie already worked for Southwest Airlines, and Don became a care manager for Magellan Behavioral Health. There are still certain aspirations that elude him. He would like to make more money, and he isn't sure about the trajectory of his career. But he has no complaints about life.

"I feel good about it."

Mike Winchell went to Baylor after he graduated from Permian and quit at the end of the 1989–90 school year because of cost and the realization that he had no future there as a football player. "Heck, I'm not going to play in the pros," he said at the time.

Winchell went to Texas Tech for a semester and then transferred to Tarleton State University in Stephenville. He graduated with a bachelor's degree in marketing in 1995. He returned to Odessa for roughly a year and then moved to the Dallas-Ft. Worth metroplex. When the *Odessa American* interviewed him in 1998, he was working as an independent surveyor in Decatur and also playing golf on the Iron Man Tour. Sponsored by the Texas Professional Golf Tour, Iron Man tournaments consist of twenty-seven holes in a single stretch. Winchell tied for fifty-fifth in 1998 and was still competing on the Iron Man Tour into the summer of 1999. He values his privacy, and during the interview he made it clear that he no longer was interested in questions relating to *Friday Night Lights*.

"People always want to talk about the book, but I don't care. That was a long time ago."

Ivory Christian had a successful freshman football season at Texas Christian University in 1989, starting two games at middle linebacker and receiving playing time in seven others. But frustrated over a strained knee and his drop in the depth chart the following year in 1990, he quit the team and left school. His father

360

prodded him to stay at TCU for the obvious athletic and educational benefits, but Ivory told him he was no longer interested in playing football.

He returned to Odessa, where he received his associate's degree at Odessa College. He worked at the Midland International Airport for several years doing plane maintenance. He then moved to Austin to work for the Texas Aircraft Pooling Board, a state agency that maintains and operates a fleet of planes for official government business. Ivory had always been ambivalent about his Permian football experience, consciously resisting any of its trappings. But on the cusp of turning thirty, he had begun to take some measure of pride in what it meant.

"Now, twelve years later, I think about it."

Boobie Miles flunked out of Ranger College at the end of the 1989–90 school year when, according to his football coach, Joe Crousen, he just stopped going to class. He returned to the Odessa-Midland area and has basically been there ever since, with the exception of a brief and unhappy stint with a semi-pro football team in Culpeper, Virginia. He has held a series of jobs over the years, most of them involving warehouse work such as driving a forklift. Most recently, he had landed a job in the Odessa area doing inventory work.

Life has not been economically easy for Boobie. I often wonder how different his fate would have been if his cleat had not gotten caught in the artificial turf of Jones Stadium that terrible August night. The moment took a fraction of a second, and yet its impact on him was forever, a brutal reminder of the very fragility of sport. But Boobie refuses to look back with self-pity on what could have been. He still loves football, although his links to Permian have understandably broken down completely. "I don't go to the games," he said.

At the end of 1998, Boobie's uncle, L. V., died of heart complications. Boobie has continued on, working to provide for a family that includes a four-year-old daughter, a three-year-old son, and twins born earlier this year. But L. V.'s absence is felt by Boobie, as it is felt by everyone who knew this uniquely fine and decent man.

"I miss him."

*   *   *

When *Friday Night Lights* was first published in September of 1990, it set off a storm of controversy in Odessa that still flares at the very mention of the book's name. Shortly after its release, I was scheduled to do a series of appearances in Odessa as part of a tour. But the trip was cancelled after several bookstore owners said that threats of bodily harm had been made against me. The owners took those threats seriously and so did I, particularly because the book's release coincided with Permian being banned from participation in the playoffs by the University Interscholastic League for conducting supervised workouts before the official start of the season. To make the tension even more palpable, Permian had been turned in by Jerry Taylor, the head coach of crosstown rival Odessa High.

The game between Permian and Odessa High had always been something of a spiritual civil war in town, but feelings now rose into the ozone as the two teams prepared to meet each other the following week. On its front page several days before the game, the *Odessa American* made a plea to the presidents of the booster clubs of both schools asking for harmony. As the situation began to receive national attention, the mayor of Odessa at the time, Lorraine Bonner, taped a public service message asking for calm. "The eyes of a nation are focused on us this week," said Bonner. "And it's up to us to reach out and pull together." The Odessa police force doubled security for the game, and a final call for peace came during the pre-game prayer to the sellout crowd of 20,000: "There's a lot of tension built up at this game tonight. Oh Lord, please give us strength to relieve the tension tonight."

There were in fact no incidents as Permian beat Odessa High that night, 24–6, to run its winning streak over the Bronchos to twenty-six years. The animosity between east and west died down, but animosity over *Friday Night Lights* has never died. The book

still evokes feelings that are raw and passionate, particularly because one of the most enduring and attractive characteristics of
West Texans is their utter contempt for moderation.

Over the years I have been accused of betrayal, and sensational-
ism, and taking information out of context, and mis-quoting. I am
not surprised by these accusations, nor am I troubled by them.
When I first arrived in Odessa, I anticipated a book very much in
the tradition of the film *Hoosiers*, a portrait of the way in which
high school sports can bring a community together. There were
elements of that bond in Odessa, and they were reflected in the
book. But along the way some other things happened—the most
ugly racism I have ever encountered, utterly misplaced educational priorities, a town that wasn't bad or evil but had lost any
ability to judge itself. It would have been a journalistic disgrace to
ignore these elements.

The book is fair and true. It was never intended as a diatribe or
an exposé. It was written instead with enormous affection and em-
pathy, because as deeply troubling as the overemphasis was on
high school football, those games were, and always will be, the
most exquisite sporting events that I have ever experienced.

For all the controversy and verbal volleys of unfairness, the
book has actually had a profoundly positive impact on Odessa. It
clearly forced certain individuals in power to look in the mirror
and examine the culture of football that had been erected. To
their enormous credit, they realized it was a reflection that had to
be altered. "I think for some people [the book] was a wake-up
call," Chuck Hourning, the public information officer for the Ector County school district, said in 1998. "I think the community
kind of reassessed itself. I don't think the community of today
would necessarily identify with the community then."

"The book was a bit like medicine," wrote the city's most re-
spected voice, *Odessa American* columnist Ken Brodnax. "Perhaps
it was a bit bitter to the taste, and it probably had some bad side effects that were hard to shake. But the dose also healed a few ills."

The result of that medicine has been a stronger academic curriculum. SAT scores for boys have improved and the number of fe-

male students taking the test has nearly doubled. The school district has spent some $5 million to upgrade technology at both high schools. Strides have also been made in establishing equal athletic programs for males and females with the $1.1 million construction of a new softball and soccer complex.

A softball and soccer complex in Odessa?

Miracles do happen.

When I was there, nothing was considered more socially acceptable than being an unabashed Permian football booster. Living, and eating, and breathing high school football had become a way of life. Today such fanatical behavior has been tempered, in part, believes Brian Chavez, because fans don't want to be associated with the kinds of extremes that were so evident in the book. "People have kind of shied away from being real avid fans," he said. Devotion is still there, but it no longer routinely rises to the level of worship, and as Brian puts it, people are more likely to "express it under their breath."

There is no doubt that the fixation on Permian football made it great. There is also no doubt the same fixation caused the educational system to suffer in the shadows. The shift in priorities was desperately needed. But as a consequence of that shift, the glory of Permian football has dropped to an all-time low.

Gary Gaines left as Permian's head coach after the 1989 season when the team won the state championship, embarking on a course that would take him to college as an assistant at Texas Tech, back to high school, and most recently to Abilene Christian University where he was named the head coach earlier this year. Gaines was replaced at Permian by assistant Tam Hollingshead, who promptly led the team to another state championship in 1991 and then left after the 1993 season to become an assistant at Texas A&M. Hollingshead was replaced by Randy Mayes, who had been an assistant.

Mayes's first two seasons were in keeping with Permian tradition as the most storied program in Texas football history. The team went to the state semifinals in 1994 and the state championship in

1995. And then it fell apart. Permian finished 3–6 in 1997, ending a string of 32 straight winning seasons. That was difficult enough, but Permian also lost to Odessa High for the first time in 32 years. There were, as usual, 20,000 people in the stands that night, and the impact of the final score was like the aftershock of some profound religious sighting in which no one could quite believe what they had just witnessed. After the game, Permian fans dressed in black sobbed on one side while Odessa High fans dressed in red sobbed on the other.

Permian ended the decade of the 1990s with perhaps its most shameful season ever. Under the once-sacred lights of Ratliff, Midland High beat Permian for the first time since 1973 in a 35–3 embarrassment. Hated sister city rival Midland Lee, on its way to a second straight state championship, toyed with the Panthers in a 34–22 victory. Players in the system began to quit at alarming rates. Attendance was down, and the team was in danger of going winless in the district before it beat Odessa High in the last game of the season. Desperate for some measure of relief, coach Mayes called the victory a "great win." But it wasn't.

I know Randy Mayes, since he had been an assistant coach at Permian when I was there. I went out to dinner with him and his wife, Cynthia. I saw him teach in the classroom. He is perhaps the biggest critic of *Friday Night Lights*. Last year in an interview with *Texas Monthly*, he called it "a novel" and said that I would "do anything to sensationalize."

Randy Mayes was not only a superb defensive coach when I knew him, but far more important, a superb teacher and husband and man. I hardly felt sorry for him during that final season of the 1990s. The job of head coach brought him singular status in the community. It brought him a *base* salary of $69,000 a year. He didn't have to bother with the educational inconvenience of setting foot in the classroom to teach a class, since his only job was football. But I could still imagine what he was going through in 1999 as the legend of Permian turned to bitter memory. I could imagine the pressure and hurt and scornful ridicule heaped on him. Because once upon a time I myself had witnessed the mercilessness of it, not with the clever eyes of a novelist, but the clear eyes of a journalist.

Football may have a slightly different place in the psyche of Odessa than it had a decade ago, but it still holds an iron grip. The sight of a boy, a high school boy, sacrificing himself in the service of team and town on a glowing field is still a powerful intoxicant, just as long as it is accompanied by the intoxicant of winning. So I wasn't surprised to learn the fate of Randy Mayes under the Friday night lights of Odessa.

He was fired.

Acknowledgments

There are many people to thank. One of them is Michael Carlisle, whose optimism and guidance became a crucial source of support for me. He is a gifted agent, but far more important than that, he is a wonderful friend. Another is my editor at Addison-Wesley, Jane Isay, whose enthusiasm for the project was infectious, and who aided me immeasurably in the painful process of trying to organize all these swirling thoughts about Odessa and high school football and American life into something coherent. Another is Gene Roberts, the executive editor of the *Philadelphia Inquirer*, who graciously gave me a leave from my job on the paper so I could pursue my journey and move to Odessa.

I could not have written this book without the townsfolk of Odessa. I have never found a group of people more down-to-earth, more honest, more willing to express their opinions without restraint. I am indebted to all of them.

I am also indebted to the Permian Panther football program. I thank Coach Gary Gaines for allowing me to become part of the team for the 1988 season. I also thank the members of his staff, assistant varsity coaches Tam Hollingshead, Mike Belew, Randy Mayes, and Larry Currie, and team trainer Tim "Trapper" O'Connell.

Above all, I thank the players themselves. It is hard for me to express the feelings that I have for them, and as I sit here back in the suburbs, I think about them all the time. I remember the first time I saw them in the field house, with no idea of what they would be like and how they would take to me, or, for that matter, how I would take to them. And I remember how I thought of them at the end, as kids that I adored.

Jerrod McDougal appears facing page xiv.

Boobie and L.V. Miles appear facing page 56.

Boobie Miles appears facing pages 57 and 202.

Mike Winchell appears facing page 76.

Don Billingsley appears facing page 77.

Ivory Christian appears facing page 118.

Brian and Tony Chavez appear facing page 180.

Gary Gaines appears facing pages 240 and 256.

Sharon Gaines appears facing page 257.

Photographs facing pages 57, 155, 241, and 257 were taken during the game against Midland Lee.

Photographs facing pages xiv and 240 were taken in the Ratliff Stadium dressing room immediately following the Midland Lee game.

The photograph facing page 274 was taken outside the field house following the Midland Lee game.